Fortuna desperata

Recent Researches in Music

A-R Editions publishes seven series of critical editions, spanning the history of Western music, American music, and oral traditions.

Recent Researches in the Music of the Middle Ages and Early Renaissance
Charles M. Atkinson, general editor

Recent Researches in the Music of the Renaissance
James Haar, general editor

Recent Researches in the Music of the Baroque Era
Christoph Wolff, general editor

Recent Researches in the Music of the Classical Era
Eugene K. Wolf, general editor

Recent Researches in the Music of the Nineteenth and Early Twentieth Centuries
Rufus Hallmark, general editor

Recent Researches in American Music
John M. Graziano, general editor

Recent Researches in the Oral Traditions of Music
Philip V. Bohlman, general editor

Each edition in *Recent Researches* is devoted to works by a single composer or to a single genre. The content is chosen for its high quality and historical importance, and each edition includes a substantial introduction and critical report. The music is engraved according to the highest standards of production using the proprietary software MusE, owned by MusicNotes, Inc.

For information on establishing a standing order to any of our series, or for editorial guidelines on submitting proposals, please contact:

A-R Editions, Inc.
Middleton, Wisconsin

800 736-0070 (U.S. book orders)
608 836-9000 (phone)
608 831-8200 (fax)
http://www.areditions.com

Recent Researches in the Music of the Middle Ages and Early Renaissance, 37

Fortuna desperata

Thirty-Six Settings of an Italian Song

Edited by Honey Meconi

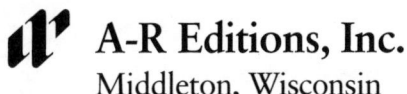

A-R Editions, Inc.
Middleton, Wisconsin

For Lewis Lockwood on his 70th birthday.

A-R Editions, Inc., Middleton, Wisconsin
© 2001 by A-R Editions, Inc.

All rights reserved. No part of this book may be reproduced or transmitted in any form by any electronic or mechanical means (including photocopying, recording, or information storage and retrieval) without permission in writing from the publisher.

The purchase of this edition does not convey the right to perform it in public, nor to make a recording of it for any purpose. Such permission must be obtained in advance from the publisher.

A-R Editions is pleased to support scholars and performers in their use of *Recent Researches* material for study or performance. Subscribers to any of the *Recent Researches* series, as well as patrons of subscribing institutions, are invited to apply for information about our "Copyright Sharing Policy."

Printed in the United States of America

ISBN 0-89579-477-2
ISSN 0362-3572

∞ The paper used in this publication meets the minimum requirements of the American National Standard for Information Sciences—Permanence of Paper for Printed Library Materials, ANSI Z39.48-1984.

Contents

Acknowledgments vii

Introduction ix
   Overview ix
   Chronology xi
   Why *Fortuna desperata?* xiv
   Variables in the Song xvi
   Conclusions xxv
   Notes on Performance xxvi
   Appendix xxvii
   Notes xxxiv

Plates xxxix

Thirty-Six Settings of *Fortuna desperata*

The Original Version 3
   1. Fortuna desperata *(a 3), uncertain* 3

Si Placet Settings 5
   2. Fortuna desperata *(a 4), anonymous* 5
   3. Fortuna desperata *(a 4), anonymous* 8
   4. Fortuna desperata/Poi che t'hebi nel core *(a 4), anonymous* 11
   5. Fortuna esperee *(a 4), anonymous* 14
   6. Fortuna desperata *(a 6), Alexander Agricola* 17

Replacement Contratenor Settings 22
   7. Fortuna desperata *(a 3), Felice?* 22
   8. Fortuna disperata *(a 3), Josquin des Prez?* 25

Settings Using the Superius 28
   9. Fortuna disperata *(a 4), Johannes Martini* 28
   10. Fortuna disperata/Sancte Petre/Oro pro nobis *(a 5), Heinrich Isaac?* 32
   11. Fortuna/Bruder Conrat *(a 4), Heinrich Isaac* 36
   12. Fortuna disperata *(a 4), anonymous* 39
   13. Fortuna disperata zibaldone *(a 4), anonymous* 43
   14. Fortuna desperata *(a 4), Jean Pinarol* 47

Settings Using the Tenor 51
   15. Fortuna desperata *(a 3), Heinrich Isaac* 51
   16. Sanctus *(a 4), Heinrich Isaac* 54

17. Fortuna desperata *(a 4), anonymous* 58
18. Esurientes implevit bonis *(a 4), anonymous* 63
19. O crux ave/Fortuna *(a 5), anonymous* 67
20. Ich stund an einem Morgen/Fortuna *(a 5), Ludwig Senfl* 71
21. Es taget vor dem Walde/Fortuna *(a 5), Ludwig Senfl* 75
22. Herr durch dein Blut (Pange lingua)/Fortuna *(a 5), Ludwig Senfl* 79
23. Virgo prudentissima/Fortuna *(a 5), Ludwig Senfl* 83
24. Helena desiderio plena/Fortuna *(a 5), Ludwig Senfl* 88
25. Nasci, pati, mori/Fortuna *(a 5), Ludwig Senfl* 94
26. Fortuna ad voces musicales *(a 4), Ludwig Senfl* 98
27. Passibus ambiguis *(a 4), Matthias Greiter* 105

Settings Using the Tenor in Mi 112

28. Fortuna desperata *(a 3), Heinrich Isaac* 112
29. Fortuna desperata *(a 4), anonymous* 118
30. Ave mater matris Dei/Fortuna disperata *(a 5), Jacquet of Mantua* 122
31. Consideres mes incessantes plaintes/Fortuna desperata *(a 5), anonymous* 126
32. Anima mea liquefacta est/Amica mea *(a 5), Cabilliau* 129
33. Fortuna *(a 4), Wilhelm Breitengraser* 133

Settings with Voices Missing 138

34. Fortuna desperata quae te dementia coepit? *(a 3), anonymous* 138
35. Fortuna *(a 4?), anonymous* 141
36. Fortuna desperata quae te dementia vertit? *(a 6), Robertus Fabri* 143

Critical Report 149

List of Sources 149
Sigla for Works Cited 153
Editorial Method 156
Critical Commentary 157
Notes 188

Acknowledgments

Many people contributed to this edition, in large ways and small, and I wish to thank them for their valuable assistance. My research on art-song reworkings, of which this is one of the results, began in earnest in 1986–87 while a fellow at Villa I Tatti; this was made possible by grants from the Leopold Schepp Foundation and the Hanna Kiel Fund. Continued research was supported by a Faculty Research Grant from Rice University and a National Endowment for the Humanities Summer Stipend. Most recently, a Lila Wallace-Reader's Digest Publication Subsidy from Villa I Tatti made possible the conclusion of this work. I am extremely grateful for the financial assistance provided by all of these sources.

Helen Eaker, Helga Felleisen, Massimo Ossi, Kristine Wallace, Harvey Yunis, and the late Susan Clark all provided assistance with translations; needless to say, any remaining faults are my responsibility. David Fallows and Martin Picker must be thanked for information of many kinds over many years, and I cannot even begin to thank Patricia Rubin for all that she has done in innumerable ways. Other individuals who have generously provided help at various times include Allan Atlas, Bonnie J. Blackburn, M. Jennifer Bloxam, Virginia Danielson, Robert Dennis, Caroline Elam, Paula Higgins, Barton Hudson, David Kidger, Kenneth Kreitner, Hiroyuki Minamino, Matthew Peattie, David Quint, Joshua Rifkin, Reinhard Strohm, Peter Urquhart, Andrew H. Weaver, and Susan Forscher Weiss. A special word of thanks goes to the Orlando Consort, who performed *Esurientes implevit bonis* (FD18) at their workshop at the Annual Meeting of the American Musicological Society in Toronto on 3 November 2000, at which time they made several helpful suggestions.

Numerous institutions have kindly given permission for the publication of music and texts from items in their collections: the Staats- und Stadtbibliothek, Augsburg; the Civico Museo Bibliografico Musicale, Bologna; the Royal Library, Brussels (for 1553 Faber); the South African Public Library, Cape Town; the Biblioteca Nazionale Centrale, Florence; the Universitätsbibliothek, Leipzig; the British Library, London; the Musikabteilung der Bayerische Staatsbibliothek, Munich (for 1534^{17}); the Universitätsbibliothek der Ludwig-Maximilians-Universität, Munich; the New York Public Library, New York; the Bibliothèque nationale de France, Paris; the Biblioteca Comunale Augusta, Perugia; the Bischöfliche Zentralbibliothek, Regensburg; the Biblioteca Casanatense, Rome; the Archivo Capitular de la Catedral, Segovia; the Stiftsbibliothek, St. Gall; the Biblioteca Apostolica Vaticana, Vatican City; the Musiksammlung der Österreichische Nationalbibliothek, Vienna (for the appropriate manuscripts as well as Canti C); the Biblioteka Uniwersytecka, Wrocław; and the Ratsschulbibliothek, Zwickau. The Herzog August Bibliothek in Wolfenbüttel very kindly supplied a reproduction of the *Fortuna desperata* version in their collection. I would like especially to thank the Biblioteca Comunale Augusta of Perugia and the British Library for their kind permission to reproduce items in their holdings as plates in this edition. I would also like to thank the libraries where I have worked extensively on this project: the Morrill Music Library and the Biblioteca Berenson at Villa I Tatti, Fondren Library at Rice University, the Van Pelt Library at the University of Pennsylvania, and the Eda Kuhn Loeb Music Library (and the Isham Memorial Library therein) at Harvard University.

I also wish to thank my beloved husband, Michel Godts, and our wonderful son, Yannick, for providing every support a scholar could wish for.

This volume is dedicated to Lewis Lockwood, who for twenty years has provided an unsurpassable model of scholar, teacher, and friend.

Introduction

Overview

The most popular Italian song of the fifteenth century was *Fortuna desperata*, both in terms of its own transmission and in its use as a model for the derivative settings it inspired.[1] For some seventy-five years composers drew on this work for their fresh creations, making this song one of the most popular of all fifteenth-century models.[2] *Fortuna desperata* survives in six masses (by Josquin, Obrecht, Appenzeller, Periquin, and two anonymous composers),[3] two keyboard works possibly derived from now-lost ensemble originals,[4] and the thirty-six ensemble settings edited here (three of which have one or more missing voices). Further, it made a brief appearance in an anonymous *J'ay pris amours* setting,[5] and it is likely to turn up again as our exploration of fifteenth- and sixteenth-century music continues. The superius, tenor, and bassus[6] all appeared in later reworkings, the last used in Josquin's mass but not in a separate ensemble setting.

Fifteen known composers, several intabulators, and a series of anonymous musicians dealt with *Fortuna desperata*; these include some of the most famous masters of the day as well as those who are known to us only by virtue of having worked with this piece. Of the great Franco-Flemish composers, Josquin des Prez, Jacob Obrecht, Alexander Agricola, Heinrich Isaac, and possibly Pierre de la Rue (if he is Periquin) used *Fortuna desperata* for one or more works. Within Italy, Johannes Martini and (possibly) Felice dealt with the model early in the history of the compositional family, and Jacquet of Mantua treated it much later, evidently influenced by one of Isaac's settings; Francesco Spinacino also provided an intabulation of the original song. A German branch of *Fortuna desperata* settings and intabulations flourished in the sixteenth century in pieces by the famous Ludwig Senfl, the less well-known group of Wilhelm Breitengraser, Matthias Greiter, Hans Buchner, and Othmar Luscinius, and the completely obscure Robertus Fabri. Another mysterious composer, Jean Pinarol, provided a single setting, as did Cabilliau and Benedictus Appenzeller. Of known composers, Isaac and Senfl are striking for their large number of works on this model.[7]

In the edition the pieces are arranged primarily by use of borrowed material: si placet versions first, then replacement contratenor settings, then works that use the superius, those that use the tenor, and those that use the tenor in mi.[8] Three incomplete works (one superius and two tenor cantus firmus settings) conclude the volume.

The simplest compositional change to the song was the addition of a si placet voice, a basic step in the modernization of a work. *Fortuna desperata* is striking among its contemporaries for the variety of si placet voices attached to it. The most common appears in FD2;[9] with the exception of the Josquin mass, this setting was the most widely circulated of any *Fortuna desperata* version, appearing at least a dozen times in contemporary sources.[10] Three other si placet altus voices, closely related to but nonetheless different from that of FD2, survive in FD3–5. In addition, Agricola's FD6 is a rare example of a triple si placet setting, with three new voices added to the original three.[11]

The two replacement contratenor settings[12] (FD7 and 8) also display significant similarities: rapidly moving new lines, the incessant use of rhythmic motives, frequent octave leaps, shifts to triplet motion, and so on.[13] Taken together, the si placet and replacement contratenor settings constitute an impressive number of works that change relatively little of the original work; i.e., the superius-tenor duet that is the core of the composition remains intact throughout. In none of the other large families of art-song reworkings (i.e., works built on *Fors seulement*, *De tous biens plaine*, *J'ay pris amours*, and so on) do we see so many pieces of such inherent stability, and no other art song has so many derivative settings so closely linked to the original.[14] If nothing else, these settings attest to both the popularity of this work and a desire to keep it in the repertory by "updating" it with a few compositional changes.

Of the remaining works in the edition—those that build on the superius or tenor—all but three are straightforward cantus firmus settings, the most common of all types of art-song reworkings (three of these—FD27, 31, and 32—use the first phrase of the tenor only).[15] Of the non–cantus firmus works, two works paraphrase the tenor (FD16, in tempus perfectum, and FD17), and one work draws material from the tenor voice (FD33). When a voice from the model is used in another work, it is normally placed in the same voice from which it came (i.e., superius in superius, tenor in tenor), untransposed, with its original note values.[16] The borrowed voice often determines the mode and sometimes the cadences of the derivative work, which at times is almost exactly as long as the original setting.[17] These procedures are also the most commonly used ones in other families of art-song reworkings; the treatment of *Fortuna desperata* conforms in this respect to generic expectations.[18]

Seven works use the superius of the original and twenty-one use the tenor. In the superius settings, only one places the borrowed melody elsewhere than the superius: Pinarol's version (FD14) transposes the tune down an eleventh and places it in the bassus. This setting is also the only work to transpose the superius. The superius cantus firmus is always used strictly, and only twice—very briefly in both cases—does the new work extend past the fifty-seven measures of the original.

Tenor borrowings exhibit somewhat more variety; fewer than half of these works are approximately as long as the original. All but one of the twenty-one works using the tenor place it in the tenor of the derivative composition; the remaining work (FD15) puts it in the superius, transposed up a fifth. Eight other works transpose the tenor. FD17 makes a conventional move down a fourth, while Greiter's setting (FD27) takes its borrowed phrase around the circle of fifths. The remaining six pieces set the work on E and essentially change the mode of the tune to Phrygian.[19] Such a switch is highly unusual for art-song reworkings, and the fact that there are six pieces that do this (FD28–33) is even more remarkable. One assumes some connection among these Phrygian settings, presumably through Isaac (to be discussed below).[20]

Fifteen of the tenor settings use the entire tenor strictly, and two of these, FD26 and 28, use the tenor twice in succession. In FD26 Senfl also uses the hexachord for additional scaffolding. As noted, three works borrow only part of the tenor. One of these is Greiter's (FD27), which takes the first five measures around the circle of fifths in an astonishing setting; the other two (FD31 and 32) present the first fifteen measures at double the normal note values and then immediately at its usual speed.[21]

Intabulations of *Fortuna desperata* settings also employ transpositions. The entire original piece was transposed in two separate intabulations, down a fourth in Berlin 40026 and more adventurously up a fourth, generating a two-flat signature, in 1507[6]. In 40026 there are also two intabulations, by Hans Buchner and Othmar Luscinius, of tenor cantus firmus settings, each of which places the tenor line, transposed down an octave, in the lowest part of the new work. These two intabulations are not included in this edition.

Aside from the Phrygian *Fortuna desperata* settings and Greiter's exploration of the circle of fifths, the pieces conform to general art-song reworking practices in their most obvious structural features. What sets *Fortuna desperata* apart from other families is its frequent—rather than merely occasional—reliance on the simultaneous use of other preexistent melodies and/or texts.

Contrafacts of the original or si placet versions link the piece to the sacred or devotional texts "O panis vite" for the incarnate Christ (FD1), "Ave stella fulgida" for the Virgin Mary (FD2), the lauda text "Poi che t'hebi nel core" for Christ (FD2 and 4), and "Virginis alme parens" for Saint Anne (FD2), as well as to the classical compilation "Quae te dementia coepit [vertit]" (FD2); the last-named text shows up again in FD34 and FD36.[22] Another piece with a classical text is FD27 ("Passibus ambiguis," concerned directly with Fortune). Other Latin texts or incipits for derivative works include "Anima mea liquefacta est" from the Song of Songs (FD32), "Ave mater matris Dei" for Saint Anne (FD30), "Esurientes implevit bonis" from the Magnificat (FD18), "Helena desiderio plena" for Saint Helena, finder of the Holy Cross (FD24), "O crux ave" (drawn from the hymn *Vexilla regis*) for the Holy Cross itself (FD19), possibly "Pange lingua" for Corpus Christi (FD22), "Virgo prudentissima" for the Virgin Mary (FD23), the litany "Sancte Petre ora pro nobis" (FD10), and "Sanctus" (FD16); these are sometimes linked with the appropriate chant models. A German devotional text, "Herr durch dein Blut," appears in FD22, joined to the famous *Pange lingua* melody.

Nor were secular tunes eschewed; they appear, sometimes bearing their texts, in FD21 (*Es taget vor dem Walde*), FD20 (*Ich stund an einem Morgen*), FD11 (*Bruder Conrat*), all German, and in FD13, a rollicking zibaldone of Italian words and melodies. Two French incipits that survive ("Fortune esperee" for FD5 and "Consideres mes incessantes plaintes" for FD31) suggest that *Fortuna desperata* must have had some circulation under French secular texts as well. Finally, there is also the mysterious text "Nasci, pati, mori" of FD25.

Many of these settings are interrelated, although not as often as we might expect. There seems to be no connection between the two works with texts for Saint Anne (FD2 and FD30), for example, and the two linked to the Holy Cross (FD19 and FD24) are problematic in certain respects. What is apparent, however, is the freedom with which the song and its derivatives fitted into the musical fabric of fifteenth- and sixteenth-century Europe: sacred, secular, liturgical, devotional, vocal, instrumental, reverent, satirical—it is difficult to find a mainstream musical trend that *Fortuna desperata* did not touch during its extended life.

Chronology

Table 3 in the appendix provides a working chronology of *Fortuna desperata*. All sources for all known versions of the piece are listed, tagged geographically by place of origin. First appearances of the versions are listed in roman type, later ones in italic. While most settings survive today in a single source (thirty-one of forty-five *Fortuna desperata* works are unica),[23] a few made multiple appearances. FD1 (the original setting and its many intabulations), FD2 (the best-known si placet version), the Obrecht mass,[24] and (even more so) the Josquin mass all enjoyed especially wide circulation. The original song circulated in ensemble or tablature form for more than fifty years after being composed, and FD2 was in circulation almost sixty-five years—a staggering longevity during a period when to most "new" meant "better." It is clear, then, that the song, both by itself and with the few changes found in the si placet and replacement contratenor settings, was very much appreciated by fifteenth- and sixteenth-century listeners. The use of the superius, tenor, and, in the case of Josquin, bassus is further testimony to the attraction of the material.

Table 3 is obviously imprecise—in some instances we know that pieces were clearly composed before the date of their first surviving source—but it does present one version of the unfolding of the *Fortuna* family. It shows the longevity of the tradition, demonstrates its very wide geographical distribution, and suggests certain patterns of transmission. It also shows how the piece and its derivatives circulated in secular and sacred manuscripts and prints, tablatures, and theoretical treatises. Several sources were especially important for transmission: Segovia, Vienna 18810, 1534[17], and the keyboard tablature Berlin 40026.

It is virtually certain that the song was composed in Florence[25] and that city keeps recurring in the song's transmission history. The poetry manuscript that contains the original version of the poem (London 16439) was compiled there, and two lauda collections containing the contrafact text "Poi che t'hebi nel core" were possibly published there (certainly the one from 1486 and maybe the one from 1496); that text continued its association with the song into the next century in two different, though related, si placet settings. Isaac, author of perhaps as many as five arrangements, came to work in Florence in 1484, and Agricola, composer of the triple si placet setting FD6, worked there in the early 1490s; both surely encountered the song in that city. Seven surviving Florentine (or probably Florentine) manuscripts transmit the original or derived settings: C.G. XIII.27 has both Isaac's FD15 and the compilation of five voices that includes the three voices of the original, the most common si placet voice (FD2), and the replacement contratenor bassus (FD7), all headed "Felice," which may refer to a Florentine composer;[26] Bologna Q17 has Isaac's FD16; Florence 121 has the original as well as Isaac's FD15; Florence 107 has a section from the Obrecht mass; and Florence 164–67, Cortona/Paris, and Florence 337 all contain the zibaldone FD13.

This last work is an especially interesting one, combining the original superius with a string of textual and musical snippets in the lower voices. This arrangement arrives forty or so years after the original song. All of its sources are definitely or probably Florentine, so in a way this setting represents Florence's farewell to the song. And a raucous one it is at that. Whereas the original poem and its textual revision[27] were deeply serious works that quite possibly reflected communal mourning, this latest venture has three lower voices whose texts are filled with double entendres and leering references. Obviously, after forty years of exposure to the most popular Italian song of the fifteenth century, someone was ready to provide a juicy send-up of the thing. That the piece appeared in at least three sources (a large number for a derivative setting) and that all of them contain complete texts suggest that Florentines were prepared to enjoy this takeoff to the fullest. Clearly, the song was not soon forgotten in its city of origin.

The song moved early to two important musical centers, Naples and Ferrara, that had close diplomatic and cultural ties to Florence.[28] Naples was probably the city that saw the compilation of the earliest surviving source to contain the original song, Paris 4379.[29] Here the original version was entered first and then the most popular si placet altus was added, apparently not long afterwards. As we shall see, the composition entered there is very close to what must have been the original version, but some changes had already crept into the work. The most obvious is the alteration of what was surely originally C in the superius line at measure 13 to a melodically insipid F to avoid parallel fifths with the lowest voice. It is important to note that alterations were appearing in the work presumably not long after it was written and that the si placet voice seems to have been added fairly soon as well. A slightly later Neapolitan manuscript, Perugia 431 (probably from the mid-1480s), also included at first an untexted and flawed version of the original three-voice composition.[30] The scribe, however, evidently gained access to a much better and more "up-to-date" copy of the piece, so the first version was crossed out and the new reading, a significantly better one of the most common si placet version, was copied on the very next opening (see plates 2 and 3).[31] This new copy contains three stanzas of text, more than any other musical source. Lastly, a still later (possibly) Neapolitan manuscript, Bologna Q16, contains another si placet setting, FD3.

The Ferrara connection also shows up very early in the history of the song, with Ferrarese court composer Johannes Martini's superius cantus firmus setting (FD9), clearly one of the earliest reworkings, appearing in the Ferrarese chansonnier Casanatense 2856.[32] This manuscript, since it was apparently compiled for the resident *piffari*, is an appropriate repository for this setting, surely a lively instrumental arrangement.[33] The Martini setting is a forerunner in another respect: superius cantus firmus settings, although fewer in number than tenor versions, tended to appear earlier than the latter. Perhaps this was because the connection to the original, via the highest sounding voice, was more audible and hence more obvious—a possible *desideratum* in such an early reworking.

Ferrara, too, was doubtless where Obrecht encountered the song during his stay in 1477/78, while Josquin may have learned it in either Ferrara or Naples in the early 1480s.[34] The *Fortuna desperata* masses by both of these composers surface in a later Ferrarese manuscript, Modena M.1.2. Obrecht's mass seems to have been modeled on Josquin's; both use C in their superius melodies and both offer additional evidence that multiple readings of the original song were in circulation early in the song's history (on the alternate readings, see below). Each of the masses was quite popular and contributed extensively to the continued presence of *Fortuna desperata* in the general musical consciousness, as the repeated appearances in table 3 show.

Another potential Ferrara connection is Paris 676, which may have originated there. This provenance is an especially intriguing possibility given that the reading of FD2 in this manuscript shares several important variants with those used by Josquin, to say nothing of this entry having two stanzas of the *Fortuna desperata* text. The other possible provenance for Paris 676 is Mantua, which had extremely close ties with Ferrara owing to the marriage of Isabella d'Este to Francesco Gonzaga in 1490.

Fortuna desperata and its derivatives soon spread to other cities in Italy, including Rome (where Josquin's mass shows up in the papal chapel manuscript C.S. 41, dating from the time of his employment there, as well as in the much later 1526 Giunta), possibly Mantua (FD4 in Florence Pan. 27), Bologna (FD12 in Bologna Q18 and the later anonymous mass in Bologna A38), and elsewhere. Venice, not surprisingly, generated numerous published versions: the Josquin mass in 1502 Petrucci and 1516 Petrucci, the Obrecht mass in 1503 Petrucci, FD2 and 4 in Canti C, an intabulation of the original for two lutes in 1507[6], and the already well-known lauda text in *Opera nova* of 1512.[35] Pesaro 1144 and Paris 27, both of which contain free intabulations of the original song, may be of Venetian origin as well.

As popular as *Fortuna desperata* was in Italy, it eventually achieved a similar, if not greater, popularity in Germanic lands.[36] By the early 1490s at the latest, Obrecht's mass was copied in the German manuscript Berlin 40021, and both the original song and a slew of derivative settings circulated in Germany, Switzerland, and Austria, sometimes with contrafact texts. Heinrich Isaac's appointment as court composer to Maximilian I (from 1497) almost certainly served as an impetus for later northern composers. Isaac was the author of possibly as many as five *Fortuna desperata* settings of considerable variety: (1) a four-voice superius cantus firmus setting where the tune was combined with motives from the popular German song *Bruder Conrat* (FD11, surviving only in a posthumous source); (2) a straightforward three-voice cantus firmus work where the tenor is placed in the superius, transposed up a fifth (FD15), appearing in the Florentine manuscript C.G. XIII.27; (3) a two-part, three-voice "Fortuna in mi" setting (FD28) transmitted in Germanic sources; (4) a supposed *Sanctus* for four voices (FD16) that paraphrases the tenor in tempus perfectum, one of the more far-reaching transformations of the material (transmitted in the probably Florentine Bologna Q17); and possibly (5) the five-voice work in Segovia (FD10) that combines the original superius with the litany chant "Sancte Petre ora pro nobis."[37] If Isaac intended to get maximum variety from his repeated reworkings, he undoubtedly succeeded. Further, he was surely a chronological as well as stylistic leader in generating the *Fortuna desperata* family, for three of the settings attributed to him appear in sources dating from the 1490s or shortly thereafter.

Of the post-Isaac settings, a large number come from Ludwig Senfl, doubtless inspired in this path by his teacher Isaac. Senfl composed even more settings than his mentor and combined the work with an even wider range of material: the chants *Helena desiderio plena* (FD 24), *Virgo prudentissima* (FD23),[38] and *Pange lingua* (FD22, transmitted with German devotional text "Herr durch dein Blut" but possibly first written with the chant text); the German popular songs *Ich stund an einem Morgen* (FD20) and *Es taget vor dem Walde* (FD21); and the pithy and unidentified "Nasci, pati, mori" text (FD25). He also wrote a hexachordally-inspired work around the tenor (FD26). Despite this wealth of material, Senfl was in certain respects less experimental than his mentor: all but the last-named work are for five voices and all use the tenor in the tenor voice, untransposed. In addition, although he was surely inspired if not prompted by Isaac himself, Senfl was clearly following his own compositional proclivities, for his output is filled with secular works using the same well-known material again and again, frequently combining one famous tune with another equally popular melody. While he certainly seems to have relished the compositional challenge of combining multiple preexistent tunes, symbolic textual interaction may also have been at work.[39]

Isaac may also have initiated the "Fortuna in mi" tradition. He was probably the first to make this unusual transposition, and his setting (FD28) was possibly known to Jacquet, who worked in Italy and whose setting (FD30) uses a form of the *Fortuna desperata* tenor identical to the one used by Isaac. The remaining four "Fortuna in mi" settings split into a Germanic pair (FD33 by Nuremberg composer Wilhelm Breitengraser and FD29, which circulated exclusively in Germanic sources; we will see another potential Isaac connection shortly) and two closely related pieces from the Habsburg-Burgundian court circle (FD32 by Cabilliau and the structurally identical, anonymous FD31). Isaac's FD28 survives in four Germanic manuscripts (two earlier intabulations and two later ensemble sources; clearly we are missing sources) and could easily have reached the Habsburg-Burgundian court through Maximilian's contacts; it is not difficult to posit a tradition inspired by his initial setting.

Maximilian's court provides still further connections to *Fortuna desperata*, specifically through several keyboard intabulations. Organist Hans Buchner was associated with Maximilian and was responsible for three intabulations: one of the anonymous FD29 "Fortuna in mi" setting, one of the original piece, and one of a work no longer traceable to an ensemble original. The widely traveled Othmar Luscinius, intabulator of possibly another no longer extant ensemble setting, worked for a while in Vienna (one of Maximilian's outposts) and knew Paul Hofhaimer, Maximilian's court organist. As will be seen below, the Luscinius and Buchner intabulations presumably of now-lost ensemble settings often use the form of the tenor favored by Isaac.

We have already mentioned the Habsburg-Burgundian court in connection with Cabilliau's work (FD32) and the anonymous FD31, the latter transmitted in the court partbooks Vienna 18746. Other works using *Fortuna desperata* are present in court-related sources. Appenzeller's Requiem appears in Montserrat 765, compiled in Brussels at the court of Mary of Hungary (the direct successor to Marguerite of Austria); Appenzeller was, of course, Mary's court composer. Earlier, Josquin's mass appeared in Vienna 11778 and movements from Obrecht's mass appeared in Florence 2439, both manuscripts coming from the scriptorium associated with the court. Josquin's mass, obviously known at court, may have inspired FD31 and Cabilliau's FD32, which follow Josquin's treatment of the cantus firmus in his *Qui tollis*. As already mentioned, the "Periquin" who composed a *Fortuna desperata* mass may be the famed court composer Pierre de la Rue. Further, some of the repertoire of the famous Segovia manuscript may have arrived in Spain with Marguerite of Austria at the time of her wedding in 1497. This manuscript contains the original song, three derivative versions (FD8–10), and Obrecht's mass. As I have pointed out elsewhere, many questions remain regarding this manuscript, including the possibility of Italian exemplars for some of its contents, but it is impossible to ignore an extremely strong Flemish presence in the collection.[40] Finally, Flemish manuscript London 35087, owned by a long-time Habsburg-Burgundian court official, contains the original version, albeit in a modernized reading.[41]

Still other parts of Europe encountered *Fortuna desperata* in one of its guises. From France we have a copy of Josquin's mass in Uppsala 76b, a keyboard intabulation of the original from 1531, and two ensemble settings (FD2 and 17) in St. Gall 462. The presumably English manuscript London 31922 contains the si placet setting FD5 with the remainder of what was probably a French contrafact text and, as we will see below, a curious amalgam of readings. The Josquin mass also appears in the late-fifteenth-century source Barcelona 5 (from Spain?), while a very late vihuela intabulation from 1552 includes the Benedictus and Pleni from his mass. Another mass section also shows up in Lisbon (1540 Vaena).

From table 3 we can observe certain compositional trends as the decades pass. As we might expect, the simpler modifications to the song—the addition of si placet voices or the substitution of a new contratenor bassus—usually take place earlier in the song's history.[42] Superius cantus firmus settings die out earlier than tenor ones, with the last examples being rather more flamboyant than the others: Fabri's extravagant but unfortunately incomplete six-voice setting (FD36) and the anonymous send-up FD13, discussed earlier. With the farewell to si placet, replacement contratenor, and superius settings, the tenor tradition takes off in earnest, in both the regular form and in the transposed "Fortuna in mi" version. Many of these tenor settings, especially later ones, use sacred or devotional texts, some accompanied by chant models. With the exception of Isaac's *Sanctus* (FD16), which paraphrases the tenor, and his "Fortuna in mi" setting (FD28), which uses the full tenor in each of its two parts, it is typically the later works that do fancy things with the tenor: paraphrase in FD17, selective borrowing in FD33, use of only part of the melody (FD31, 32, and 27; the latter, of course, sends its borrowed material around the circle of fifths), and twofold presentation of the cantus firmus (FD26, 31, and 32; the latter two present it initially in doubled note values). This is additional evidence that the further away chronologically composers were from the original song, the more likely they were to experiment with it (e.g., combining it with another melody or treating it in a less straightforward manner).

Fortuna desperata settings continue to be composed or copied into the 1540s and 1550s, demonstrating an astonishing longevity for a compositional tradition. While many of the final appearances of works are in theoretical treatises, we also find a presumably tenor cantus firmus setting (FD34), another motet (FD32), and two full masses (Appenzeller's Requiem and an anonymous mass). One of the very last works, Matthias Greiter's setting of a text by Ovid (FD27) is one of the most spectacular, for it takes the first phrase of the tenor and whirls it around the circle of fifths, visiting all the flats along the way and requiring B♭♭s at the end. This blatant example of humanistic text painting shows how far the original song had traveled in the seventy-five or more years of its existence.

Fortuna desperata, then, covers a wide range over the decades, with newly-derived compositions surfacing at regular intervals over a span of many years. The new pieces are sprinkled among recopyings of many of the earlier ones; both the original version and the most common si placet setting are still being intabulated in the 1520s, and Josquin's mass appears in full twice at the end of the 1530s and piecemeal thereafter; indeed, it appears to close out the tradition. Although settings were initially concentrated in Italy, Obrecht's mass was known in Germany by the early 1490s, with si placet settings showing up there around the same time or shortly thereafter, and a slew of versions surfaced in Spain by the end of the century. The geographical spread continued well into the sixteenth century, although the last Italian source is Giunta's Josquin mass print of 1526. Ironically, this preeminent Italian song fell out of favor there long before it disappeared from elsewhere in Europe.

One final observation is that derivative versions almost always identify the work as belonging to the *Fortuna desperata* complex in some way or another—the only ensemble versions that do not are three works with a Latin text or incipit: Isaac's *Sanctus* (FD16), the setting within a Magnificat (FD18), and Greiter's *Passibus ambiguis* (FD27).[43] This is entirely in keeping with the traditions of art-song reworkings, where recognition of the connection to the original song was apparently considered important.[44]

Why *Fortuna desperata*?

One could easily infer from the extensive literature on *Fortuna desperata* that the song was fatally flawed (those parallel fifths! those diminished triads!) and that symbolic reference or homage to the original composer was the main purpose behind its reuse.[45] Common sense alone suggests, however, that dozens of scribes and composers would not continue to lavish their time and effort on a piece for almost eighty years were it not of considerable interest in its own right.[46] Further, as is true for many of the most famous models for art-song reworkings, the composer of *Fortuna desperata* cannot be determined.[47] Although previously thought to be Busnois, his authorship cannot be confirmed,[48] nor can that of any of the suggested alternatives,[49] making it highly unlikely that the derived versions were intended as homage to the original author. Thus, while the use of *Fortuna desperata* as symbol was certainly invoked at least sometimes in derivative settings and while we can indeed see composer connections among particular reworkings (especially regarding Isaac and Senfl), some of the credit for the song's longevity on its own and as model surely stems from its purely musical strengths.

The simplicity of *Fortuna desperata* is deceptive, for this is surely a work where the whole is greater than the sum of its parts. The work has the typical structure of a three-voice composition from the latter half of the fifteenth century, an independent superius-tenor duet to which a contratenor (bassus) has been added. The superius and tenor each have the range of a ninth, and the tenor is pitched a fifth below the superius. The third voice is slightly wider in range—a tenth—and lies a fourth below the tenor. As will be discussed further, it was transmitted at times in C clef and at times in F, and gradually came to assume the name of bassus rather than contra. Functioning as a rhythmic and harmonic filler, the bassus is less graceful than the other voices and, with the exception of the Josquin mass, was not used as a cantus firmus in reworkings. It also raises some questions of performer's accidentals and fifteenth-century harmonic preferences—questions that seem to have been raised then as well as now (see below).

Edward Lowinsky pointed out the connection in contemporary music theory between Fortune and the Lydian mode (the male Fortune, Jupiter) as well as the Hypolydian mode (the female Fortune, Venus); Bartolomeo Ramos de Pareia makes this link in his *Musica practica*.[50] Although Ramos was writing after the composition of *Fortuna desperata*, this symbolic relationship also could have been intended in the work. The superius fits perfectly in Hypolydian while the tenor is an exact fit for Lydian; the bassus is closest to Hypolydian. This symbolism may also explain the occasional transmission of these voices without the expected signature of one flat (see below): although the fifth and sixth modes usually flatted the B at this time, they are, theoretically, modes without any accidentals.

The first and last cadences (mm. 15 and 57) are on F, with the sole remaining cadence (m. 36) on A. These are all classic suspension cadences formed by superius and tenor. The first cadence is also an octave leap cadence, with bassus going up to middle C. The second cadence is the weakest of the three, as we might expect, with bassus moving up a step from its E (or E♭, as it sometimes is indicated) to F, undercutting the A of the other two voices. The final cadence was doubtless originally written like the first, with an octave leap in the bassus to form a closing F-C fifth; this is what the earlier sources have. Later sources replaced the octave with a leap upward of a fourth,[51] conforming to the shift in cadential tastes; this later change has the virtue of ending the piece as it began, with an octave F.

In addition to these cadences there is thwarted cadential motion in measures 30–31, where the superius and tenor appear to be about to converge on F. The superius, however, veers off to A, starting a new syntactic unit and proceeding in parallel motion with the bassus. After the cadence at measure 15—a place where the bassus motion soon leads the song forward—there is no strong harmonic resting place until the final cadence. This lack of strong cadences helps propel the music forward; rest is provided rhythmically rather than harmonically.

The texture is largely homophonic, but is handled with a mastery that belies the outward simplicity of its surface. Essentially the work alternates between homorhythmic sections and those featuring more varied activity; indeed, one of the marvelous qualities of this piece is its perfect pacing. Through a combination of harmonic, rhythmic, and textural devices, we are led ever onward in a seemingly inevitable manner. Little is demanded of the listener except sheer enjoyment; there are no complex rhythms or polyphonic intricacies to follow, and the appeal is direct. This apparent simplicity is the reason the song has received so much adverse criticism over the years; only an attempt to understand the song's musical appeal reveals the subtleties of its construction.

The song opens with a homorhythmic section of breve–semibreve–semibreve–breve that captures the listener's attention with its sure footing. Pure homorhythm then recurs in measures 9–13, 25–29, 32–34, 49–51, and 53–55. Working at the same time is a brilliant rhythmic ebb and flow. Homorhythmic sections often coincide with points of greater rhythmic stasis, including breves and dotted breves, and provide a point of repose before the onset of renewed rhythmic activity. The rhythmic motion is on the slow side; there are relatively few minims (the first occur in m. 6 in the bassus) and even fewer semiminims. The greatest rhythmic activity occurs in roughly the third quarter of the piece, and the composer handles the rhythm of the last section extremely well. The activity of measure 45 seems about to be repeated in measure 48—indeed, in some sources it is—but the composer puts on the brakes, slowing down to three consecutive measures of breves, a rhythmic holding pattern before the work picks up speed again in measure 52 to lead to the final cadence. The rhythmic holding back is especially effective in the superius line, for it coincides with the scalar rise from the lowest note in its range, middle C; the increase in speed in measure 52, emphasized by the semibreve rest preceding it, heightens the sense of a drive to the goal. A similarly effective use of a semibreve rest is found in both the superius and tenor lines in measure 45, where they leap back into motion after consecutive breves in measures 39–40.

The voices are clearly delineated in terms of range, with little crossing of parts. Crossing occurs between the bassus and tenor only in measure 5 and during the cadential section at measures 15–17; it occurs between the superius and tenor in measures 24 and 40–42. In these instances, the voice crossing helps to contribute to harmonic stability, since the lines merely exchange pitches (starting at mm. 23 and 39); this effect is aided by sustained bassus pitches in measures 23–24 (C), 39–40 (A), and 42 (D). Other appealing voice interplay is seen in the use of contrasting motion within a homorhythmic texture as the piece opens, followed immediately by rhythmic imitation (the superius pattern of mm. 4–7 is picked up by the tenor in mm. 6–9).

xv

Melodically, both superius and tenor display fine craftsmanship. Both lines are smooth, with much conjunct motion and no awkward leaps, and both have gently rising and falling contours. Although neither has a large range, each exploits it well. Both begin the second section of the work (after the cadence in m. 15) with a move to their highest range, the superius starting on C and cresting to D in measure 20, and the tenor in imitation a fifth below (unique in this work, and exceedingly rare in contemporary Italian music) at measure 21, an octave higher than last heard, and reaching its highest pitch first at measure 24 and again in 27. The bassus even makes a subtle reference to this imitation: in measures 16–17 it outlines the shape that the superius (mm. 20–21) and tenor (mm. 24–25) will soon take, and many sources, including Paris 4379, have a superius line exactly matching the bassus here (see below). The superius, starting one last climb in measure 29, returns to its lower range after the cadence in measure 36 before settling on its final F.

One factor in the smoothness of the superius line is the frequent reiteration of the pattern semibreve–semibreve–breve (or a close variant thereof) seen, for example, in measures 18–19, 20–21, 24–25, 26–27, and 29–30 and present almost from the start (mm. 2–3, 6–7, and so on). Smoothness and a sense of internal unification are also enhanced when the top two voices move in thirds at several points—measures 9–13, 25–31 (less strictly at the close there), 33–34, 42–46, 47–50—and then in sixths just before the close (mm. 54–55). Simply put, superius and tenor are each well-constructed and memorable,[52] and the beguiling melodic and rhythmic simplicity of their lines would make them appealing prospects for borrowing even without any textual associations.[53]

Variables in the Song

Although *Fortuna desperata* was undoubtedly composed in Florence, the earliest surviving source, Paris 4379, is non-Florentine.[54] Despite this, in pitch and rhythm it comes very close to presenting what was probably the original form of the song. Both tenor and bassus, for example, contain very commonly used versions of their respective lines, and nothing in any of the three voices is a unique reading. The superius, moreover, differs in only two places from the most common reading: at measure 13, where it has the F substituted for the original C, and the final cadence, which underwent many changes over the years as the piece was continually modernized. Paris 4379 has therefore been used (with slight modifications) as the primary source for FD1.[55] Paris 4379 also includes the most common altus si placet voice, added slightly later to the same folios, and consequently was chosen as the primary source for FD2 as well. This choice has the advantage of providing the same touchstone for the comparison of voice parts among multiple sources of FD1 and FD2.

Text and Underlay

The original poem for *Fortuna desperata* was part of a new flowering of Tuscan poetry from the 1470s, when Florentines began to compensate for their neglect of the vernacular in favor of classical Latin during the earlier decades of the century.[56] Not coincidentally, we see an increase in the number of composed settings of Italian poetry, of which *Fortuna desperata* is one example, at just about this same time. The original poem appears in a single source, the Florentine poetry manuscript London 16439, which was possibly compiled within a decade of the poem's composition (see plate 1):[57]

Fortuna disperata,
Iniqua & maladecta,
Che di tal Donna electa
La fama ha dineg[r]ata.[58]
    Fortuna disperata,
    Iniqua & maladecta.
Sempre sia bestemmiata,
La tua perfida fede,
Che in te non ha merzede,
Ne fermeza fondata.
    Fortuna disperata,
    Iniqua & maladecta.
O morte dispietata,
Inimica & crudele,
Amara piu che fele,
Di malitia fondata.
    Fortunata disperata,
    Iniqua & maladecta.

*

Hopeless fortune,
Unjust and cursed,
Who has denied [defamed] the reputation
Of so distinguished a lady.
    Hopeless fortune,
    Unjust and cursed.
May your treacherous faith
Always be cursed,
For there is no mercy in you,
Nor fixed constancy.
    Hopeless fortune,
    Unjust and cursed.
O pitiless death,
Hostile and cruel,
More bitter than bile,
Founded in malice.
    Hopeless fortune,
    Unjust and cursed.

In the manuscript the poem is called a "canzonetta intonata antica," acknowledging that a musical setting was known and, moreover, that it was not a new one. Although anonymous, the poem was closely linked to Medici circles.[59]

The original poem presents three stanzas, each of which is followed by a refrain that repeats the first two lines of the first stanza. No musical source contains a poetic refrain of such length; the closest provide a repeat of only the opening line of text (more on this below). Secondly, none of the musical sources contains the three stanzas as given in London 16439. The texted sources all contain the first stanza, with minor variants as noted in table 1, where, with the exception of Perugia 431, the sources are given in approximate chronological order. Two musical sources contain more text: Paris 676 and Perugia 431 both contain a second stanza, and Perugia 431 contains a third. In each case, however, the second stanza opens with the first two lines of the original poem's third stanza and then veers off to new material, while the third stanza in Perugia 431 is entirely new—and structurally weak, although emotionally powerful.[60] The surviving musical sources are thus somewhat removed from the original poem, suggesting that the textual changes occurred relatively early in the song's history.

Two interesting textual variants appear in the first stanza. The first, the switch between "denigata" and "denigrata," strongly influences the meaning of the text. Has Fortuna denied (*denigata*) or defamed (*denigrata*) the reputation of the lady in question? Besmirched her honor or taken her at too young an age?[61] Of the seven texted musical sources, five (including the probable earliest, Paris 4379) have "denigata" and only the two with the most text (Perugia 431 and Paris 676) have "denigrata." In Perugia 431, however, the text originally read "denigata" but the *r* was then added to turn it into "denigrata." London 16439 is no help here, for "dinegata" was changed to "dinegrata" in it as well.

The other textual variant has no effect on meaning but raises some interesting stemmatic questions; this is the switch from "disperata" to the much more common "desperata," a switch we can see, once again, occuring very early in the song's transmission.[62] Italian dictionaries say little about the latter other than describing it as an archaic form of "disperata," but "disperata" has a very strong link to Florence. This link may not be surprising in that classical Italian grew out of Tuscan; in any event, all but one Florentine source uses it, including the one for the original poem, surely making it the original reading. C.G. XIII.27 is the only Florentine source to use "desperata"; interestingly, there are other points in the song's reading there that suggest some distance from the original. Curiously, Segovia uses "disperata,"[63] which might be evidence for the use of Italian exemplars, as mentioned above. Also, the use of the original form "disperata" fits nicely with the demonstration below that Segovia presents underlay that is probably closer to the original reading than is that of any other texted source. It is certainly tempting to see use of "disperata" as evidence of a closer link to the original reading—it is found in the very early manuscript Casanatense 2856, for example. It is possible, however, that a manuscript could carry over some features of an original reading (e.g., "disperata") while ignoring or changing others (e.g., the switch from C to F in the superius).

The first stanza is not syntactically complete, so it is striking that most texted sources have only that portion of the poem. Possibly the text was memorized; certainly both the superius and tenor melodic lines are extremely easy to memorize. This may account for the many partially texted or untexted readings (some of which, of course, appear in manuscripts that never added any text). Perhaps the incompleteness of the first stanza led to a falling off of any kind of texting. Yet another possible explanation comes from a consideration of the subject of the poem. Perhaps it was too specific to continue to be used—and we have already noticed the very extensive list of contrafacts and additions of differently texted material.

The underlay for *Fortuna desperata* presents a variety of problems. Because text underlay in the fifteenth century was particularly fluid,[64] no single solution can be claimed as definitive, and *Fortuna desperata* presents its own special set of problems. Indeed, as is obvious from table 1, the various manuscripts that texted the work did so in continually shifting ways. Nonetheless, certain points lead towards a viable solution that quite possibly matches fifteenth-century practice.

First, the question of underlay means most specifically underlay to the superius part (and more often in the original three-part version than in its si placet form). Only one source, London 35087, texts the tenor and bassus parts. As it turns out, text is fairly easy to underlay to the tenor line, and we will return to that line below. The bassus seems less likely to have received texted performance (though the scribe of London 35087 obviously felt it deserved it). At the same time, the lack of text does not preclude wordless vocal performance of any given part.

Seven sources present the superius line with text: Paris 4379 (ca. 1470–85; probably Naples), Perugia 431 (probably ca. 1485; Naples or vicinity), Segovia (northern repertoire probably before 1497), Paris 676 (1502; Ferrara or Mantua), London 35087 (pre-1509;

Bruges?), Florence 167 (ca. 1520; Florence), and Cortona/Paris (ca. 1519–23; Florence). As mentioned above, all sources are at least somewhat distant, either geographically or temporally, from the lost original.

Table 1 shows the layout of the words in the various sources that present a texted superius. The far left column lists the measures that begin syntactic units in the melodic line. The column for each source aligns the text as it appears in the manuscript with these various units; usually, but not always, the text corresponds precisely to the beginning of a unit. When it does not I have placed the text next to the closest unit. The first word or words of each line of text is presented in italics for each source, so that the breakdown of lines is readily apparent. Perugia 431 runs the text through the voice parts without any pretense about matching underlay; that is, it writes out the first stanza underneath the superius part, begins the second stanza at measure 53 of the superius and continues writing it through the tenor line, which is directly below the superius (see plate 2). The texts for the two stanzas as they appear in Perugia 431 are therefore given as poetry in the last column of table 1.[65]

The first thing to note is that the four earlier sources (including Perugia 431) do not generally repeat text (exceptions to be noted below), while the later ones (London 35087, Florence 167, and Cortona/Paris) have more repetition of text. In this respect these later manuscripts reflect their time: early-sixteenth-century music, in general, is more likely than fifteenth-century music to have textual repetition written into the source, resulting in less melismatic vocal lines.

Surprisingly, there is greater agreement as to where new lines of text begin than one might have expected. Five of the six sources place the second line at measure 17; the only exception is the late and geographically distant London 35087. The third line most often starts at measure 31 (in Segovia, Paris 676, and Florence 167, the last source from Florence); two other sources place it earlier, but in different positions, and Cortona/Paris puts it later. Similarly, three sources (Paris 4379, Segovia, and London 35087) begin the fourth line at measure 38. Not surprisingly, these most popular places to commence new lines of text, which probably reflect the original texting, coincide with the strongest internal cadences: measure 17 follows the extremely clear cadence on F in measure 15; measure 31 coincides with a thwarted cadence on F; and measure 38 follows a clear A cadence in measure 36. This plan is followed by the much-maligned Segovia codex.

Concerning how much of the text to repeat, again the sources provide some clues. Both the earliest source (Paris 4379) and the two Florentine ones (Florence 167 and Cortona/Paris) repeat the initial "Fortuna," and Paris 676 leaves a tantalizing space under the music beginning at measure 4 that likewise suggests textual repetition there. Certainly it is musically very satisfying to repeat the initial word.

TABLE 1
Texting in Superius of *Fortuna desperata*

m.	Paris 4379	Segovia	Paris 676	London 35087	Florence 167	Cortona/Paris	Perugia 431[a]
1	*[F]Ortuna*	*fortuna*	*fortuna*	*Fortuna*	*Fortuna*	*Fortuna*	Fortuna desperata
4	fortuna desperata	disperata	desperata	desperata	fortuna disperata	Fortuna disperata	Iniqua et maledecta che da tal domna electa
12				*Iniqua*			La fama ai deneg[r]ata
17	*Iniqua*	*iniqua*	*Iniqua* e maledeta	maledicta	*Iniqua* et maladetta	*iniqua* et mala	fortuna desperata
22	e maledeta	et maledicta		*che dital*	Iniqua et maladecta		O morte despietata iniqua e crudele
26	che de tal			dona		decta	che alta piu che stella
31	dona elleta	*che de tal* done electa	*Che de Tal* dona electa	electa	*che di tal* donna eletta		ma si abassata .f.d.
38	*la fama*	*la fama*		*la fama*	Eletta	*che di*	
41	ay denegata	ay denegata	*La fama* tua	la fama	*La fe mha*	tal donna	
44				ay	denegata	electa	
47			hai denigrata	denegata			
52	fortuna desperatta	fortuna disperata	ta	ay denegata	La fe mha denegata	*La fe mhai* dinegata	

[a] The text in Perugia 431 is not aligned with the music; see plate 2.

Repetition at the close presents another series of problems. It seems clear that some kind of textual refrain was intended; in addition to the two-line refrain provided in the poetic source, the three earliest texted sources (Paris 4379, Perugia 431, and Segovia) each bring back the words "Fortuna desperata" at the beginning of the last phrase (m. 52). The next source chronologically, Paris 676, ends the work with the suggestive syllable "ta," which might refer to a repetition of "denigrata" but could also be the tail end of a repeated "fortuna desperata." Once again, then, we see later sources altering the work's presentation to match contemporary trends; by the early sixteenth century, such textual repetition at the close of a piece was not the norm.

The problem then is how much text to repeat at the end and where to put it. The poem as it appears in the Florentine poetic source, London 16439, is described as a *canzonetta intonata* (a song set to music), but the textual repetition of the first two lines at the conclusion is difficult to link up with the music. The final phrase that begins at measure 52 does not have enough notes to accomodate the text, and moving the textual refrain back to measure 47, the next logical starting point, destroys the symmetry that phrase has with measure 44. Two scenarios thus present themselves: either the scribe of London 16439 erred by presenting a bit too much text for the refrain, or the original did include the full two lines, somewhat awkwardly set to the closing measures, which early on were trimmzed to a single line linked to the final phrase.[66] I am inclined toward the former idea.

On the basis of these observations, then, the edition of FD1 lays out the text corresponding to the four major divisions of the superius line, with the initial two words recurring at the end. Possible internal repetitions are suggested in brackets; performers are, of course, free to ignore them. Although I have indicated ligatures as they appear in the source, I have not always observed them in providing underlay. I take this liberty for two reasons. First, we know that perfomers themselves broke ligatures as necessary. Second, the melodies circulated with constant changes in both rhythmic values and use of ligatures, indicating that this extremely popular work was treated with considerable freedom by scribes and surely performers as well. I am availing myself of the same freedom. Similarly, the underlay for the tenor line of FD1 is added not according to how it appears in London 35087, its sole texted source, but to provide a textual counterpart to the prevailing musical homophony in the work. Alternative textings and underlays for the superius line are found in FD2 (based on Paris 4379) and FD13 (following Florence 167).

Accidentals

Just as with underlay, we have a great variety of accidentals notated in the song, both as signature accidentals and as additions to individual pitches. The superius was most often notated without a B♭ in the signature, while the tenor almost always flatted the B in the signature. Sources for the bassus are almost evenly divided between those that flat the B and those that do not, with the latter occuring somewhat more often, but usually later. The most common combination was therefore flats in the tenor and bassus signatures and none in that of the superius, a pattern followed by Paris 4379, the oldest source, as well as, to a certain extent, the notorious Segovia.[67] Interestingly enough, this use of partial signatures sometimes carries over to derivative pieces, where the borrowed *Fortuna* line is distinguished by a different signature from its surrounding voices (e.g., FD15, 17, 22–24, and 26).

Despite the lack of B♭ in the signature, the superius line surely flatted its individual Bs, as suggested editorially in the edition. The B in measure 27 was often specifically flatted, even when there was a signature accidental, as in Leipzig 1494, fol. 162v (FD2). In measure 54, the B was flatted about half of the time when there was no flat in the signature. None of the other Bs ever received flats other than those indicated in the signature. This is not to say that flats were not added by the performer—they doubtless often were—but we can say that the superius made a gradual transition from a written identity without a flat to one with it.

The tenor, as already mentioned, almost invariably flats its Bs via a signature accidental. Exceptions are the Frankfurt 20 manuscript and the first entry in Perugia 431. In measure 35, Wolfenbüttel 78 and Augsburg 142a also lack a B♭, since the signature accidental has dropped out at this point. Of some interest is the E in measure 44. Paris 676 flats this; no other small-scale ensemble source does,[68] nor does the Josquin mass, but the Obrecht mass, which uses the tenor frequently, almost universally flats this pitch. Since nothing in the writing at this point (including solmization) requires flatting this E, we can assume two separate traditions of hearing this line, one (more common) without the flat and the other with it. This is akin to the superius C/F traditions for measure 13, to be discussed in more detail below, and the existence of multiple traditions, as we shall soon see, characterizes the bassus line as well.

Because the bassus presents the greatest inconsistency and therefore the most problems, the relevant accidental information is presented in table 2, where the sources are presented in approximate chronological order. Whether or not the bassus B was flatted in a signature accidental, all Bs surely would have been flatted in performance. The questions thus deal with the Es in measures 8, 27–28, 35, and 55.

The E in measure 8 is infrequently flatted in ensemble sources: London 35087 (FD1), London 31922 (FD5), and Zwickau 78/2 (FD2), all sixteenth-century sources, are the only ones to flat that pitch. Six intabulations, also somewhat later in date, similarly read E♭ at that point. Of the many sources for the Josquin mass, only one (the very late print 1539[2]) flats the E and then only on the first appearance of the cantus firmus, not the second. In the original and in si placet settings, flatting the E removes the diminished fifth between the bassus and the tenor B♭ at that moment. The question here—the same one that will be asked for the Es in measures 27–28, 35, and 55—is whether that diminished interval was acceptable or intolerable to contemporary ears. Recent research suggests that the interval was tolerated more often than we might expect.[69] We have already seen that explicit flatting of the note was confined to later sources, and we shall soon see that the later comparable situations are treated inconsistently in the manuscripts. Unless we assume that diminished intervals were always unacceptable—which does not seem to be the case—the sources for measure 8 suggest that it was more likely sung as an E♮ in the early history of the song and that it moved towards a flatted performance as time wore on.

The E in measures 27–28 is held against the superius B♭ for a much longer time than in measure 8 (a dotted breve as opposed to a semibreve) and is flatted much more often in the sources. Of the non-mass sources, fourteen have an explicit flat at that point.[70] Four more sources, indicated with "no" in table 2, are notated without flats but sound against an altus E♭ and thus must have been flatted. In the Josquin masses, this E (transposed to B) is always flatted in its first cantus firmus appearance and is almost always flatted the second time around; it remains natural in only a single, late manuscript. This leaves only a half-dozen sources that might have generated an E♮ at that point.

Measure 35 presents a situation strongly comparable to that of measure 27: the E is often flatted in the sources as well, although not quite as frequently as in measure 27. What is striking is the treatment in sources for the Josquin mass, which are unanimous here: in the first appearance of the cantus firmus, the E (B in transposition) is always flat; the second time around it is always natural (the surrounding voices would permit E♭ [B♭] as readily as E♮ [B♮]). This is highly suggestive of two performance traditions for this passage in the original version.

The E in measure 55 of the bassus voice is, in general, flatted less often than any other. Only three ensemble sources (all from the sixteenth century) provide an explicit flat here: Paris 676 (FD2), Augsburg 142a (FD6), and London 35087 (FD1). A fourth source, London 31922 (FD5) provides a ♭ sign several breves before the actual pitch that seems to belong to it; in any event, a simultaneous E♭ in the altus at this point would require a similar pitch in the bassus. In addition, only three intabulations present an unequivocal flat here, although it is likely that the highly rewritten version in Pesaro 1144's second setting makes reference to an E♭ reading. The place where this E is most often flatted, then, is in Josquin's mass (where, transposed, the corresponding pitch is a B). On the first appearance of the cantus firmus in his mass, five sources, including the two earliest, flat the E (B), while six sources leave it alone. Even more striking is the second appearance of the cantus firmus, where seven sources (including all five of the earliest ones) provide a flat, leaving only four unaltered. This second cantus firmus appearance is even more noteworthy given that the cantus firmus E (B) enters against a sustained B♮ in the superius. Again, there seem to have been two traditions here, with the unflatted E much more common, but the flatted version known early enough for Josquin (or his scribes) to have followed it.

With the bassus Es, then, we see something of a pattern: the longer the potential dissonance with another voice, the more likely that a source will indicate a flat. In measure 27, the most frequently flatted E, we are dealing with a dotted breve. Measure 35 is flatted next most often; here we have a potential breve dissonance with the tenor, versus a semibreve dissonance with the superius A if the bassus is flatted. In measures 8 and 55 the dissonance only lasts a semibreve, and these Es receive far fewer flats. In measure 55, flatting the E creates a linear problem with the preceding A—unless that A is also flatted, but this requires flatting the simultaneous A in the superius—so this place gets the fewest flats of all (if we exclude the Josquin mass, which presents a special case).

Another point to observe is the lack of consistency within many individual sources. Florence Pan. 27 and Cape Town Grey flat the two interior Es but not the outer ones. Neither Perugia 431 setting has any written E♭s at all, nor does the first Leipzig 1494 setting (fol. 62), C.G. XIII.27, Basel F.X.10, and St. Gall 462, while Paris 27, 1507[6], London 35087, the first Berlin 40026 intabulation, and probably London 31922 (all later sources) flat everything. Bologna Q16, Canti C, and Florence 121 flat measure 35 but none of the others, while Paris 4379, Segovia, and Wolfenbüttel 78 flat measure 27 but none of the others. Paris 676 flats the last two, and the second Berlin 40026 intabulation flats the first two. Augsburg 142a flats all but measure

TABLE 2
Use of E♭ in Bassus Voice

Source	m. 8 E♭	mm. 27–28 E♭	m. 35 E♭	m. 55 E♭
Paris 4379	no	yes	no	no
Perugia 431 (FD1)	no	no	no	no
Perugia 431 (FD2)	no	"no"	no	no
Josquin 1[a]	no[b]	yes	yes	see table 3[c]
Josquin 2[a]	no	yes[d]	no	see table 3[e]
Bologna Q16	no	no	yes	no
Leipzig 1494 (fol. 62)	no	"no"	NA	no
C.G. XIII.27	no	no	no	no
Segovia	no	yes	no	no
Pesaro 1144, pp. 31–35	no	NA	NA	yes?[f]
Florence Pan. 27	no	yes	yes	no
Basel F.X.10	no	no	no	no
Paris 676	no	"no"	yes	yes
Canti C	no	"no"	yes	no
Wolfenbüttel 78	no	yes	no	no
Paris 27	yes	NA	yes	yes
Augsburg 142a	no	yes	yes	yes
Cape Town Grey	no	yes	yes	no
1507[6] [g]	yes	yes	yes	yes
London 35087	yes	yes	yes	yes
Florence 121	no	no	yes	no
St.Gall 462	no	no	no	no
London 31922	yes[h]	yes	yes	yes?[i]
Berlin 40026 (FD1)[j]	yes	yes	yes	yes
Berlin 40026 (FD2)	yes	yes	no	NA
Munich 718	yes	yes	yes	no
Zwickau 78/2	yes	yes	yes	no
1531[5]	yes	yes	no	no

Sources given in italics are intabulations. "No" indicates that E is natural in the source but that it sounds against an E♭ in the altus and hence must receive a flat. NA = not applicable; the pitch is altered so that neither E♮ nor E♭ are present.

[a] Josquin 1 and 2 refer to the two appearances of the transposed bassus that is used as the cantus firmus in the Sanctus of his mass. These references are to the tranposed versions, i.e., E♭ in the model = B♭ in the mass. The F♯ of the cantus firmus in the mass is equivalent to a B♭ key signature.

[b] Only one of eleven sources, the late print 1539[2], flats this note.

[c] Six sources use the natural reading here; five use the flat. These five include the two earliest (C.S. 41 and Barcelona 5), as well as Modena M.1.2, Munich 3154, and 1516 Petrucci.

[d] Only one of eleven sources, the later manuscript Vienna 11778, uses the natural reading here.

[e] Four sources use the natural reading here, while seven use the flat. These seven include all the earliest sources (C.S.41, Barcelona 5, 1502 Petrucci, Modena M.1.2, Munich 3154) as well as Vienna 11778 and 1539[2]. Despite this pedigree, the natural version is surely correct since the cantus firmus (tranposed so the pitch here is B) enters against a sustained B♮ in the superius.

[f] The part is very heavily rewritten, but there is a prominent E♭ in the bassus voice close to the end, surely intended as an equivalent.

[g] Accidentals are the transposed equivalent, i.e., A♭ for E♭ and E♭ for B♭.

[h] Flat actually appears before the E in measure 6 (see plate 5).

[i] A flat on the E space appears many breves before this actual E and presumably refers to it (see plate 5). In any event, a simultaneous E♭ in the altus would require a flat in the bassus as well.

[j] Accidentals are the transposed equivalent, i.e., B♭ for E♭ and F for B♭.

8, while Munich 718 and Zwickau 78/2 flat all but measure 55. The sources for the Josquin mass—and possibly therefore Josquin himself—are inconsistent on the two appearances of the cantus firmus.

What does all this mean? In general, the later the source, the more likely the Es will be flatted, and the longer the dissonance, the more likely flats will be explicitly added to avoid it. Did the scribes simply become more explicit about notating an earlier practice, or were they increasingly critical about diminished fifths that performers had previously shrugged off? Did they become less confident that the performers could be trusted to add preferred accidentals? As pointed out earlier, there seem to have been traditions for both E and E♭ in both measure 8 and measure 55, and the same may be true of the interior Es as well. In other words, just as with the E in measure 44 of the tenor line, there was variety in contemporary performance of the Es in the bassus line. Confirmation of this comes from examination of intabulated versions: although all sources are consistent in flatting measure 27, the second Pesaro 1144 reading does not flat measure 8 while others do; the second Berlin 40026 version and 1531[5] do not flat measure 35 while others do; and Munich 718 and 1531[5] do not flat measure 55 while others do.

Taken as a whole, then, *Fortuna desperata* visually moves away from the partial signatures of the fifteenth century to the unified ones of the sixteenth and similarly becomes increasingly explicit in its signing of accidentals, lessening the ambiguity of earlier sources. In both the tenor and bassus we can trace variant traditions in the performance of accidentals; joined to the C/F traditions of the superius line, we have still more evidence that the song had a fluid life, one not restricted to a single form of rendition.

Clefs

All superius parts with one exception (Wolfenbüttel 78, which uses G3) are transmitted in C1 clef, while the tenor and especially the bassus are associated with more than one clef. When untransposed, the tenor is usually in C3 clef; exceptions are Paris 4379 (the earliest source), Paris 676, and Augsburg 142a, which use C4. Since both Paris 4379 and Paris 676 also notate the bassus using C4, this suggests an intellectual perception or connection of the work, at least here, with a fading tradition, that of two equal lower voices against a separate and higher superius. This linked cleffing is especially interesting because the bassus is really in a different range than the tenor; it lies about a fourth lower.

C4 was the most frequently used clef for the bassus, and four of the earliest appearances of the song (Paris 4379, the two Perugia 431 settings, and FD3 in Bologna Q16) present the voice this way. While C4 is retained in some later sources,[71] others, especially those from the north, use an F clef instead—usually F3, but on two occasions (Basel F.X.10 and St. Gall 462) the exceedingly rare F2. In other words, the presentation of the lowest voice shifted to create a stronger visual contrast with the tenor—a more "modern" presentation that is in keeping with a general tendency to bring the piece up to date.

Similarly, the bassus voice shows a change in nomenclature in most later sources.[72] Although lacking designation in several sources, it is called "contra" in Paris 4379; this is changed to "bassus," "contrabassus," or similar designations in sources that contain a si placet voice. Yet even two manuscripts without a si placet voice—Wolfenbüttel 78 and Munich 718—use "bassus" ("Ba" in the case of Wolfenbüttel 78). Only Florence 121 still uses the term "contra."

Melody and Rhythm

The superius line in Paris 4379 presents the most common reading in every respect except for the use of F instead of the surely original C at the beginning of measure 13, and for the final cadence.[73] The C reading is clearly superior melodically—both Josquin and Obrecht use it—and it appears in more than half of the sources that contain the superius line, including some very early ones.[74] The change to F, favored by the more pedantic and used to avoid parallel fifths with the bassus, obviously occurred not long after the song's composition and appeared regularly. Unfortunately, it cannot function as a separative variant; it is clear that the song was so well known (as remarked above, it is incredibly easy to memorize the two upper voices) that scribes might have changed back and forth from C to F at will. An excellent demonstration of this is Martini's superius cantus firmus setting (FD9). In its earlier source, Casanatense 2856 (prepared in Ferrara where Martini was working), the superius appears with a C. In the later Segovia manuscript the C has been changed to F—unnecessarily so, since the bassus part here is not the original and there are no parallel fifths to be avoided. The scribe clearly knew the F version of the tune (and as table 3 shows, F was used for all the *Fortuna desperata* pieces in the Segovia manuscript except for Obrecht's mass, where, given the structure of the mass, I would argue that it would have been less evident to the scribe that the superius melody was being used).[75] Conversely, one can easily imagine a scribe encountering an F version, thinking "no, that's not how it goes," and changing it back to C.

The change from C to F is the most significant of the variants, resulting in a melodic contour greatly diminished in quality. No other change appears as frequently, and all others are of the seemingly casual sort readily occurring in any piece's transmission. Some of these changes, however, possibly resulted from a desire for unification with the tenor line; see below.

Aside from the C/F switch, the most widespread superius variants were as follows: (1) "ties"[76] were added or deleted in passages such as measures 1–2, 5–6, 9–10, 17–18 (the most frequent place for this kind of change, with fifteen sources tying the C), and 27–28; (2) intervals in measures 20–21 and 29 were often filled in (especially the former, with fourteen ensemble appearances, as well as the Josquin and Obrecht masses, filling in the B);[77] (3) a popular "cadential" variant appeared eleven times in measure 35;[78] (4) the final cadence, particularly open to change, circulated with seven readings: the older style under-third cadence of Paris 4379 consistently gave way to forms of the more modern leading-tone cadence.[79]

Josquin used the superius in his mass in both the Agnus (using the first phrase only) and the Credo, where it is presented four times. The internal readings of the four Credo appearances are mostly consistent; only the first laying-out of the melody in the Credo varies from the other three.[80] Aside from that, Josquin's superius differs in five places from the Paris 4379 reading. In two of these places—measure 48 and the final cadence—it shares the reading of the Casanatense 2856 version of FD9, an extremely early form of the superius. In measure 20 it fills in the line, as do many other sources, and in measure 29 it uses a reading also found in Florence 121 (FD1), Leipzig 1494 (FD2, fol. 62), FD14 (both sources), St. Gall 463 (FD2), and Munich 718 (FD1). As mentioned before, Josquin always uses the C reading in measure 13.

Obrecht uses as his superius a version identical to that of Paris 4379 except in four places: (1) measure 13, where it uses C; (2) measure 20, where it has a unique variant; (3) measure 48, where it shares a variant with the earlier version of Martini's FD9 (Casanatense 2856);[81] (4) the final cadence, where the variant also appears in FD5 (London 31922), FD8 (Segovia), FD14 (Canti C and the derivative Munich 1516), the Wolfenbüttel 78 reading of FD1, and the Zwickau 78/2 reading of FD2. Obrecht's superius thus differs from Josquin's in only three spots.

The two composers are also remarkably close in their tenor lines. Josquin uses the tenor once in his Kyrie, three times in the Gloria, and once in the final Agnus. These five appearances are remarkably consistent: only the Agnus differs when it introduces a very popular variant (tying the notes) in measures 21–22. Otherwise, Josquin's tenor reading is identical to that of Paris 4379 with two exceptions: measure 7, where it reads as a breve instead of two semibreves (a very common variant), and measure 48, where its reading is shared only by the Regensburg C120 reading for FD29 and Hans Buchner's intabulation—a striking variant also found in the Obrecht mass.

In his mass, Obrecht uses the complete tenor nine times as well as once in part. The nine appearances do not always agree with each other, nor do all the sources agree on the readings, further evidence that the song was not carved in stone. The main differences with Paris 4379 are as follows: (1) in measure 7, Obrecht always uses a breve, a very popular variant; (2) measure 21 is usually as in Paris 4379, but in Kyrie II it is tied to measure 22, also a popular variant; (3) measure 24 most often appears as in Paris 4379, but in the Osanna it uses a popular variant found in Paris 676 (FD2) and many other sources; (4) measure 27 is usually like Paris 4379, but it sometimes reads like Paris 676 and several other sources; (5) measure 29 circulates with three different readings in the Obrecht mass, all found in other sources (including Paris 4379); (6) measure 47 is sometimes tied to measure 48 in Obrecht, a very rare variant only found in FD8; (7) in measure 48 itself, Obrecht's reading matches Josquin's and the two late works cited above.

So we again have several possibilities with the Obrecht mass. He may have known more than one version of the song and used variants found therein at will as he composed the mass, or he may have introduced variants of his own into the song. Perhaps scribes, doubtless quite familiar with the song, altered its appearance in the mass to match the version that they knew. Obrecht certainly knew a version of the tenor identical to Josquin's, but he preferred to flat the E in measure 44, as noted above, and the superius lines also differ slightly between the two masses.

Regarding the tenor line in general, it has considerably fewer variants than the superius, which is striking considering that it appears in far more sources owing to its more frequent use. Senfl's settings agree almost one hundred percent of the time in their tenor readings,[82] and these readings often, though not always, are linked with those of Isaac's pieces as well as works in Germanic sources. Isaac's readings are largely unified, though not quite to the extent of Senfl's. Although Paris 4379 frequently presents the most common reading of the tenor, a number of variants that were introduced at a slightly later stage of the song's history were ultimately used more often.

Measure 7 appeared as a breve in both the Josquin and Obrecht masses and as early as the 1490s in ensemble settings. This reading was adopted by Senfl and many others,[83] and eventually it became more widespread than the two semibreves used earlier. The tie in measures 9–10 was sometimes dropped, just as with the superius line, but superius and tenor are not always in agreement in later sources about untying this note. The same is true for the opening of the imitative phrase starting in measure 17 of the superius and measure 21 of the tenor. Neither opening is apparently tied in the original; later sources often tie the superius but even more often tie the tenor here. The tied tenor note, used by Isaac and Senfl, essentially displaces the untied form as the norm. The third between measures 19–20 of the superius and measures 23–24 of the tenor is filled-in in most Isaac sources, in two Germanic ones (Frankfurt 20 [FD1] and Zwickau 78/2 [FD2]) and in London 31922 (FD5).[84]

In Paris 4379, measure 20 of the superius and measure 24 of the tenor present different readings of the supposedly imitative line. While a respectable number of later superius sources fill in the third to match the tenor, none of the tenor sources is changed to mimic the superius. Instead, more than half the sources introduce a different rhythm here, a dotted semibreve followed by two semiminims. All of the Senfl and Isaac sources, numerous Germanic sources (including the Luscinius and Buchner intabulations), Jacquet's FD30, Paris 676 (FD2), London 31922 (FD5) and sometimes Obrecht's mass use this new version. Two Germanic sources (for FD36) and London 31922 (FD5) even introduce this rhythmic variant in the corresponding superius passage (m. 20).

Superius and tenor are homorhythmic in measures 27–28 in Paris 4379; a few sources break the tie in either superius or tenor, but only Paris 676 (FD2) and Munich 718 (FD1) do it in both.[85] Measure 29, on the other hand, is another place where superius and tenor are not in parallel motion in Paris 4379. A few sources change the superius to match the tenor here, and others change the tenor to match the superius. More frequently the tenor rhythm was altered to the dotted semibreve and two semiminims used so often in measure 24 of the tenor. Again, more than half the sources use this reading, starting with FD2 in Perugia 431 and including all of Senfl's and Isaac's settings, the Luscinius and Buchner intabulations, and several others such as London 31922 (FD5) and Zwickau 78/2 (FD2). Three manuscripts (London 31922 and Zwickau 78/2 again as well as Vienna 18810 for Isaac's FD11) adopt this reading for the superius, thus providing more homorhythm.

The tenor line is frequently altered in measure 30, usually breaking the breve into two semibreves. This change occurs in almost all the Senfl sources and in two others, including St. Gall 462 (FD2); the superius line is similarly altered in two manuscripts (St. Gall 462 being one, which thus again maintains the homorhythm). Several other sources use a cadential type of motion here that occurs in Isaac's versions as well as in London 31922 (FD5), Jacquet's FD30, the independent Luscinius and Buchner intabulations, and FD19 (arguing against Staehelin's suggestion that it is by Senfl).[86]

Measure 48 is another place where the tenor usually appears in a changed version. Three sources adopt the even, descending minims that occur in the superius, creating homorhythm with that voice in two cases.[87] Most often the tenor appears as a stepwise descending line with the rhythm dotted minim–semiminim–minim–minim: almost all Senfl and Isaac sources[88] as well as several others (Frankfurt 20 [FD1], London 31922 [FD5], Jacquet's FD30, FD35, and the Luscinius intabulation) use this. Another common variant is D–C–B as dotted semibreve and two semiminims, appearing in nine sources. In two of these (Perugia 431 and Zwickau 78/2 [both FD2]), the superius adopts this rhythm as well for more homorhythm. Several other variant readings also appear at this point, including the unusual one used by Josquin and Obrecht.

With the superius and tenor, then, the changes are largely of the same kind and often, although not always, maintain imitation or homorhythm or create new instances of the latter. Yet certain passages, such as measures 29 or 48, remain more often without parallel motion. Although the superius has more alterations overall, tenor variants are more widespread, owing to the frequent use of that voice by Isaac and Senfl (in most cases, the latter was surely introduced to the variants by the former). In general, both the superius and tenor have variants that circulate frequently within Germanic sources; these often show connections as well to Jacquet's motet (surely via Isaac's Italian presence) and, curiously, the reading of FD5 in London 31922, a presumably English manuscript where the French incipit of FD5 already implies a continental link. As we will see shortly, this source also has readings related to Josquin's bassus.

Although the bassus voice appears in fewer sources than superius or tenor, it has a large number of variants, most of which appear in a single source. Of the ones that appear in multiple sources, the most common occur in measure 6 (a change to four minims) and measures 23–24 (a change to tied Cs). Measures 37 and 41 also display dotted rhythms in several sources. Perhaps most striking of the changes in the bassus are those of the final cadence. Middle C is the most common cadential pitch, but five sources replace that with the F below. One source gives the F below that as final, another gives the C an octave below middle C, and one source gives the A below middle C. Finally, Perugia 431 (FD2) gives both middle C and the F below that, providing the ultimately more fashionable F alternative early on. Contemporary musicians clearly felt free to alter the ending, as we have

xxiv

already seen in the case of the superius. Once again the trend is for modernization, with the original octave-leap cadence (suitable for its time) brought up to date by the substitution of F as the final pitch.

Josquin's bassus looks like that of Paris 4379, with four differences: (1) measures 5–6, where Josquin uses a variant found only in London 31922 (FD5); (2) measures 10–11, where Josquin ties the notes across the barline—again, as does London 31922 (FD5); (3) measures 21–22, where the long of Paris 4379 is changed to a breve–semibreve rest–breve—again, the same reading as London 31922, and one that also appears in Paris 676; (4) measure 57, where Josquin's bassus ends on an F, already given as an alternate final as early as Perugia 431.

Variants and Authenticity

Although I have already noted places where lack of agreement in cantus firmus lines can argue against an attribution, it is worth pausing to consider the trustworthiness of this method as a determinant of authenticity. This is a much more complex question than has previously been assumed. Until recently, lack of conformity between readings has been taken as a blow against authenticity. The fuller picture of variants made possible by this edition, however, shows that such a conclusion is perhaps hasty. We will briefly look at *Fortuna desperata* as used by Josquin, Isaac, and Senfl regarding this question.

For Josquin, the differences between the superius and tenor of FD8 (Segovia) and those used in his mass have been used as evidence against his authorship of FD8. Knowing what we do now, though, about the song's transmission, we can place those differences in context. The critical commentary to this work in the *New Josquin Edition* lists differences between the readings.[89] As is apparent from what I have presented here, neither the use of F as opposed to C in measure 13 of the superius melody nor the presence of a flat in the superius key signature of FD8 (which does not extend through the entire piece) can be used as separative variants for *Fortuna desperata*. Of the remaining variants, curiously, each one that appears in the superius of FD8 (with the exception of the final cadence) also appears in the superius of the reading of FD1 in Segovia. While it would be wrong to say that Segovia's scribe always copied the superius melody in exactly the same way—we can see selected differences in the superius parts of FD9 and FD10— this is nonetheless a striking point that should give us pause, especially given other similarities in the Segovia readings pointed out above. Was the scribe influenced in copying the superius of these two pieces, which of course have between them only one line's difference (unlike FD9 and 10, which have three

and four different voices respectively)? Yet at the same time, the two places where FD8's tenor differs from Josquin's[90] are not duplicated in the tenor of Segovia's FD1.[91]

Senfl is very consistent in his tenor readings: except for obvious copying errors, there are just two differences in any of the sources for his works, both in the late theoretical print 1553 Faber. In only two places does the tenor of FD19, suggested by Martin Staehelin as Senfl's,[92] diverge from Senfl's tenor, but one of these, measure 30, is a very significant spot since it aligns the reading with Isaac's tenor. Curiously, Senfl's tenor itself differs from Isaac's in three important places (mm. 23, 25, and 30).

Isaac is involved in several authenticity problems with both his superius settings and his tenor settings. FD10 has been questioned, and its superius disagrees with that of the readily accepted FD11 in eight possibly significant places (as noted above, the reading of m. 13 cannot be used as a separative variant). For the tenor settings, FD16 (*Sanctus*) cannot receive a proper comparison since it presents a paraphrased version of the melody. A comparison of FD15 and 28, on the other hand, reveals much closer but still not exact tenor readings (two differences).

At first glance, then, we would seem to want to reject FD10 as inauthentic. Let us step back briefly, however, and examine something else: the superius line of Martini's FD9 setting as it appears in Casanatense 2856 and Segovia. There are ten differences between these two readings (not including the C/F difference in m. 13), two more than found between FD10 and 11. Further, FD11 survives only in a posthumous source. Can we be sure that it presents the original form that Isaac knew, or did variants creep in over the decades? Clearly, considerable differences between readings are not necessarily damning, and we should proceed with caution as we evaluate these works.

Conclusions

Fortuna desperata, then, is a composition that underwent a fair amount of change even without taking its reworkings into account, and many of these alterations dressed the song in a more up-to-date guise. Its cleffings changed so that the bassus was easily distinguished visually from the tenor; no longer did it look like an old-fashioned work with two equal lower voices under the higher superius. The bassus came to be known specifically as that and not as a contratenor, even without the presence of an altus. Partial signatures gave way to flats in all voices, with internal flats more frequently indicated: the work generally shifted from one of potentially ambiguous harmonies to one of explicitly stated accidentals, at least in part in keeping with the overall musical shift towards greater clarification of pitch that took place in the decades after the composition of *Fortuna desperata*. While the only major melodic alteration was the substitution of F for C in measure 13 of the superius, numerous less significant ones took place in all three voices, sometimes increasing, sometimes maintaining, and sometimes decreasing the precision of imitation and frequency of homorhythm between the superius and tenor. The final cadence changed from an under-third to a leading-tone cadence and from an octave-leap to an ascending-fourth ("V-I") bassus movement.

Textual changes were dramatic, with the original poem drastically altered to the reading found in Perugia 431; the refrain was possibly changed from two lines to one, and it eventually disappeared altogether, another modernization. Partially to compensate for the loss of the refrain, later sources had a greater amount of internal textual repetition, and London 35087 underlaid all three voices, again making the song look up-to-date (and "equal-voiced") in that respect. In other words, the song was not treated as a static, untouchable entity, but rather freely altered to match prevailing tastes as the decades went by. While there is definitely a Germanic bent to many of the later variants, aided by Isaac's important role in the complex, it is difficult if not impossible to generate an accurate stemma for the song, doubtless because of the very popularity of the song and the willingness of scribes to substitute their memory of the song for what they might have had before them.

What conclusion can we draw from this study? *Fortuna desperata* was both beloved on its own and reworked again and again for purposes of symbolism, homage, sheer love of the song's sound, and other factors we will never be able to recover. The actual pitches of the song were volatile, undergoing change through the decades at the hands of composers, performers, and scribes. More than one version of each of the voices circulated, which hinders precise pinning down of its exact lines of transmission but frees us as performers in our choices of underlay, accidentals, and the exact contour of the melodic lines. By bringing this beautiful song and its fascinating derivatives together in a new edition it is hoped that modern performers and scholars will fall under the spell of this music, just as composers—and doubtless audiences as well—did so many centuries ago.

Notes on Performance

Questions of performing media are among the most important facing musicians who wish to play fifteenth- and sixteenth-century music, but they are questions for which few firm answers are known. We are aware that there was instrumental performance of music that originated as vocal, and we are beginning to experiment with vocal performance of music previously considered instrumental. Since no precise indications of instrumentation (or even the exact voices to be used) are given in the manuscripts and prints that contain this music, we can (and should) approach it with considerable freedom.

Performers should not necessarily restrict themselves to singing only what has text in this edition. Text can be added to untexted parts, or these parts can be performed vocally on a neutral syllable or perhaps even with solfege syllables. Likewise, instrumentalists can perform texted lines. What is most important is maintaining a balance among the parts; this is chamber music, with equal importance attached to each line, and one performer to a part will normally be most satisfactory. By the same token, performers will probably not go wrong with a homogenous sound reflecting this equality, although using different types of instruments or a mixture of voices and instruments seems to have been practiced as well in the fifteenth and sixteenth centuries. Certainly the borrowed melody should not be obscured, no matter what the choice of performing medium.

A similar flexibility should be maintained regarding musica ficta and text underlay, as both were flexible in their day. The ficta offered in the edition is a starting place; those tolerating less or more dissonance may wish to make some changes, especially since in some of the pieces no happy solutions to individual problems were found. Similarly, the text underlay fits the music closely in some works and less well in others. With the original song and its si placet settings, the variety in ligature use among the different sources virtually guarantees that different performances took place back then, and we should likewise feel free to experiment.

Recent overviews of current thought on the problems of ficta and underlay (as well as much more about the performance of music of this time) can be found in *Companion to Medieval and Renaissance Music*, ed. Tess Knighton and David Fallows (London: J.M. Dent, 1992; reprint edition, Berkeley: University of California Press, 1997); another important guide to performing early music is *Performance Practice: Music Before 1600*, ed. Howard Mayer Brown and Stanley Sadie (New York and London: W.W. Norton, 1989).

Appendix

Fortuna desperata Chronology

Complete library sigla and references for the dating and provenance of the manuscripts and prints are given in the critical report. FD numbers refer to the number of the piece in this edition. Roman type is used for entries under the earliest date associated with each piece; usually that coincides with the work's earliest surviving source. Italic entries indicate later sources for pieces. Attributions and headings or incipits are given as they appear in the sources. (F) or (C) indicates the pitch of the superius line at measure 13 of the original setting or its equivalent for those versions that use the superius. (E) or (E♭) readings refer to the pitch in the bassus line at measure 54 of the original setting or its equivalent; sources for the Josquin mass contain a reference for each of the two appearances of the transposed cantus firmus, i.e., the E or E♭ references actually indicate whether the Josquin source has B or B♭.

TABLE 3
The Chronology of the *Fortuna desperata* Settings

	Manuscript, Print, or Event	*Fortuna desperata* Settings and Related Material
1470	Paris 4379 (ca. 1470–85; probably Naples, possibly Rome)	FD1/FD2 (F): original version *a 3* (*Fortuna disperata*) to which the si placet altus of FD2 was added later to make a setting *a 4*. No attribution. (E)
1475	Death of Ser Felice di Giovanni Martini in Florence (between 26 June and 14 August 1478)	Possible *terminus ante quem* for original composition, most common si placet voice (FD2), or FD7.
	Casanatense 2856 (ca. 1479–81; Ferrara)	FD9 (C): superius cantus firmus setting *a 4* (*Fortuna disperata*). Attribution: Jo[hannes] martini (ca. 1440–97/98).
1480	Perugia 431 (1480–90, probably ca. 1485; Naples or vicinity)	*FD1 (F): original version a 3 (Fortuna desperata), crossed out. No attribution. (E)*
		FD2 (F): si placet setting a 4 (Fortuna desperata). No attribution. (E)
	1484: Isaac arrives in Florence	
1485	*Iesus. Laude facte* (1486; Florence)	lauda text:[a] *PO chi tebbi nel core* "Cantasi come Fortuna disperata." Attribution: Francesco d'Albizo.
	Before Obrecht mass (Naples? Ferrara? before 1487–88?)[b]	mass *a 4* (C) by Josquin des Prez (?–1521)
	Obrecht in Italy (1487–88)	mass *a 4* (C) by Jacob Obrecht (1457/58–1505) written then? (Ferrara?)
	London 16439 (between autumn 1487 and 25 March 1488? Florence)	original text of *Fortuna disperata*
	Berlin 40021 (mass paper 1489–93; Germany)	Obrecht mass *a 4* (C): [Missa] O Fortuna. No attribution. First surviving source.
1490	Bologna Q16 (1490s; probably Naples or Rome)	FD3 (C): si placet setting *a 4* (*Fortuna disperata/desperata*). No attribution. (E)

xxvii

Table 3 continued
The Chronology of the *Fortuna desperata* Settings

	Manuscript, Print, or Event	*Fortuna desperata* Settings and Related Material
	Leipzig 1494 (ca. 1490–1504; possibly Leipzig)	FD2 (C): si placet setting *a 4* (*Fortuna / Virginis alme parens*). No attribution. (E)
		FD2 (F): si placet setting *a 4* (*Ave stella fulgida*). Superius and altus only. No attribution.
	1491: Agricola returns to Florence	
	C.G. XIII.27 (1492–94; Florence)	FD2/FD7 (F): si placet setting *a 4* (FD2) with additional voice that forms replacement contratenor setting *a 3* (FD7) (*Fortuna desperata*). Attribution: felice (d. 1478?). (E) Possibly posthumous first surviving source for FD7.
		FD15: tenor cantus firmus setting *a 3*; original tenor in superius, transposed up a fifth (*Fortuna desperata*). Attribution: Ysach (ca. 1450–1517)
	C.S. 41 (ca. 1492–95; Rome)	Josquin mass *a 4* (C): [*Missa*] *fortune desperata*. Attribution: Josquin des pres. First surviving source. (E♭/E♭)
1495	*Laude facte* (1496? Florence?)	lauda text: *PO chi tebbi nel core* "Cantasi come Fortuna disperata"
	Segovia (northern repertoire probably pre-1497; Spain)	FD1 (F): original version *a 3* (*Fortuna desperata*). Attribution: Anthonius busnoys (ca. 1430–92). (E)
		FD8 (F): replacement contratenor setting *a 3* (*Fortuna disperata*). Attribution: Josquin du pres.
		FD9 (F): superius cantus firmus setting *a 4* (*Fortuna disperata*) Attribution: ysaac; but by Martini.
		FD10 (F): superius cantus firmus setting *a 5* (*Fortuna disperata / Sancte petre / Ora pro nobis*). Attribution: ysaac.
		Obrecht mass *a 4* (C): [*Missa*] *Fortuna disperata*. Attribution: Iacobus hobrecht.
	Bologna Q17 (post-1497 and possibly post-1500; northern Italy, probably Florence or vicinity)	FD16: Sanctus *a 4*; uses tenor paraphrased in tempus perfectum. Attribution: ysac.
	Barcelona 5 (late 15th century; place of origin unknown)	Josquin mass *a 4* (C). Without title or attribution. (E♭/E♭)
	Pesaro 1144 (pre-1500? Venice?)	?FD1 (C): very free lute intabulation of superius? (*Fortuna*). No attribution.
		FD1 (C): free lute intabulation of original ([*for*]*tuna displ[erata]*). No attribution. (E♭?)
1500	Frankfurt 20 (ca. 1500; Frankfurt?)	FD1 (F): original version *a 3* (*Fortuna desperata / O panis vite*). Superius and tenor only. No attribution.
	Florence Pan. 27 (early 16th century; northern Italy, probably Mantua)	FD4 (C): si placet setting *a 4* (*Fortuna desperata / Poi che te hebi nel core*). No attribution. (E)
	Tarazona 3 (early 16th century; probably Seville)	Periquin mass *a 4*: *Missa Fortuna disperata*. Attribution: Periquin (?Pierre de la Rue, ca. 1452–1518).
	Basel F.X.10 (ca. 1500–1510; Basel)	FD2?: si placet setting *a 4* (*Fortüna*). Bassus only. No attribution. (E)
	Paris 676 (1502; Ferrara or Mantua)	FD2 (C): si placet setting *a 4* (*Fortuna desperata*). No attribution. (E♭)
	1502 Petrucci (1502; Venice)	Josquin mass *a 4* (C): [*Missa*] *Fortuna desperata*. In print *Misse Josquin*. (E/E♭)

Table 3 continued
The Chronology of the *Fortuna desperata* Settings

	Manuscript, Print, or Event	*Fortuna desperata* Settings and Related Material
	Bologna Q18 (ca. 1502–6; Bologna)	FD12 (C): superius cantus firmus setting *a* 4 (Fortuna disperata). No attribution.
	1503 Petrucci (1503; Venice)	Obrecht mass *a* 4 (C): [Missa] Fortuna desperata. In print *Misse Obreht*.
	Canti C (1504; Venice)	FD2 (F): si placet setting *a* 4 (Fortuna desperata). No attribution. (E) FD14 (C): superius cantus firmus setting; original superius in bassus, transposed down an eleventh (Fortuna desperata). Attribution: Jo[hannes] Pinarol (fl. 1504).
1505	Wolfenbüttel 78 (ca. 1505; probably southern Germany)	FD1 (F): original version *a* 3. No text or attribution. (E)
	Paris 27 (ca. 1505; Venice?)	FD1 (F): lute intabulation of original superius; lower voices extremely free (Fortuna desperata). No attribution. (E♭)
	Modena M.1.2 (ca. 1505; Ferrara)	Josquin mass *a* 4 (C): [Missa] fortuna desperata. Attribution: Iosquin. (E♭/E♭) Obrecht mass *a* 4 (C): without title. Attribution: Ia. Hobreth.
	Florence 2439 (ca. 1505–8; Habsburg-Burgundian court scriptorium)	Obrecht mass *a* 4, excerpts only: Kyrie II, Sanctus, Osanna; each title is "Fortuna." Each attribution: Hobrecht.
	Augsburg 142a (1505–14; Augsburg)	FD6 (C): triple si placet setting *a* 6 (Fortuna desperata). Attribution: Allexannderr A (Alexander Agricola, ca. 1446–1506). Possibly posthumous first surviving source. (E♭)
	Cape Town Grey (pre-1506; northern Italy)	FD2 (F): si placet setting *a* 4 (Poi che t'hebi nel core). No attribution. (E)
	Munich 3154 (1506/7; probably Innsbruck, possibly Augsburg)	Josquin mass *a* 4 (C). No title or attribution. (E♭/E♭)
	1507[6] (1507; Venice)	FD1 (C): intabulation for two lutes of original version, transposed up a fourth (Fortuna desperata). Attribution for transcription: Francesco Spinacino (fl. 1507). (E♭)
	London 35087 (pre-1509; Bruges?)	FD1 (C): original version *a* 3 (Fortuna desperata). No attribution. (E♭)
1510	Florence 121 (ca. 1510; Florence)	FD1 (C): original version *a* 3 (Fortuna desperata). No attribution. (E) FD15: tenor cantus firmus setting *a* 3; original tenor in superius transposed up a fifth. No text or attribution, but by Isaac.
	1510 Obrecht (ca. 1510; Basel)	Obrecht mass *a* 4 (C): Missa super Fortuna desperata. Attribution: Ja. Obrecht.
	St. Gall 462 (1510, with additions to 1530; Paris, with additions in Glarus)	FD2 (C): si placet setting *a* 4 (Fortuna desperata quae te dementia vertit). No attribution. (E) FD17: setting *a* 4; original tenor paraphrased in tenor, transposed down a fourth (Fortuna desperata). No attribution.

TABLE 3 continued
The Chronology of the *Fortuna desperata* Settings

	Manuscript, Print, or Event	*Fortuna desperata* Settings and Related Material
	Florence 107 (1510–13; Florence)	Obrecht mass *a 4*, excerpts only: *Christe,*[c] *Pleni,*[c] *Benedictus,*[c] *Agnus II.*[c] No attribution.
	London 31922 (ca. 1510–20; probably London)	FD5 (C): si placet setting *a 4* (*Fortune esperee*). No attribution. (E, but E♭ in altus)
	St. Gall 464 (ca. 1510–20; possibly Basel)	FD36 (C): superius cantus firmus setting *a 6* (*Fortuna*). Superius and bassus only. Attribution: Robertus Fabri (?–?)
	Wrocław 428 (ca. 1510–30 and perhaps ca. 1516; possibly Frankfurt an der Oder or vicinity)	FD18: tenor cantus firmus setting *a 4* (*Esurientes implevit bonis*). No attribution.
	Opera nova (1512; Venice)	Lauda text: *PO chi thebbi nel core* "Cantasi come Fortuna disperata"
	St. Gall 530 (ca. 1512–21; Konstanz)	FD29: keyboard intabulation of tenor in mi cantus firmus setting (*Fortuna in mi*). Attribution for transcription: Maister Hansen Buchnerus (1485–1538). Obrecht mass *a 4* (excerpt only: *Benedictus*[c]): "Imprepel frantaz sequitur." No attribution.
	Basel F.IX.22 (1513 [prima pars] and 1515 [secunda pars]; Basel and/or Freiburg)	FD28: keyboard intabulation of tenor in mi cantus firmus setting (*Fortuna in mi*). Prima and secunda partes presented separately. Attribution: Isac (prima pars only).
	Florence 196 (after 24 June 1514)	Lauda text: *Poi ch'io t'ebbi nel core*[d]
1515	Vatican 11953 (ca. 1515–16; court of Maximilian I)	FD19: tenor cantus firmus setting *a 5* (*O crux ave*). Bassus only. No attribution.
	Uppsala 76b (ca. 1515–35; France, possibly Troyes or vicinity)	Josquin mass *a 4* (C). No title or attribution. (E/E)
	1516 Petrucci (1516; Venice)	Josquin mass *a 4* (C): [Missa] *Fortuna desperata* in *Liber primus Missarum Josquin*. (E♭/E)
	Before death of Isaac (1517)	FD11 (C): superius cantus firmus setting *a 4* (*Fortuna / Bruder Conrat*) by Isaac.
	Bologna Q19 (ca. 1518; northern Italy)	FD30: tenor in mi cantus firmus setting *a 5* (*Ave mater matris dei / Fortuna disperata*). Attribution: Jachet (1483–1559).
	Regensburg C120, first part (ca. 1518–19; court of Maximilian I, Innsbruck?)	FD19: tenor cantus firmus setting *a 5* (*O crux ave / Fortuna*). No attribution.
	Cortona/Paris (ca. 1519–23; Florence)	FD13 (F): superius cantus firmus setting *a 4* (*Fortuna disperata*). Superius, altus, and tenor only. No attribution.
1520	Florence 164–67 (ca. 1520; Florence)	FD13 (F): superius cantus firmus setting *a 4* (*Fortuna disperata zibaldone*). No attribution.
	Florence 337 (ca. 1520; probably Florence)	FD13: superius cantus firmus setting *a 4* ([F]*Ortuna desperata*). Bassus only. No attribution.
	Regensburg C120, second part (ca. 1520–21; southern Germany, possibly Augsburg)	FD29: tenor in mi cantus firmus setting *a 4* (*Fortuna desperata*). No attribution.
	Berlin 40026 (ca. 1520–24; Pforzheim)	FD1 (C): florid keyboard intabulation of original, transposed down a fourth (*Fortuna in ut*). Attribution: H[ans] B[uchner]. (E♭)

TABLE 3 continued
The Chronology of the *Fortuna desperata* Settings

	Manuscript, Print, or Event	*Fortuna desperata* Settings and Related Material
		FD2 (F): keyboard intabulation of si placet setting (*Fortuna quatuor in fa*). No attribution.
		FD28: keyboard intabulation of tenor in mi cantus firmus setting (*Fortuna in mi*). Secunda pars only. No attribution, but by Isaac.
		Keyboard intabulation of unknown tenor cantus firmus setting *a 3*; original tenor in lowest voice (*Fortuna in fa*). Attribution: M[agister] O[thmar] N[achtigall] (= Luscinius [ca. 1478/80–1537]).
		Keyboard intabulation of unknown tenor cantus firmus setting *a 3*; original tenor in lowest voice (*Fortuna in fa*). Attribution: H[ans] B[uchner] (1483–1538).
	Modena IV (ca. 1520–30; probably Modena)	*Je pris amors* setting *a 4*; contains brief quote of a superius/tenor motive from *Fortuna desperata*.[e] No attribution.
	Vienna 11778 (1521–34 and probably ca. 1521–25; Habsburg-Burgundian court scriptorium)	Josquin mass *a 4 (C)*: *Missa Fortuna desperata*. Attribution: Josquin. (E/E♭)
	Vienna 18746 (1523; Habsburg-Burgundian court scriptorium)	*FD31*: tenor in mi cantus firmus setting *a 5* (*Consideres mes incessantes plaintes / Fortuna desperata*). No attribution.
	Munich 718 (1523–24; Ingolstadt?)	*FD1 (C)*: intabulation of original for viols *a 3* (*Fortuna*). No attribution. (E)
1525	Bologna A38 (ca. 1525; Bologna)	anonymous mass I *a 4* (*Missa de fortuna Disperata*)
	1526 Giunta (1526; Rome)	Josquin mass *a 4 (C)*: [*Missa*] *Fortuna desperata* in *Liber primus Missarum Josquin*. (E/E)
	Munich 328–31 (by 1527; probably Augsburg)	*FD29*: tenor in mi cantus firmus setting *a 4* (*Fortuna*). Superius, tenor, and bassus only. No attribution.
		FD35: tenor cantus firmus setting *a 4*? (*Fortuna*). Superius, tenor, and bassus only. No attribution.
1530	Zwickau 78/2 (1531; probably Zwickau)	*FD2 (C)*: si placet setting *a 4*. No text or attribution. (E)
	1531[5] (1531; Paris)	*FD1 (C)*: keyboard intabulation of original (*Fortuna desperata*). No attribution. (E)
	Vienna 18810 (by 1533; Augsburg or Munich)	FD11 (C): superius cantus firmus setting *a 4* (*Fortuna / Bruder Conrat*). Attribution: henricus ÿsaac. Posthumous first surviving source.
		FD20: tenor cantus firmus setting *a 5* (*Ich stund an ainnem morgen / Fortuna*). Attribution: Ludovicus Sennfl (ca. 1486–1542/43).
		FD23: tenor cantus firmus setting *a 5* (*Virgo prudentissima / Fortuna*). Attribution: Ludovicus Sennfl.
		FD24: tenor cantus firmus setting *a 5* (*Helena desiderio plena / Fortuna*). Attribution: Ludovicus Sennfl.
		FD25: tenor cantus firmus setting *a 5* (*Nasci, pati, mori / Fortuna*). Attribution: Ludovicus Sennfl.
	1534[17] (1534; Nuremberg)	FD20: tenor cantus firmus setting *a 5* (*Ich stund an einem morgen / Fortuna*). Attribution: Ludovicus Senfflius.
		FD21: tenor cantus firmus setting *a 5* (*Es taget vor dem Walde / Fortuna*). Attribution: Ludovicus Senfflius.

TABLE 3 continued
The Chronology of the *Fortuna desperata* Settings

	Manuscript, Print, or Event	*Fortuna desperata* Settings and Related Material
		FD22: tenor cantus firmus setting *a 5* (*Herr durch dein Blut / Fortuna*). Attribution: Ludovicus Senfflius.
		FD26: tenor cantus firmus setting *a 4* (*Fortuna ad voces musicales*). Attribution: Ludovicus Senfflius.
		FD33: setting *a 4*; draws on tenor in mi (*Fortuna*). Attribution: Guiliel. Breitteng[raser] (ca. 1495–1542)
1535	Zwickau 78/3 (ca. 1535–45; probably Zwickau)	FD28: tenor in mi cantus firmus setting *a 3* (*Fortuna*). No attribution, but by Isaac. First ensemble appearance.
	1537 Heyden (1537; Nuremberg)[f]	*FD26: tenor cantus firmus setting a 4 (Fortuna ad voces musicales).* Attribution: Ludovici Senflij.
	TVC (1538; Nuremberg)	*FD28: tenor in mi cantus firmus setting a 3* (handwritten addition: *Fortuna desperata*). Secunda pars only. Attribution: H. Isac (handwritten addition).
		Josquin mass a 4, excerpt only: Pleni.[c] No text or attribution.
		Obrecht mass a 4, excerpt only: Pleni.[c] No text or attribution.
	1539[1] (1539; Nuremberg)	*Josquin mass a 4 (C): [Missa] Super Fortuna Desperata.* Attribution: Iosquin. (E/E)
	1539[2] (1539; Nuremberg)	*Josquin mass a 4 (C): [Missa] Fortuna.* Attribution: Iosquin. (E/E♭)
1540	1540 Heyden (1540; Nuremberg)[f]	*FD26: tenor cantus firmus setting a 4 (Fortuna ad voces Musicales).* Attribution: Ludovici Senflij.
	1540 Vaena (1540; Lisbon)	*Josquin mass a 4, excerpt only: keyboard intabulation of Beneditus qui venit.*[c] No text. Attribution: Jusquin.
	Munich 1516 (ca. 1540; probably Augsburg)	*FD14 (C): superius cantus firmus setting a 4; original superius in bassus, transposed down an eleventh (Fortuna desperata).* No attribution, but by Pinarol.
	Montserrat 765 (ca. 1540; Brussels)	Requiem mass *a 4* by Benedictus Appenzeller (ca. 1480/88–after 1558)[g]
	St. Gall 463 (ca. 1540 or slightly later; Glarus or vicinity)	*FD2 (C): si placet setting a 4 (Fortuna desperata quae te dementia cepit;* Index: *Fortuna desperata antiquum).* Superius and altus only. No attribution.
		FD34: setting *a 3*; probably tenor cantus firmus setting (*Fortuna desperata quae te dementia coepit*). Superius only. No attribution.
		FD36 (C): superius cantus firmus setting a 6 (Fortuna desperata quae te dementia vertit). Superius, altus, and vagans only. Attribution: Robertus Fabri (?–?).
1545	Herdringen 9821 (ca. 1545–50?; probably Germany)	anonymous mass II *a 4*: *Missa Fortuna*. Based on tenor in mi; Kyrie and Sanctus only.
	1547 Glarean (1547; Basel)[f]	*FD26: tenor cantus firmus setting a 4 (Fortuna ad voces Musicalis).* Attribution: Litavico Senflio Tigurino.
		Josquin mass a 4, excerpt only: Agnus. Attribution: Iodoco Prat.
1550	Before death of Greiter (1550)	FD27: tenor cantus firmus setting *a 4* (*Passibus ambiguis*) by Greiter.

TABLE 3 continued
The Chronology of the *Fortuna desperata* Settings

	Manuscript, Print, or Event	*Fortuna desperata* Settings and Related Material
	1552[35] (1552; Salamanca)	*Josquin mass a 4, excerpts only: intabulation for vihuela of Benedictus*[c] *and Pleni.*[c] *No texts. Title for Benedictus: Missa de fortuna desesperata. Attribution for both excerpts: Iusquin.*
	1553 Faber (1553, Basel)[f]	*FD26: tenor cantus firmus setting a 4 (Aliud vocum exercitium ad Fortunam). Attribution: Ludovico Senfflio.* *FD27: tenor cantus firmus setting a 4 (Passibus ambiguis). Attribution: Matthaeo Greitero (ca. 1495–1550). Posthumous first surviving source.*
	1554[9] (1554; Antwerp)	FD32: tenor in mi cantus firmus setting *a 5 (Anima mea liquefacta est / AMica mea Fortuna desperata)*. Attribution: Cabbiliau (ca. 1518–?).
	1554 Zanger (1554; Leipzig)[f]	*Josquin mass a 4, excerpt only: Christe (Exemplum augmentationis Iosquini ex Misse, Fortuna). No text.*
1555		
1560	Stuttgart 26 (ca. 1560; Bavaria)[f]	*Josquin mass a 4, excerpt only: Kyrie I (Exemplum alterationis Josquini fortuna).*
	1563 Wilphlingseder (1563; Nuremberg)[f]	*Josquin mass a 4, excerpt only: Agnus I. Incipits in tenor and bassus only; otherwise no text. Attribution: Iodoci Pratensis.*

[a]This table includes all lauda sources that contain *cantasi come* indications for *Fortuna desperata*. The following sources for the lauda text may or may not have such an indication and are not included in the table: according to A. Feist, "Mitteilungen aus älteren Sammlungen italienischer geistlichen Lieder," *Zeitschrift für romanische Philologie* 13 (1889): 115–85, (1) Venice, Biblioteca Nazionale Marciana, MS 78; (2) Munich, Bayerische Staatsbibliothek, MS it. 240; (3) *Laude devote composte da diverse persone spirituali* (Venice, 1556); (4) *Libro di Laude* of uncertain date [Feist's Item E, p. 117]; and according to Lodovico Frati, "Giunte agli 'Inizii di antiche poesie italiane religiose e morali' a cura di Annibale Tenneroni," *Archivum Romanicum* 2 (1918): 185–207, 325–43, esp. 342, (5) [no library given], MS Gambalunghiano 206 D IV, p. 29.

[b]The dating and provenance of Josquin's and Obrecht's masses remain uncertain. Josquin may have been in both Ferrara and Naples in the early 1480s; see Edward E. Lowinsky, "Ascanio Sforza's Life: A Key to Josquin's Biography and an Aid to a Chronology of His Works," in idem, ed., *Josquin de Prez: Proceedings of the International Josquin Festival Conference* (London, New York, and Toronto: Oxford University Press, 1976), 33–76; reprinted in idem, *Music in the Culture of the Renaissance and Other Essays*, ed. Bonnie J. Blackburn (Chicago and London: University of Chicago Press, 1989), 541–64. My sources for information on the Obrecht and Josquin masses, including the dates of their sources, are the editions by Barton Hudson; see Jacob Obrecht, *Collected Works*, New Obrecht Edition, ed. Chris Maas, vol. 4, *Missa De tous biens playne; Missa Fors seulement; Missa Fortuna desperata*, ed. Barton Hudson (Utrecht: Vereniging voor Nederlandse Muziekgeschiedenis, 1986); and Josquin des Prez, *The Collected Works of Josquin des Prez*, New Josquin Edition, Critical Commentary to vol. 8, *Masses Based on Secular Polyphonic Songs: Missa Faysant regretz, Missa Fortuna desperata*, ed. Barton Hudson (Utrecht: Vereniging voor Nederlandse Muziekgeschiedenis, 1996).

[c]Not a cantus firmus section.

[d]According to Giulio Cattin, the *cantasi come* is "Fortuna desperata." See idem, "I 'Cantasi come' in una stampa di laude della Biblioteca riccardiana (Ed. r. 196)," *Quadrivium* 19, no. 2 (1978): 38.

[e]See the introduction for more information on this work.

[f]Theoretical treatise.

[g]Information from David Fallows, *A Catalogue of Polyphonic Songs, 1415–1480* (Oxford: Oxford University Press, 1999), 520.

Notes

1. *Fortuna desperata* is frequently (and incorrectly) described as a chanson and is then criticized for not looking like one. For further discussion of this issue see Honey Meconi, "Poliziano, *Primavera*, and Perugia 431: New Light on *Fortuna desperata*," in *Antoine Busnoys: Method, Meaning, and Context in Late Medieval Music*, ed. Paula Higgins (Oxford: Clarendon Press; New York: Oxford University Press, 1999), 486.

2. See Honey Meconi, "Art-Song Reworkings: An Overview," *Journal of the Royal Musical Association* 119 (1994): 1–42.

3. The best modern edition of the mass by Obrecht can be found in Jacob Obrecht, *Collected Works*, New Obrecht Edition, ed. Chris Maas, vol. 4, *Missa De tous biens playne; Missa Fors seulement; Missa Fortuna desperata*, ed. Barton Hudson (Utrecht: Vereniging voor Nederlandse Muziekgeschiedenis, 1986), 49–91. For Josquin, see Josquin des Prez, *The Collected Works of Josquin des Prez*, New Josquin Edition, vol. 8, *Masses Based on Secular Polyphonic Songs: Missa Faysant regretz, Missa Fortuna desperata*, ed. Barton Hudson (Utrecht: Vereniging voor Nederlandse Muziekgeschiedenis, 1995), 31–69. None of the other four masses has been edited; they are found respectively in Montserrat 765, Tarazona 3, Bologna A38, and Herdringen 9821. (Source sigla are identified in the critical report.) All masses are for four voices; the Bologna A38 mass expands to five voices in the Credo, and only the Kyrie and Sanctus survive for the Herdringen 9821 mass. For a succinct summary of the Josquin and Obrecht masses, see M. Jennifer Bloxam, "Masses Based on Polyphonic Songs and Canonic Masses," in *The Josquin Companion*, ed. Richard Sherr (Oxford: Oxford University Press, in press), 151–209. I am grateful to Professor Bloxam for kindly sharing a copy of her essay prior to its publication. On the Periquin mass, see Kenneth Kreitner, "Franco-Flemish Elements in Tarazona 2 and 3," *Revista de musicología* 16 (1993): 2567–86.

4. An intabulation attributed to Othmar Luscinius is in Berlin 40026, fols. 133v–135. A setting ascribed to HB (Hans Buchner) is in the same tablature, fols. 135v–136v. Modern editions of these can be found in *Die Orgeltabulatur des Leonhard Kleber*, 2 vols., ed. Karin Berg-Kotterba, Das Erbe deutscher Musik, vols. 91–92 (Frankfurt: Henry Litolff, 1987), 2:64–67 and 2:67–70, respectively. Both works are three-voice tenor cantus firmus settings, with the original tenor transposed down an octave and appearing in the lowest voice. The Luscinius work is specifically labeled "tenor pedaliter," instructing the performer to play the melody on the pedals; the Buchner setting is simply labeled "Tenor in Basso."

5. A modern edition is in *J'ay pris amours: Twenty-Eight Settings in Two, Three, and Four Parts*, ed. Richard Taruskin, Ogni Sorte Editions, RS 5 (Miami: Ogni Sorte, 1982), 45–47; see his comments on page 4. The quotation appears in the superius, measures 6–7; the borrowed material is the imitative motive of the original version (superius, mm. 17–21; tenor, mm. 21–25).

6. I use this term for the lowest voice of the original composition.

7. See the recent article by Martin Picker, "Henricus Isaac and *Fortuna desperata*," in *Antoine Busnoys*, 431–45.

8. As we shall see, there are rough chronological implications to this arrangement, with earlier settings tending to appear earlier in the edition.

9. FD numbers refer to the numbers assigned to the pieces in this edition.

10. In the case of missing partbooks (e.g., Basel F.X.10) and intabulations, it is often difficult to tell exactly what setting of *Fortuna desperata* is transmitted in a given source. Neither the Josquin nor the Obrecht mass always circulated in complete form; a variety of individual sections were transmitted as well.

11. The only other triple si placet setting currently known is one for *O rosa bella*, which has been edited in John Dunstable, *Complete Works*, 2d, rev. ed., prepared by Margaret Bent, Ian Bent, and Brian Trowell, Musica Britannica, vol. 8 (Royal Musical Association and American Musicological Society; London: Stainer and Bell, 1970), 133–34.

12. Although I refer throughout to the lowest voice of the original setting as the bassus, the name it eventually came to be called, settings that replace this voice are designated "replacement contratenor settings," as is usual in the scholarly literature.

13. These techniques are used frequently in other replacement contratenor settings of the time; see, for example, the settings in *J'ay pris amours: Twenty-Eight Settings*, 10–13.

14. See Meconi, "Art-Song Reworkings," 26–36.

15. See ibid., 4–5.

16. Duple meter is retained in all but one case (FD16).

17. See FD9, 10, 11, etc.

18. I bring up this point since most discussions of the work focus on the symbolic treatment of the material and overlook the fact that precisely the same techniques are used in non–*Fortuna desperata* pieces. While composers may indeed have intended symbolic interpretations, they still took care to satisfy purely musical and generic expectations. On art-song reworkings in general, see Meconi, "Art-Song Reworkings."

19. In addition to these ensemble settings, the Herdringen 9821 anonymous mass is based on "Fortuna in mi".

20. Two scholars who emphasize the symbolic function of Fortune discuss theoretical and symbolic aspects of the Phrygian transposition; see Julie E. Cumming, "The Goddess Fortuna Revisited," *Current Musicology* 30 (1980): 7–23; and Alfred Loeffler, "Fortuna desperata: A Contribution to the Study of Musical Symbolism in the Renaissance," *Student Musicologists at Minnesota* 3 (1968–69): 1–30. The frequency of transposition varied considerably within different families of art-song reworkings. *Fors seulement* has twenty works using transposition, *J'ay pris amours* has eight, and *De tous biens plaine* has only three. No matter what family, Phrygian was not a popular choice for transposition.

21. This is, of course, the same technique Josquin uses in the Qui tollis of his very widely circulated mass. Given that the mass was copied at the Habsburg-Burgundian scriptorium around the same time as FD31 and that the composer of FD32 worked for the court, the structural similarity of these later works hardly seems coincidental.

22. The sources containing these pieces are closely related. St. Gall 462 has the *Fortuna desperata* version in it with the contrafact text; compiled in Paris and owned by Johannes Heer, it was later taken to Glarus when Heer returned home. Glarus was also the home of Heer's friend Aegidius Tschudi, owner

and compiler of St. Gall 463, which contains the other FD2 contrafact with this text as well as FD34 and 36. Only St. Gall 464, which contains FD36, stands slightly outside this circle; it was acquired by Tschudi, but copied outside of Glarus, probably in Basel. Significantly, here FD36 contains only the incipit "Fortuna" and no other text.

23. The fourteen works appearing in more than one source are the original version FD1 and the most common si placet version FD2, Martini's superius cantus firmus setting FD9, the Florentine zibaldone setting FD13, Pinarol's superius cantus firmus setting FD14 (the Munich 1516 version is copied directly from the Canti C version), an Isaac tenor cantus firmus setting (FD15), the anonymous *O crux ave / Fortuna* (FD19), Senfl's *Ich stund an einem Morgen / Fortuna* (FD20), his *Fortuna ad voces musicales* (FD26; later copies are all in theoretical treatises), Isaac's two-part "Fortuna in mi" work (FD28), an anonymous "Fortuna in mi" setting (FD29), Fabri's six-voice superius cantus firmus setting (FD36), and the Josquin and Obrecht masses.

24. This work appears in an unusually large number of sources for an Obrecht mass.

25. See Meconi, "Poliziano, *Primavera*, and Perugia 431."

26. Almost all scholars, including myself, have equated "Felice" with Ser Felice di Giovanni Martini, who died in Florence between 26 June and 14 August 1478. If this identification is correct, then at least some part of *Fortuna desperata* was written before 14 August 1478 at the latest. Whether this part is the original song, the most popular si placet altus, or the replacement contratenor that survives only in C.G. XIII.27 is impossible to determine. In any event, David Fallows (personal communications of 22 December 1994 and 15 January 1995) has cautioned that the identification of the attribution with the earlier musician is not ironclad.

27. Discussed in Meconi, "Poliziano, *Primavera*, and Perugia 431."

28. See Lewis Lockwood, "Music at Florence and Ferrara in the Late Fifteenth Century: Rivalry and Interdependence," in *La musica a Firenze al tempo di Lorenzo il Magnifico: Congresso internazionale di studi, Firenze . . . 1992*, ed. Piero Gargiulo, Quaderni della Rivista italiana di musicologia, no. 30 (Florence: Leo S. Olschki, 1993), 1–13; and Allan W. Atlas, "Aragonese Naples and Medicean Florence: Musical Interrelationships and Influence in the Late Fifteenth Century," ibid., 15–45.

29. On a possible Neapolitan textual influence, see Meconi, "Poliziano, *Primavera*, and Perugia 431," 469.

30. It is possible that the scribe was working from a texted exemplar but had not gotten around to adding the text before abandoning this version.

31. The placement of the voices, however, is very strange here: the superius and tenor are on the left side of the opening, as expected, but the bassus is above the altus on the right side. Was the scribe working from an exemplar on which the altus voice was itself a later addition? The opening also contains the indication "In ciascum parte e data fortuna desperata etc" (in each part is given fortuna desperata etc.); see plate 2. This suggests that the scribe was working from a completely (and apparently more traditionally) texted exemplar.

32. If the composer "Felice" associated with FD7 is the same person as "Felice di Giovanni Martini," would that connect him to Johannes Martini, providing another Florence-Ferrara connection? Picker also brings up this point in "Henricus Isaac and *Fortuna desperata*," 435.

33. The most recent information on the manuscript is summarized in Lockwood, "Music at Florence and Ferrara," 10–13.

34. Bloxam makes the enticing suggestion that the mass might be connected to the annual Ferrarese *ventura* (search for fortune), instituted by Ercole I d'Este and held since 1473; see "Masses Based on Polyphonic Songs," 171–72. Curiously, Pietro Aaron (*Libri tres de institutione harmonica*, fol. 39v) says he knew Isaac, Agricola, Josquin, and Obrecht in Florence; perhaps the last two were there at one point. As Bonnie Blackburn has pointed out (private communication), Aaron is writing while Isaac and Josquin are still alive; would he have taken liberties with the truth? On Aaron's biography, see *A Correspondence of Renaissance Musicians*, ed. Bonnie J. Blackburn, Edward E. Lowinsky, and Clement A. Miller (Oxford: Clarendon Press; New York: Oxford University Press, 1991), 74–100.

35. All but the lauda text were published by Petrucci.

36. Derivative settings of *Fortuna desperata* in Germanic lands are usually tenor cantus firmus works in the German tenorlied tradition.

37. On Isaac's settings, see Picker, "Henricus Isaac and *Fortuna desperata*."

38. Isaac also set a mass on this chant as well as a six-voice motet, the latter using a paraphrased text. Senfl also wrote his own separate motet setting on this chant.

39. The unexplained dates incorporated into three of his settings (FD23–25) may be symbolic or may refer to a specific commission or some other kind of patron interaction; we cannot draw any firm conclusions without more information.

40. See Meconi, "Art-Song Reworkings," 15–16. Working independently, Emilio Ros-Fábregas also argued for an early date for the northern repertoire, with Prince Juan (Marguerite of Austria's future husband) as one of the most likely candidates for ownership; see idem, "The Manuscript Barcelona, Biblioteca de Catalunya, M.454: Study and Edition in the Context of the Iberian and Continental Manuscript Traditions," 2 vols. (Ph.D. diss., City University of New York, 1992), 1:206–23. Joshua Rifkin's attempt to discredit a possible Habsburg-Burgundian connection for Segovia is based on misunderstandings of the repertoire of the Habsburg-Burgundian court manuscripts as well as La Rue's position therein; see idem, "Busnoys and Italy," in *Antoine Busnoys*, 524–27.

41. Rifkin, "Busnoys and Italy," 532 n. 114 brings up the very interesting possibility that Obrecht brought the song north with him when he returned from Ferrara. If he did, though, the version in London 35087 was not the one with which he was working, for it differs from that used in his mass in precisely the places that generate the greatest individuality: measures 20, 48, and 56 in the superius and measures 7, 21, 27–28, 47, and 48 in the tenor.

42. FD5, in London 31922 (ca.1510–20), is last to appear. Agricola's triple si placet setting (FD6) may well date from his time in Florence in the 1490s.

43. The Josquin and Obrecht masses are not always properly identified. As time goes on, the name "Fortuna" is used in preference to "Fortuna desperata."

44. See Meconi, "Art-Song Reworkings," 25. *Fortuna desperata* works generally eschew allusion in favor of direct acknowledgment of their material, e.g., FD1 in Frankfurt 20 has a contrafact Latin text in the tenor but the incipit for the superius is "fortuna desperata."

45. I discuss these views in Meconi, "Poliziano, *Primavera*, and Perugia 431," 494–97. Bibliography on the symbolic aspects of Fortuna (sometimes disparaging *Fortuna desperata* as a work in its own right) includes Loeffler, "Fortuna desperata"; Cumming, "The Goddess Fortuna Revisited"; Picker, "Henricus Isaac and *Fortuna desperata*"; Edward E. Lowinsky, "The Goddess Fortuna in Music,

with a Special Study of Josquin's *Fortuna d'un gran tempo*," *Musical Quarterly* 29 (1943): 45–77; reprinted with revisions in idem, *Music in the Culture of the Renaissance and Other Essays*, ed. Bonnie J. Blackburn (Chicago and London: University of Chicago Press, 1989), 221–39 (subsequent references are to the revised version); and idem, "Matthaeus Greiter's *Fortuna*: An Experiment in Chromaticism and in Musical Iconography," *Musical Quarterly* 42 (1956): 500–519; 43 (1957): 68–85; reprinted with revisions in idem, *Music in the Culture of the Renaissance*, 240–61 (subsequent references are to the revised version). An important exception to this general tendency in discussions of *Fortuna desperata* is Reinhard Strohm, *The Rise of European Music, 1380–1500* (Cambridge: Cambridge University Press, 1993), 620, who, with his usual perception, recognizes the power of the music.

46. This is not to say that symbolism was never invoked by the use of *Fortuna desperata*; visual and literary images of fortune pervaded fifteenth- and sixteenth-century culture (see the bibliography above) and the numerous contemporary compositions dealing with Fortune (not just *Fortuna desperata*) are their musical counterparts. Rather, it is to acknowledge that *Fortuna desperata* was chosen again and again in preference to other musical Fortune works because of its inherent aural quality.

47. See Meconi, "Poliziano, *Primavera*, and Perugia 431," 489–94.

48. See ibid. The lengthy attempt by Rifkin, "Busnoys and Italy," to discredit him does not answer the main points raised in Meconi, "Poliziano, *Primavera*, and Perugia 431." If Segovia is such a poor source for Busnois, how does it manage to get the other piece attributed to him right? Why should an Italian song look like a French chanson or follow the same transmission patterns? Why must we assume that Busnois was at the Burgundian court during the lengthy period of missing paylists when we can prove that La Rue, in a comparable situation, was demonstrably absent during certain periods? More sophisticated stylistic analysis of the kind I recommended to solve the Busnois problem (ibid., 489) may be forthcoming in Mary Kathleen Morgan, "The Three-Voice Chansons of Ockeghem and Busnoys" (Ph.D. diss., University of Pennsylvania, in progress).

49. My original suggestion of Felice as possible composer (first made in Honey Meconi, "Poliziano, Parisina, and Perugia 431: New Light on *Fortuna desperata*" [paper presented at the Twenty-Second Conference on Medieval and Renaissance Music, University of Glasgow, July 1994]) has received—doubtless contrary to his intentions—less rather than more support from Rifkin, "Busnoys and Italy," 568–69, who unfortunately does an excellent job of showing how composers of replacement voices—at least in scribal eyes—assumed "authorship" of original works. Quasi-analogous situations—FD6 and the six-voice *O rosa bella* setting mentioned above—show that sometimes the composer designation applies to the original song and sometimes not, reinforcing my conclusion that the composer of the song may be forever unconfirmed; see Meconi, "Poliziano, *Primavera*, and Perugia 431," 494.

50. Ramos is quoted with translation in Lowinsky, "The Goddess Fortuna," 237.

51. The F is presented as an alternative in conjunction with C as early as the second Perugia 431 entry.

52. One might argue that these lines are the most memorable of any of the art songs that generated the large families of reworkings.

53. *Fortuna desperata* shares certain traits of construction with Ockeghem's *Fors seulement*, including an extensive reliance on parallel motion and relatively little use of short note values. Just as with *Fortuna desperata*, I suspect the smoothness of line was one factor in the appeal of Ockeghem's very popular work.

54. One wonders how many early Florentine manuscripts containing *Fortuna desperata* may have perished on Savonarola's bonfires in the 1490s. The exact date of Paris 4379 is not known; within the manuscript, the song is in neither the earliest nor the very latest section. Its readings in general are better than those in either of the two versions in Perugia 431, which is almost certainly later because of its inclusion of music by Isaac, who arrived in Italy in 1484, and text by Serafino dall'Aquila, born in 1466.

55. There are numerous differences between this reading and that of the considerably later and rather altered London 35087. Because the latter appeared in the old Josquin edition (see the critical commentary for FD1) and hence received widespread use, many scholars have an erroneous impression of the song, which in London 35087 contains unique readings for both the tenor and bassus.

56. See Meconi, "Poliziano, *Primavera*, and Perugia 431," 478.

57. London 16439, fol. 75v. On the appearance of this poem in the manuscripts, see ibid., 483.

58. The *r* was added later; for further discussion of this change, see ibid. and below.

59. See Meconi, "Poliziano, *Primavera*, and Perugia 431."

60. The text for stanzas 1 and 2 from Paris 676 and stanza 3 from Perugia 431 along with a translation are given in the critical commentary for FD1.

61. See Meconi, "Poliziano, *Primavera*, and Perugia 431," 483.

62. Although "disperata" was surely used in the original song, "desperata" is used for most of this edition both in deference to the near universal scholarly use of this form as well as the wider circulation of the original version and its derivatives with this spelling.

63. Other non-Florentine sources to do so are Casanatense 2856, Bologna Q16, Bologna Q18 (all relatively early), and Bologna Q19, which has a reading linked to Isaac in several ways.

64. See Honey Meconi, "Is Underlay Necessary?" in *Companion to Medieval and Renaissance Music*, ed. Tess Knighton and David Fallows (London: J. M. Dent, 1992; Berkeley: University of California Press, 1997), 284–91.

65. As mentioned above, Perugia 431 carries the indication that text was originally given for each part, at least in the exemplar the scribe was using.

66. The more of a refrain that is added, of course, the more closely the song observes the syllabic norm of contemporary Italian works.

67. Segovia supplies a flat for the second of three systems of the superius; one might interpret this as a local accidental, but solmization requirements would keep it in effect for the remainder of the line.

68. The equivalent spot is flatted in the intabulations of FD1 in Paris 27 and Berlin 40026, but not in the intabulation of FD2 in the latter manuscript.

69. See Peter Urquhart, "False Concords in Busnoys," in *Antoine Busnoys*, 361–87, as well as the bibliography cited therein. One thinks also of the astonishing diminished triad outlined melodically in the contratenor in the opening duet of Ockeghem's famous *Fors seulement*. Was this a fifteenth-century equivalent of Mozart's "Dissonance" Quartet, or was it accepted without further thought?

70. In Paris 4379 the flat is far to the left and at first appears to be a signature flat. While it is plausible that the E in measure 35 would be flatted, it is extremely unlikely that

those in measures 37 or 41 would be (especially given the E♮ in the tenor at measure 41), which means that the accidental must apply to measure 27 only.

71. Cape Town Grey uses C5.

72. The change of name is usually, but not always, tied to a change in clef, i.e., when the lowest voice uses an F clef, it is usually called "bassus."

73. The Josquin and Obrecht masses have been checked for their readings of the three voices, but the other masses have not.

74. Twenty-five sources use C while sixteen use F. This count does not include the Josquin or Obrecht masses, which always use C.

75. Segovia's scribe also uses the same superius variants in measures 20 and 35 for his readings of FD1 and 8–10.

76. The use of this anachronistic terminology is purely for the sake of convenience.

77. Aside from the Josquin mass, the most common form of this variant is found in the Florentine manuscript Florence 121 (FD1), the northern Italian manuscript Florence Pan. 27 (FD4), Canti C and its derivative Munich 1516 (FD14), Segovia (FD1, 8–10), and the northern manuscripts Frankfurt 20 (FD1) and St. Gall 462 and 463 (both FD2). London 31922 (FD5) and St. Gall 463 and 464 (both FD36) use a different rhythm for these pitches, as does the Obrecht mass, but there with a unique variant: semibreve D–dotted minim C–semiminim B. Curiously, Rifkin, "Busnoys and Italy," 532–33 and 543, presents Segovia's reading as unusual rather than common, even though it can be traced back as far as the Josquin mass.

78. This variant appears in the Florentine source Florence 167 (FD13), Isaac's FD11 in Vienna 18810, the Segovia readings for FD1 and FD8–10, London 31922 (FD5), and the northern sources Wolfenbüttel 78 (FD1), St. Gall 462 and 463, and Zwickau 78/2 (all FD2). Again, Rifkin, ibid., seems to think Segovia's reading here is aberrant.

79. Except for this cadence and the choice of pitch in measure 13, however, the Paris 4379 reading was always the most common.

80. The variants occur in two places: the equivalent to measure 24, where it has a breve instead of two semibreves—a variant also found in London 31922 (FD5), Florence 121, Segovia (both FD1), and others—and measure 38, where it shows a rhythmic change known from Perugia 431 (FD2).

81. This variant occurs in other sources as well: both of those for FD14, both for FD36, and London 31922 (FD5).

82. Excluding a few obvious mistakes, the only different reading is in the treatment of measures 30 and 32–33 in the 1553 Faber source for FD26.

83. It appears as a breve in Isaac's FD28 but not in his FD15.

84. In pieces that use the tenor only, it is also filled-in in FD29 (Munich 328–31 only), FD30 (Jacquet's motet in Bologna Q19), and the Luscinius and Buchner intabulations not edited here.

85. The constraints of the notation appear to be responsible for the break in Munich 718.

86. See the discussion in the critical commentary for FD19.

87. London 35087 (FD1) and Paris 676 (FD2). The third instance occurs in the tenor cantus firmus setting FD19.

88. The exception is Isaac's FD28 in Zwickau 78/3, which concludes with a downward leap of a third.

89. See Josquin des Prez, *The Collected Works of Josquin des Prez*, New Josquin Edition, vol. 27, *Secular Works for Three Voices: Critical Commentary*, ed. Jaap van Benthem and Howard Mayer Brown (Utrecht: Vereniging voor Nederlandse Muziekgeschiedenis, 1991), 77.

90. Ibid. errs in marking measure 21 as different; Josquin uses the same version in his Agnus.

91. Not enough of the tenor is used in FD31, suggested as Josquin's, to use this as a determinant of authenticity.

92. Martin Staehelin, "Möglichkeiten und praktische Anwendung der Verfasserbestimmung an anonym überlieferten Kompositionen der Josquin-Zeit," *Tijdschrift van de Vereniging voor Nederlandse Muziekgeschiedenis* 23 (1973): 86.

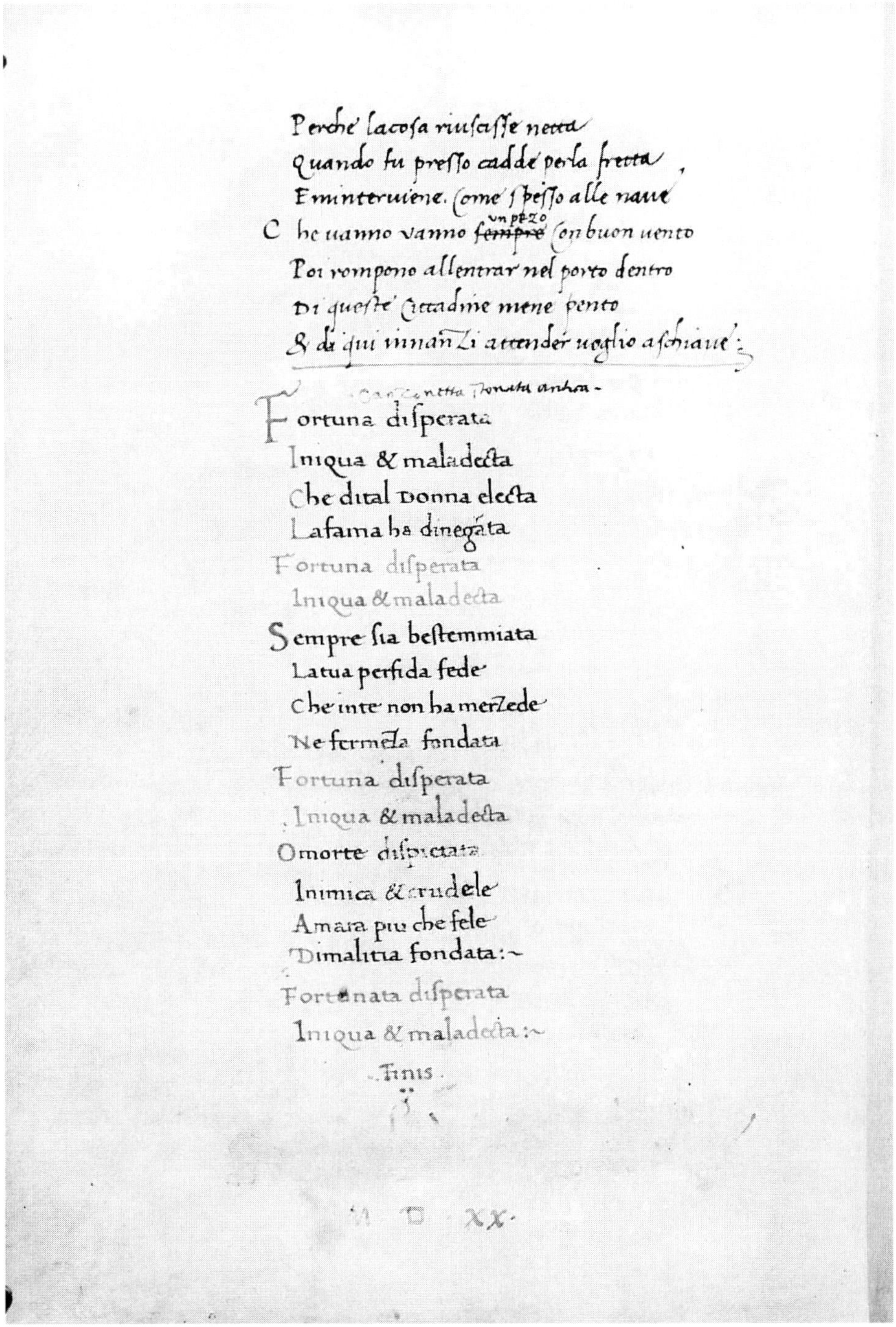

Perché la cosa riuscasse netta
Quando fu presso cadde per la fretta
E m'interviene come spesso alle navi
Che vanno vanno sempre (un pezo) con buon vento
Poi rompono all'entrar nel porto dentro
Di queste cittadine mene pento
& di qui innanzi attender voglio a schiave

Fortuna disperata
Iniqua & maladecta
Che di tal donna electa
La fama ha dinegata
Fortuna disperata
Iniqua & maladecta
Sempre sia bestemmiata
La tua perfida fede
Che in te non ha merzede
Ne ferme la fondata
Fortuna disperata
Iniqua & maladecta
O morte dispietata
Inimica & crudele
Amara piu che fele
Di malitia fondata:~
Fortunata disperata
Iniqua & maladecta:~
Finis

M D XX.

Plate 1. *Fortuna disperata*. London, British Library, Reference Division, Department of Manuscripts, MS Additional 16439, fol. 75v. Reproduced by permission of the British Library.

Plate 2. *Fortuna desperata* (FD2), superius and tenor. Perugia, Biblioteca Comunale Augusta, MS 431 (G.20), fol. 84v (old foliation 94v). Reproduced by permission of the Biblioteca Comunale Augusta.

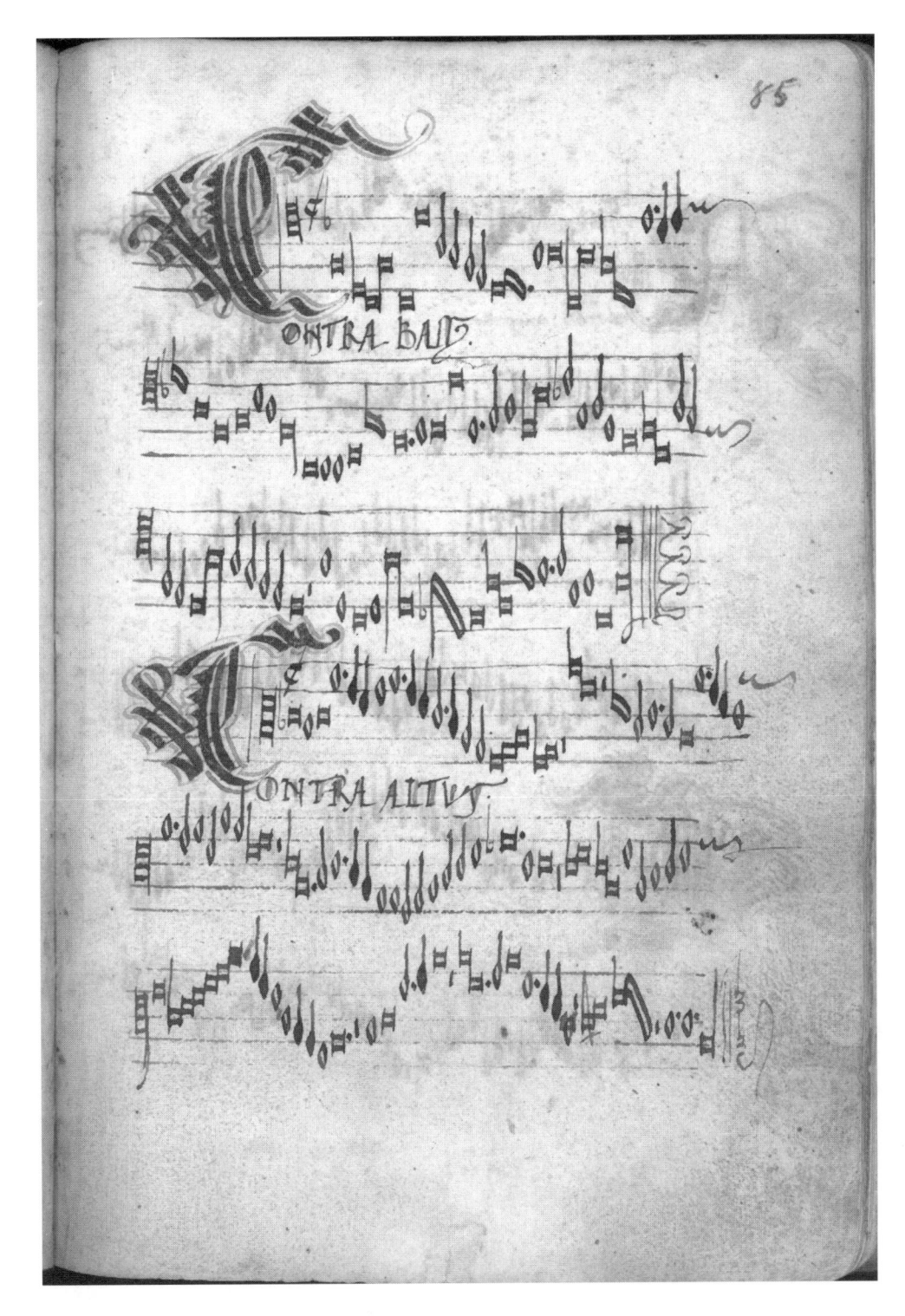

Plate 3. *Fortuna desperata* (FD2), bassus and altus. Perugia, Biblioteca Comunale Augusta, MS 431 (G.20), fol. 85 (old foliation 95). Reproduced by permission of the Biblioteca Comunale Augusta.

Plate 4. *Fortune esperee* (FD5), superius and tenor. London, British Library, Reference Division, Department of Manuscripts, MS Additional 31922, fol. 4v. Reproduced by permission of the British Library.

Plate 5. *Fortune esperee* (FD5), altus and bassus. London, British Library, Reference Division, Department of Manuscripts, MS Additional 31922, fol. 5. Reproduced by permission of the British Library.

Thirty-Six Settings of *Fortuna desperata*

The Original Version
1. Fortuna desperata

Paris 4379, fols. 40v–41 [n11v–n12]　　　　　　　　　　　　　　　　　　　　　　　　　　uncertain

29
-de- cta,] Che, de tal do- - na e- - le-
-de- - cta, Che, de tal do- - na e- le-
36
-cta, La fa- ma, [la fa-
-cta, La fa- ma, la fa-
43
-ma] ai de- - ne- gra- ta, [ai de- - ne- gra- ta.]
-ma ai de- - ne- gra- ta, ai de- ne- gra- ta.
50
For- tu- - na de- spe- ra- ta.
For- tu- - na de- spe- ra- ta.]

Si Placet Settings
2. Fortuna desperata

Paris 4379, fols. 40v–41 [n11v–n12]

anonymous

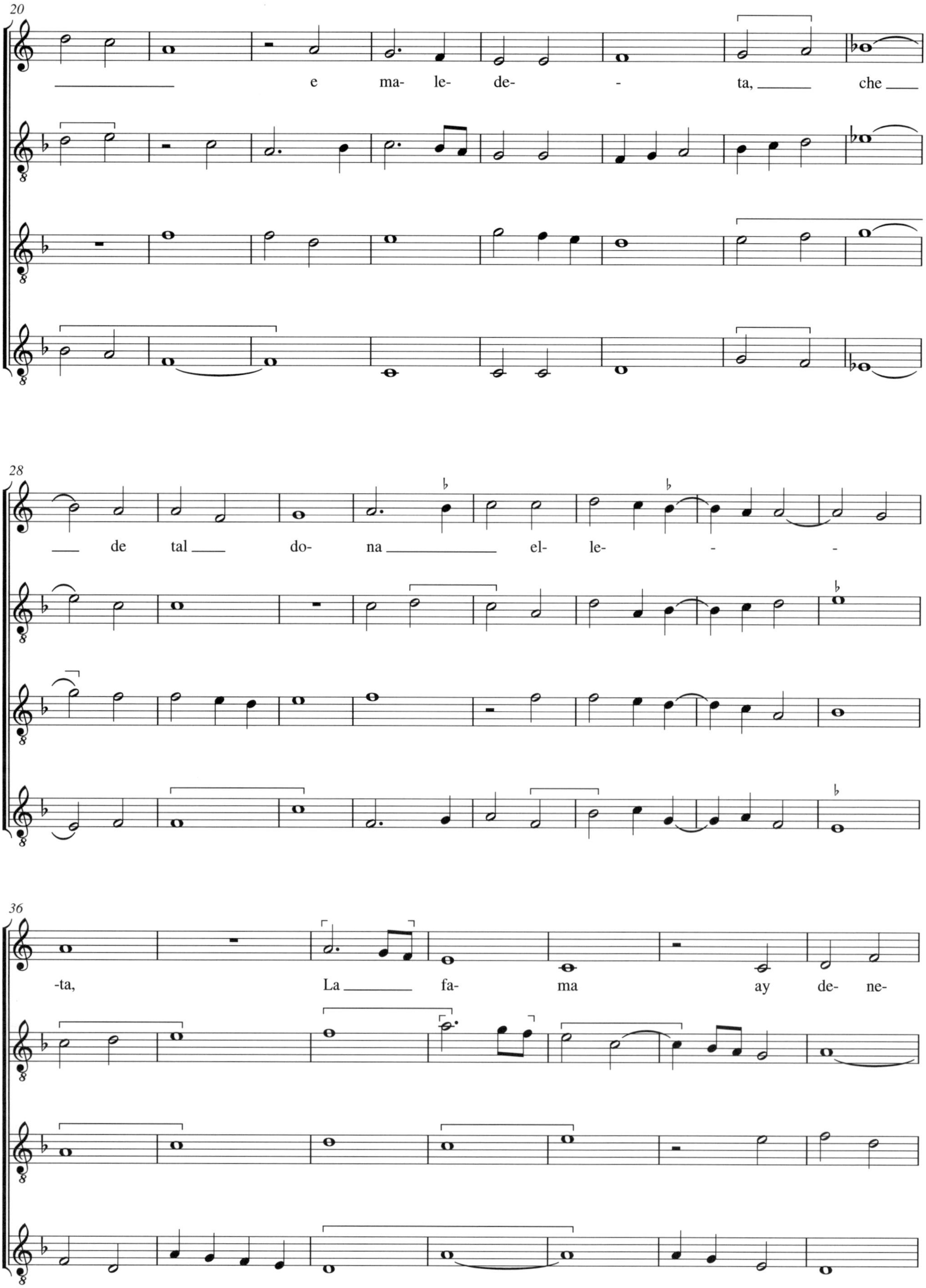
20
e ma- le- de- - ta, che
28
de tal do- na el- le- - -
36
-ta, La fa- ma ay de- ne-

-ga- - - - -ta.

For- tu- na de- spe- rat- ta.

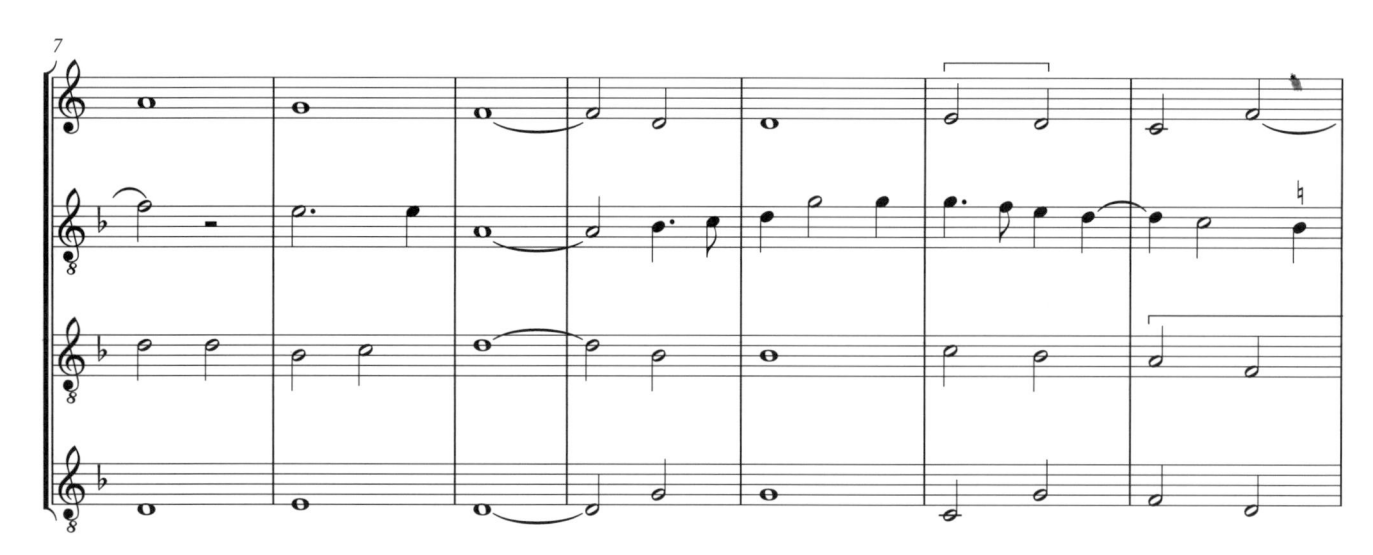

3. Fortuna desperata

Bologna Q16, fols. 117v–118

anonymous

9

10

4. Fortuna desperata / Poi che t'hebi nel core

Florence Pan. 27, fols. 22v–23 — anonymous

e pi - o, Cre - - scie tan-
-to il _____ di- si - - o,
Che gli ar- de a tut- te,

a l'ho- - re, [a l'ho- - - -re,] a tut- - te a l'ho- - re.

5. Fortune esperee

London 31922, fols. 4v–5 (no. 2)

anonymous

15

16

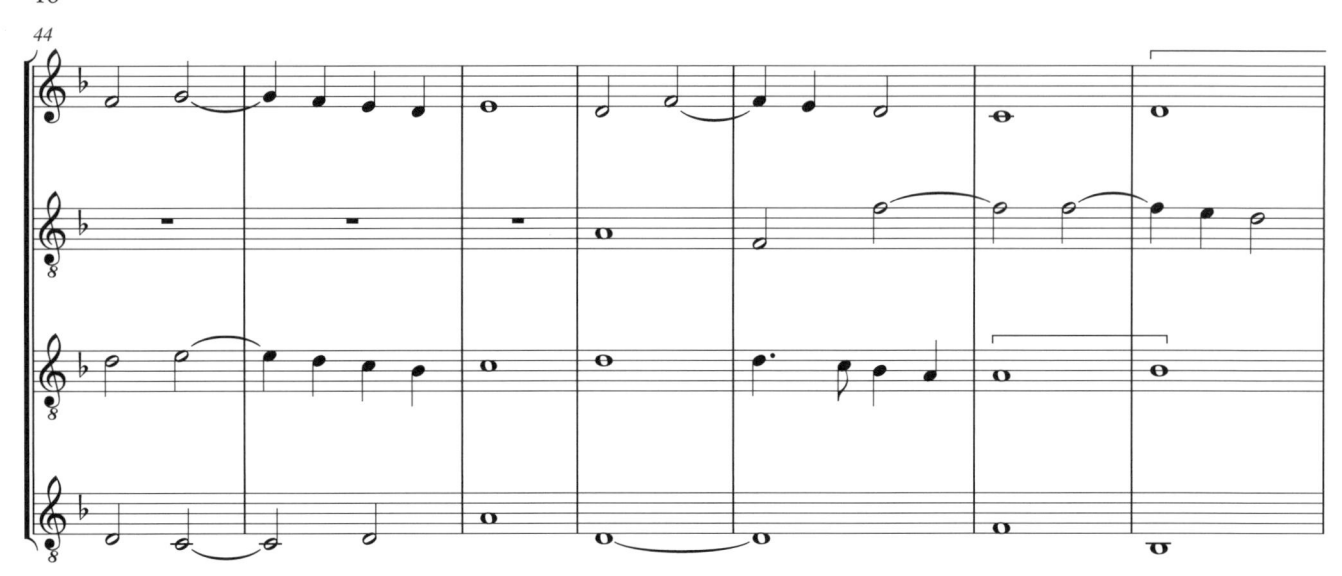

6. Fortuna desperata

Augsburg 142a, fols. 46v–47   Alexander Agricola

18

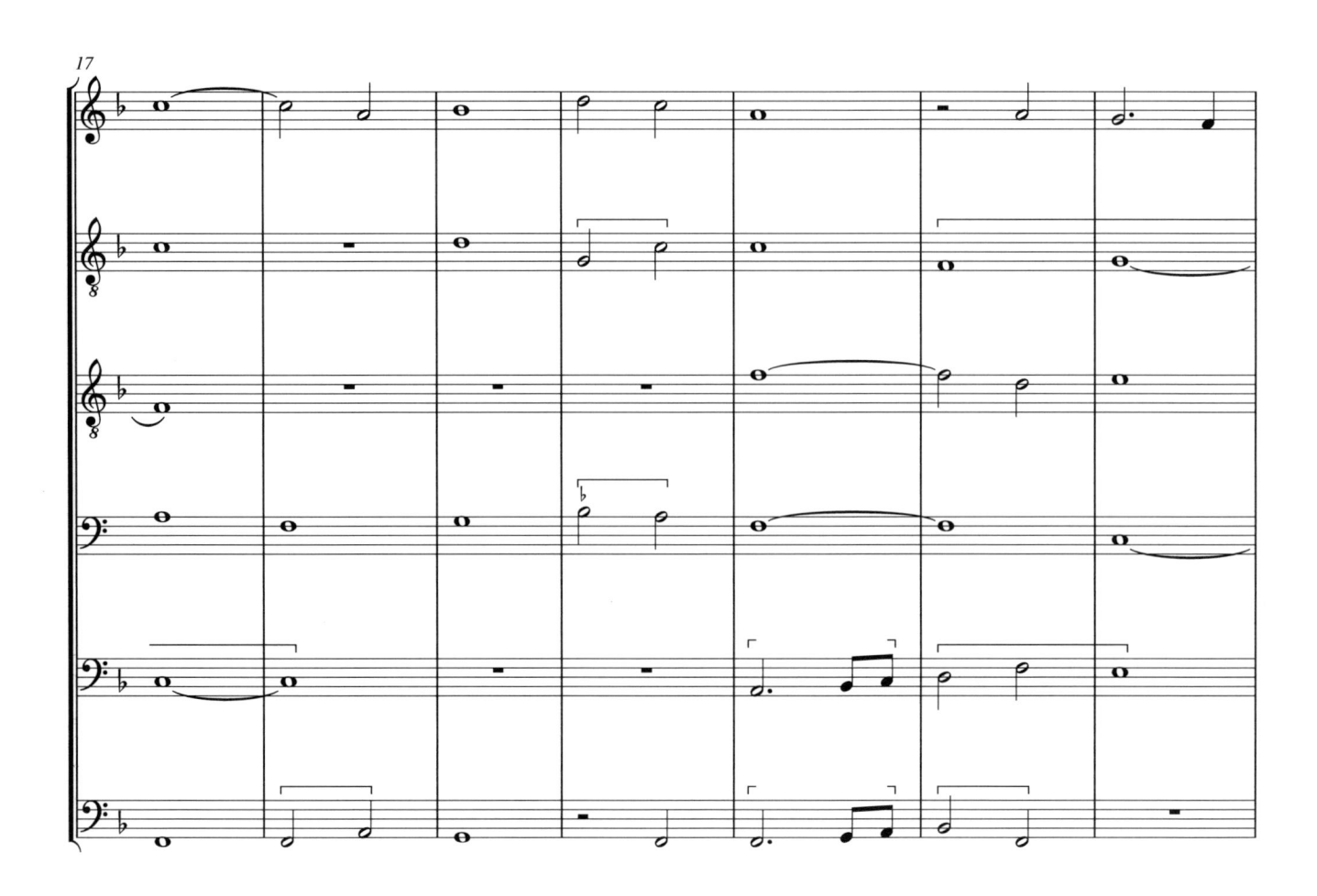

19

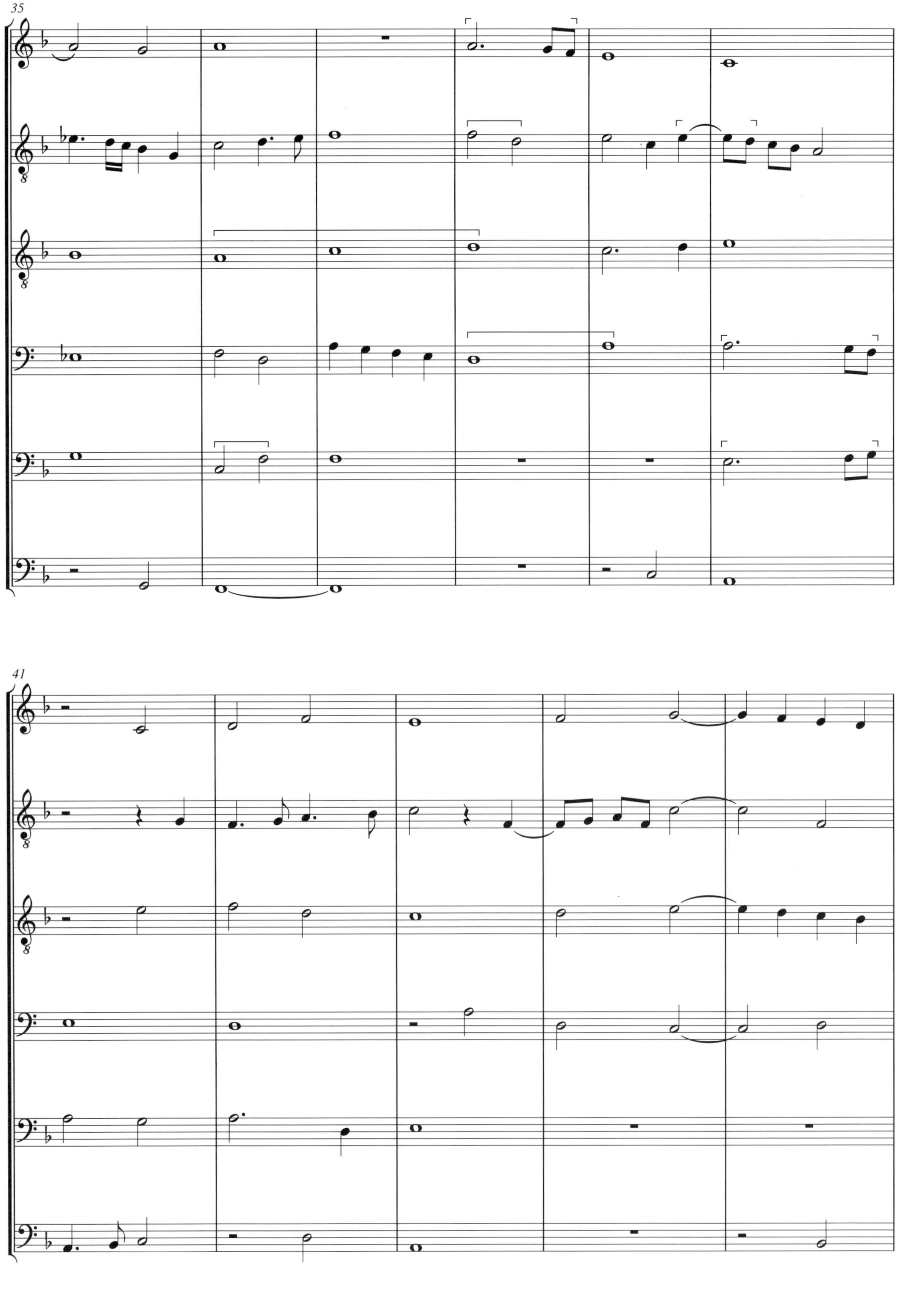
35
41

21

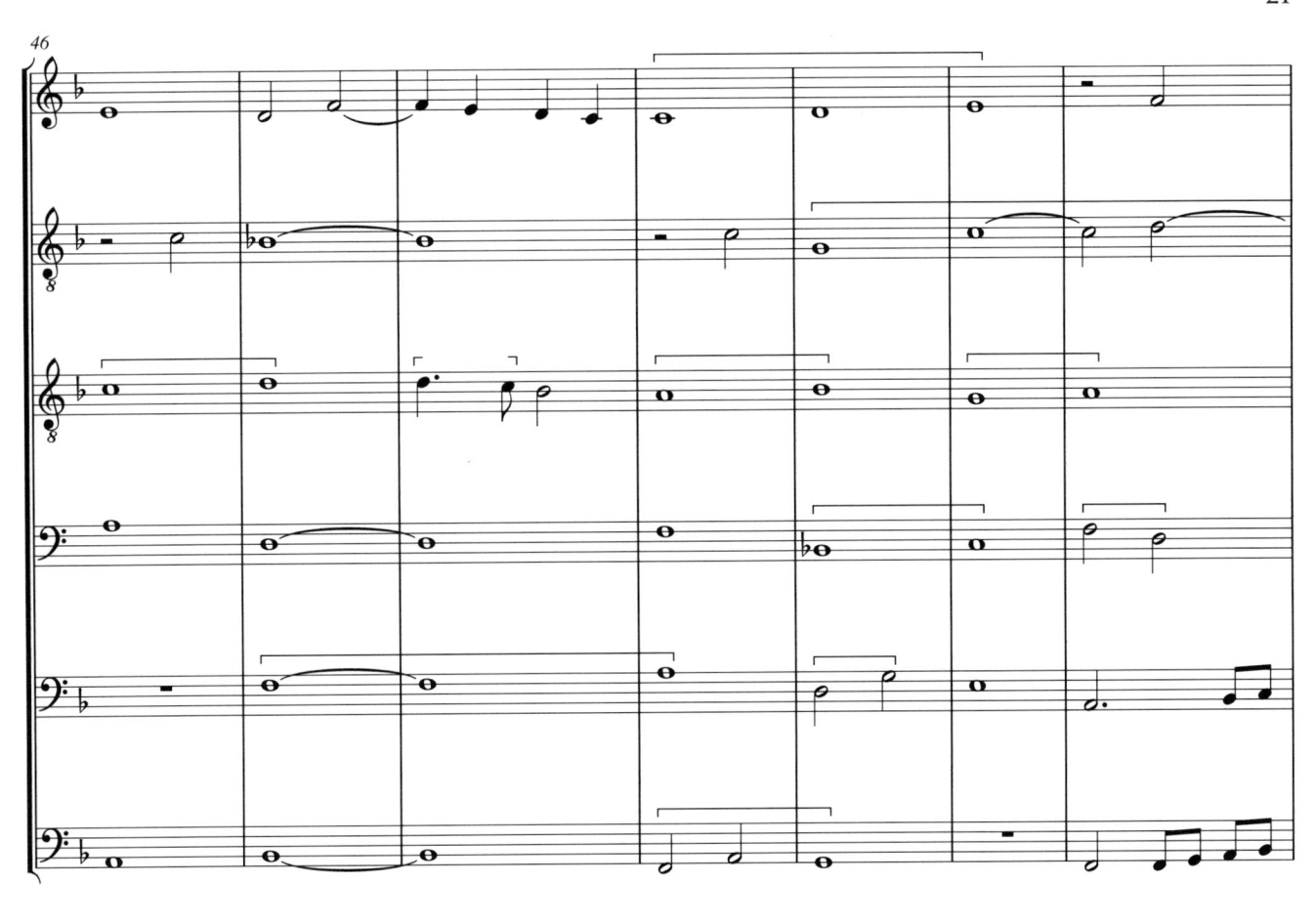

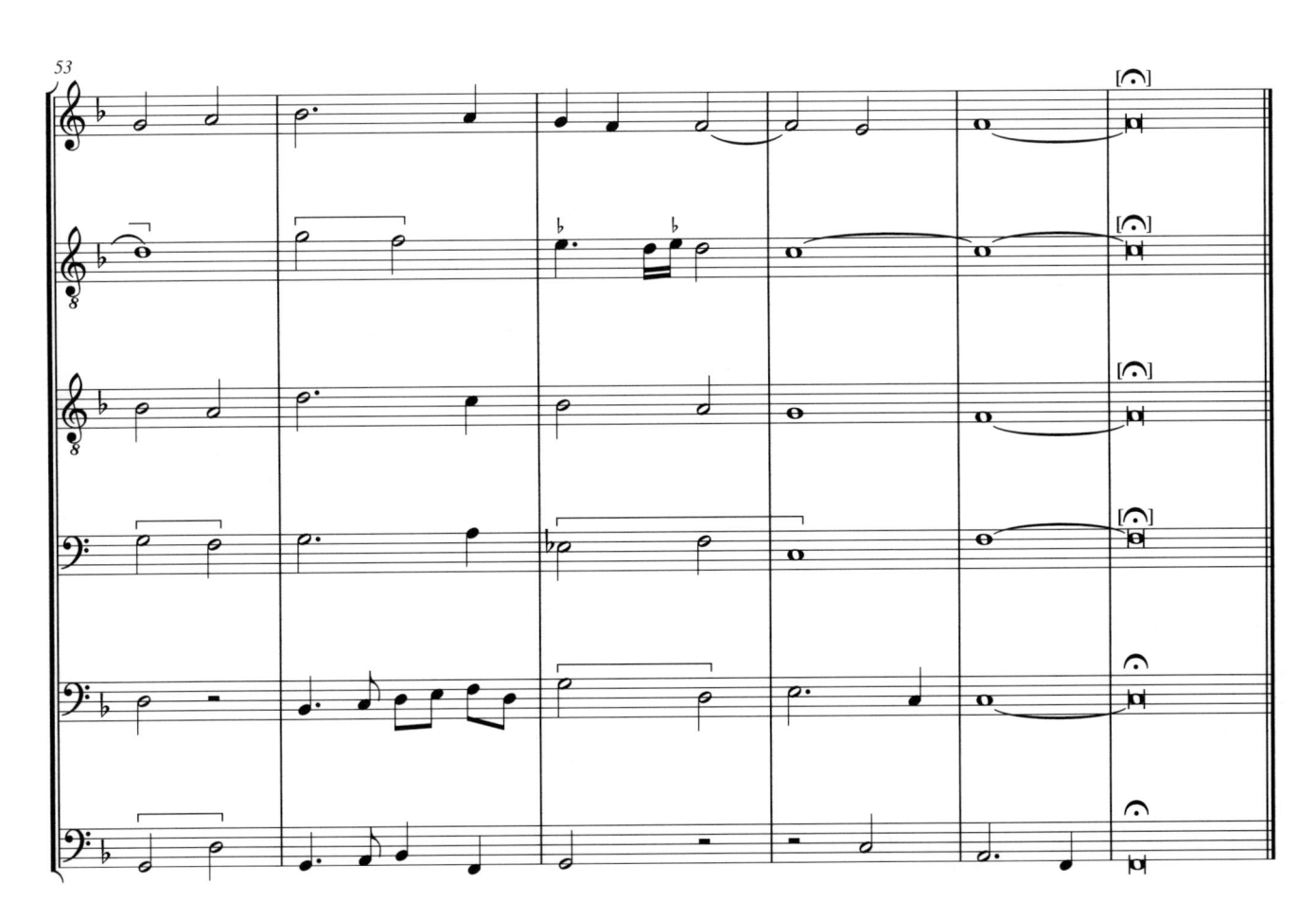

Replacement Contratenor Settings
7. Fortuna desperata

C.G. XIII.27, fols. 56v–57 [63v–64]

Felice?

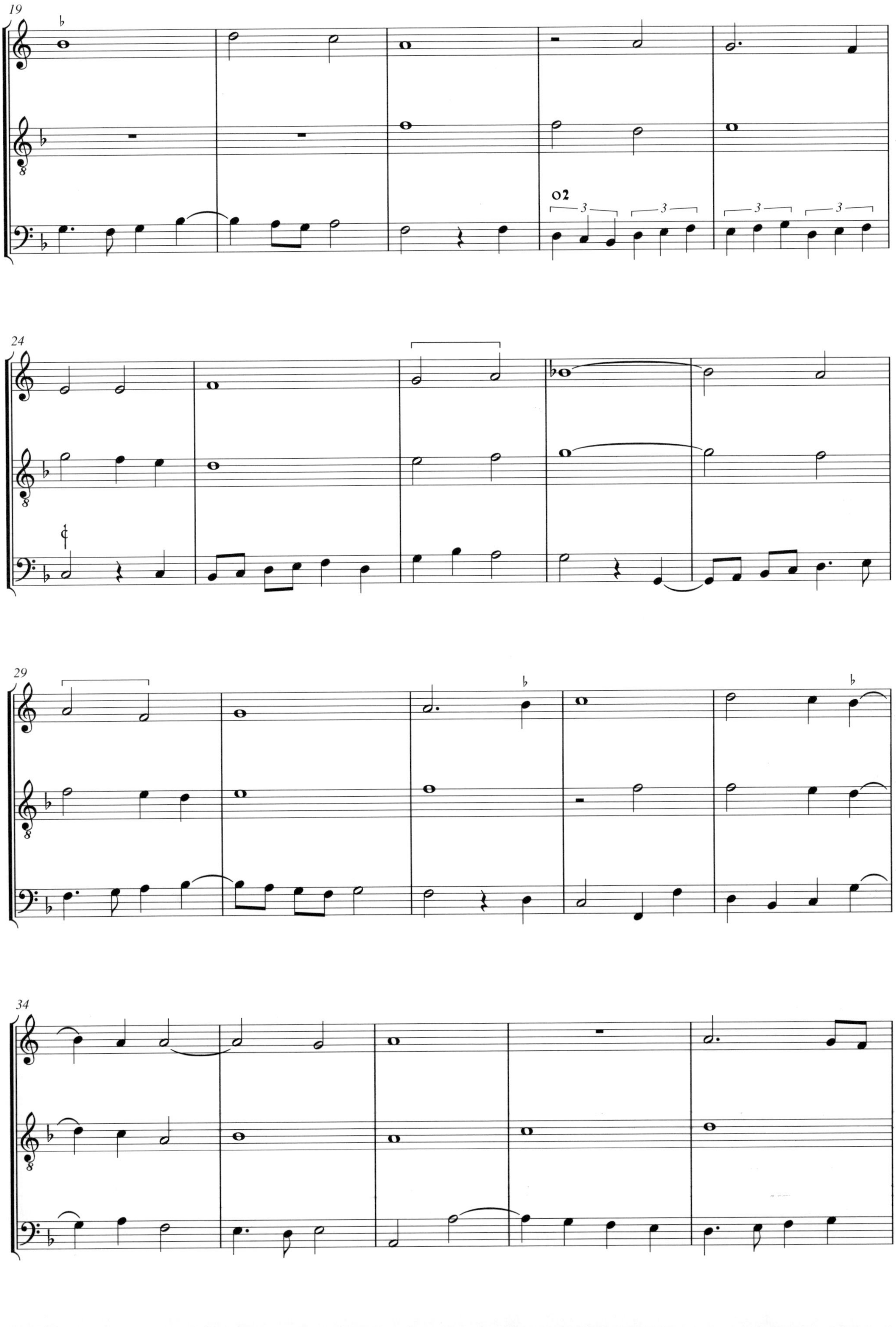
19
o2
3
24
29
34

24

8. Fortuna disperata

Segovia, fol. 182v

Josquin des Prez

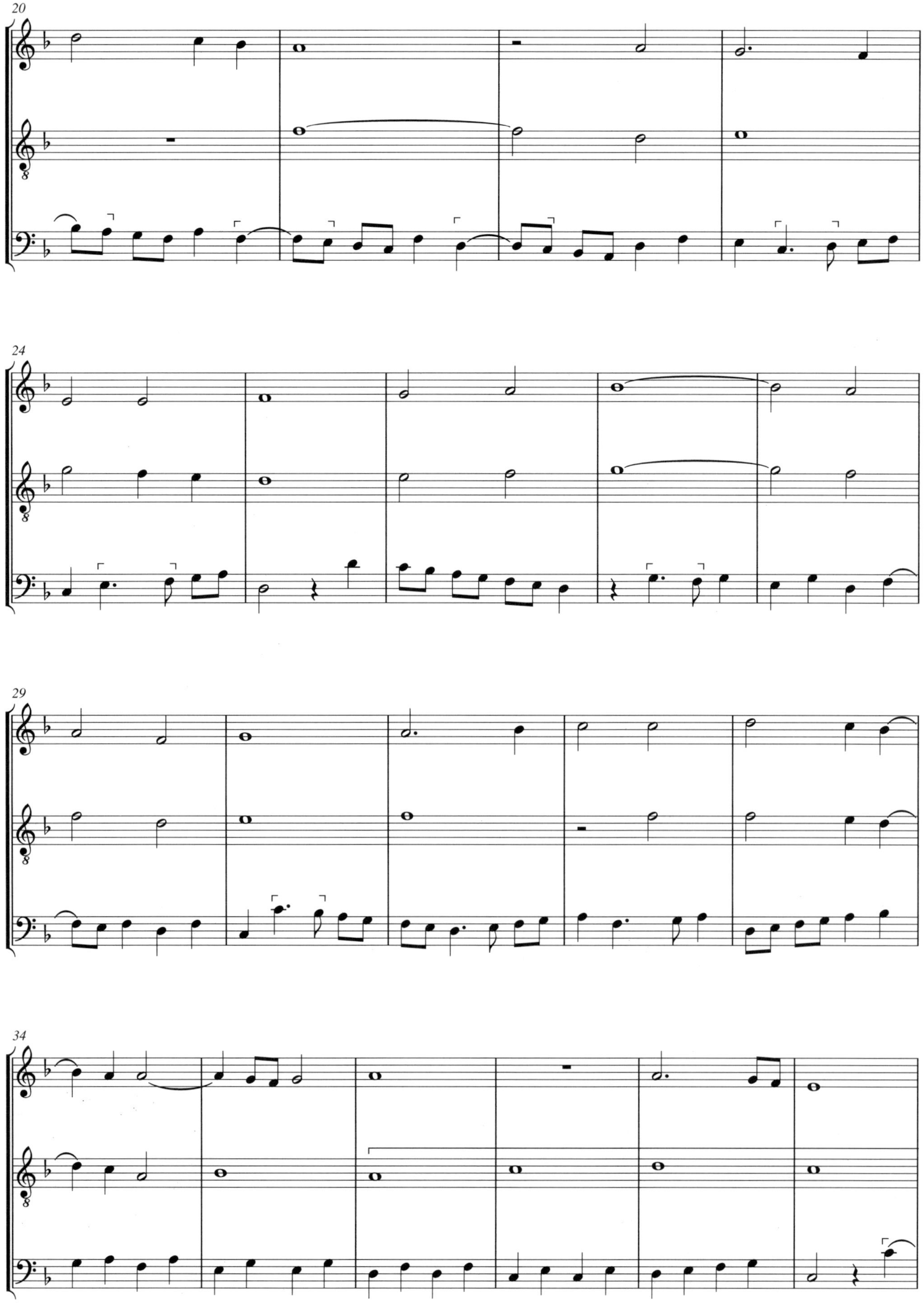
20
24
29
34

27

Settings Using the Superius
9. Fortuna disperata

Casanatense 2856, fols. 147v–149 (no. 102)

Johannes Martini

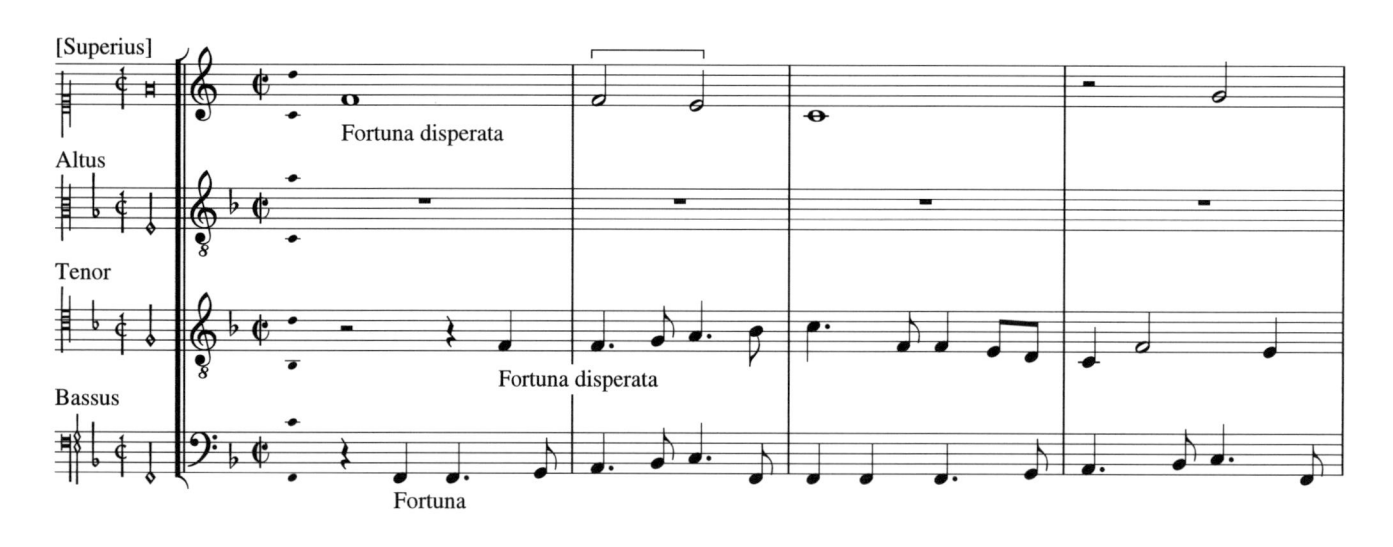

29

Secunda pars

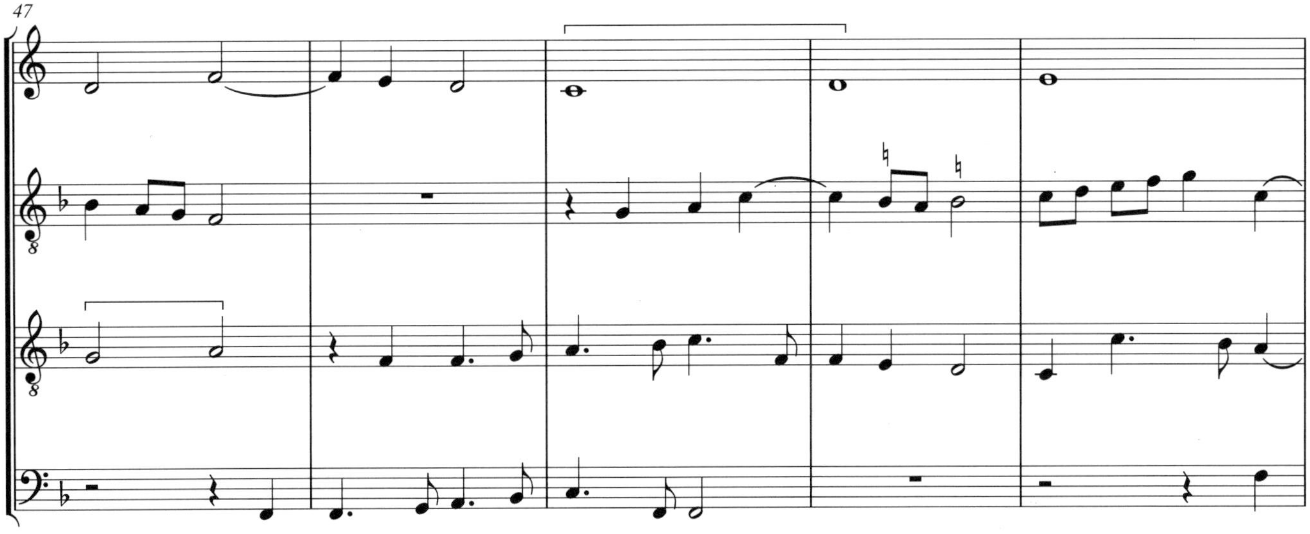
47

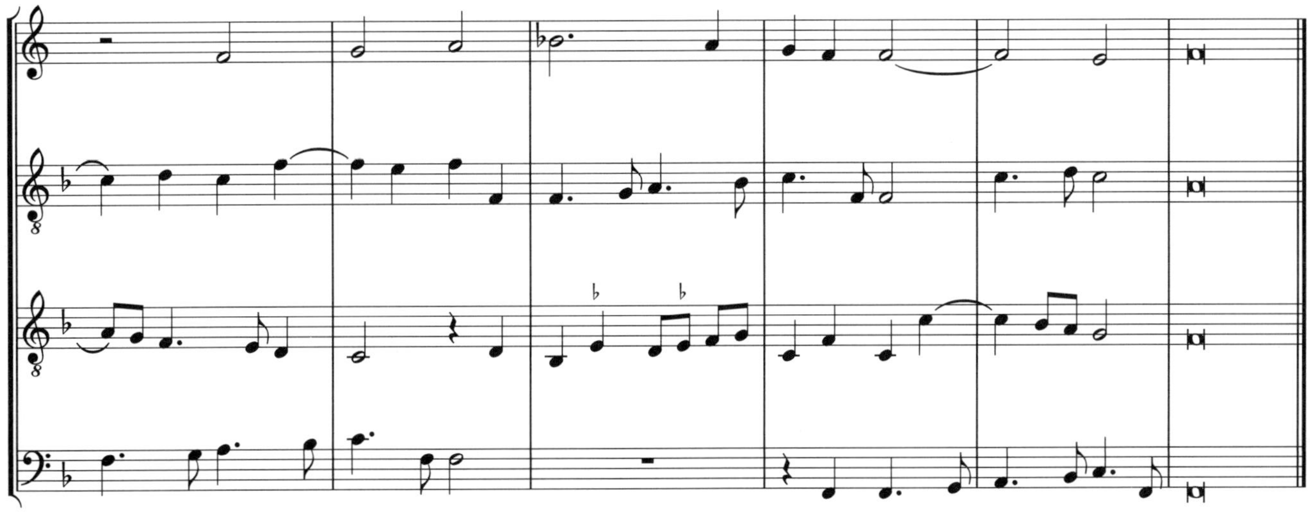
52

10. Fortuna disperata / Sancte Petre / Ora pro nobis

Segovia, fols. 117v–118

Heinrich Isaac?

33

33
San- cte Mat- thae- e,
-ra pro no- bis.
38
San- cte Ja- co- be,
o- ra pro no- bis. o-
43
San- cte Thad- dae- e,
-ra pro no- bis. o- ra pro no-

35

11. Fortuna / Bruder Conrat

Vienna 18810

Heinrich Isaac

Discantus fols. 22v–23

Fortuna Bruder Conrat

Contratenor fols. 19v–20

Bruder Conrat Super fortuna

Tenor fols. 20–20v

Bruder Conrat Super fortuna

Bassa vox fols. 20–20v

Bruder Conrat Super fortuna

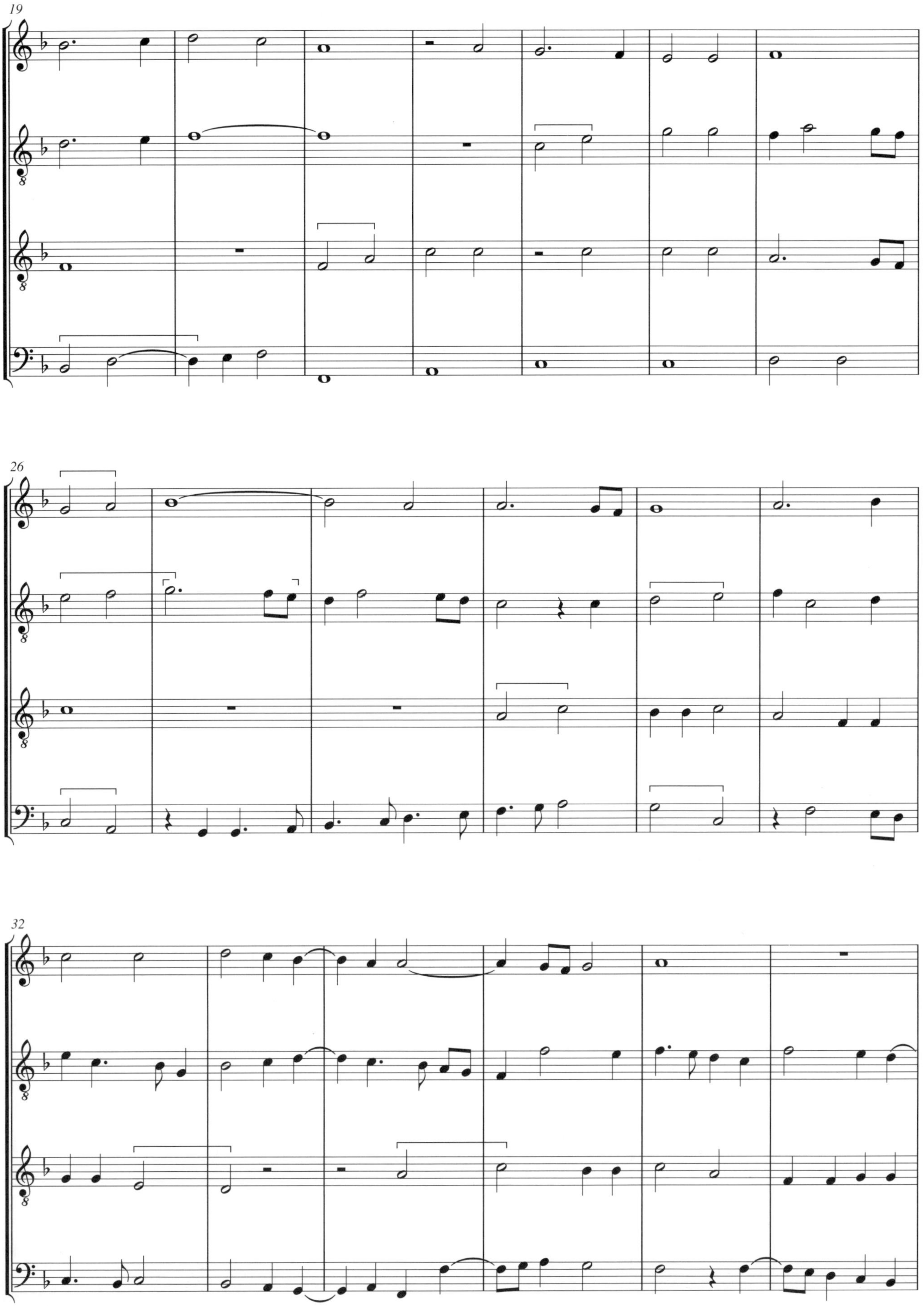
19
26
32

38

12. Fortuna disperata

Bologna Q18, fols. 28v–29 — anonymous

Fortuna disperata

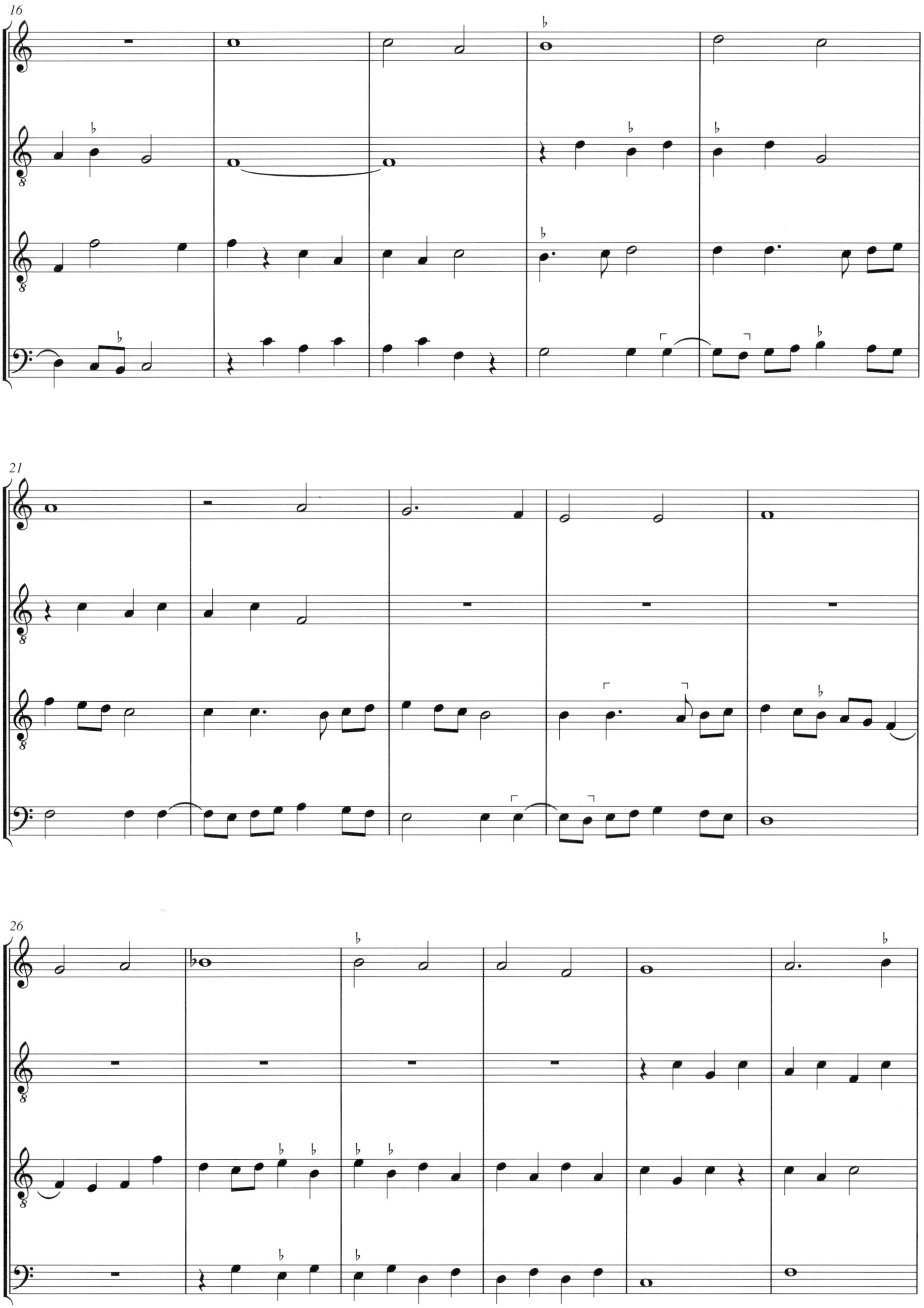
16
21
26

41

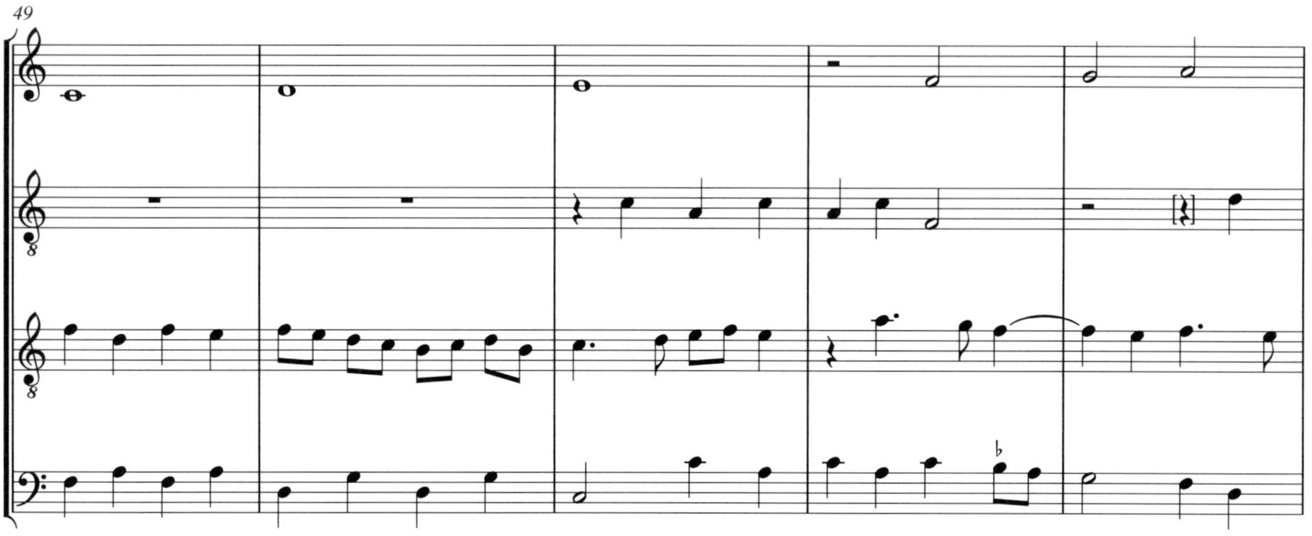
49

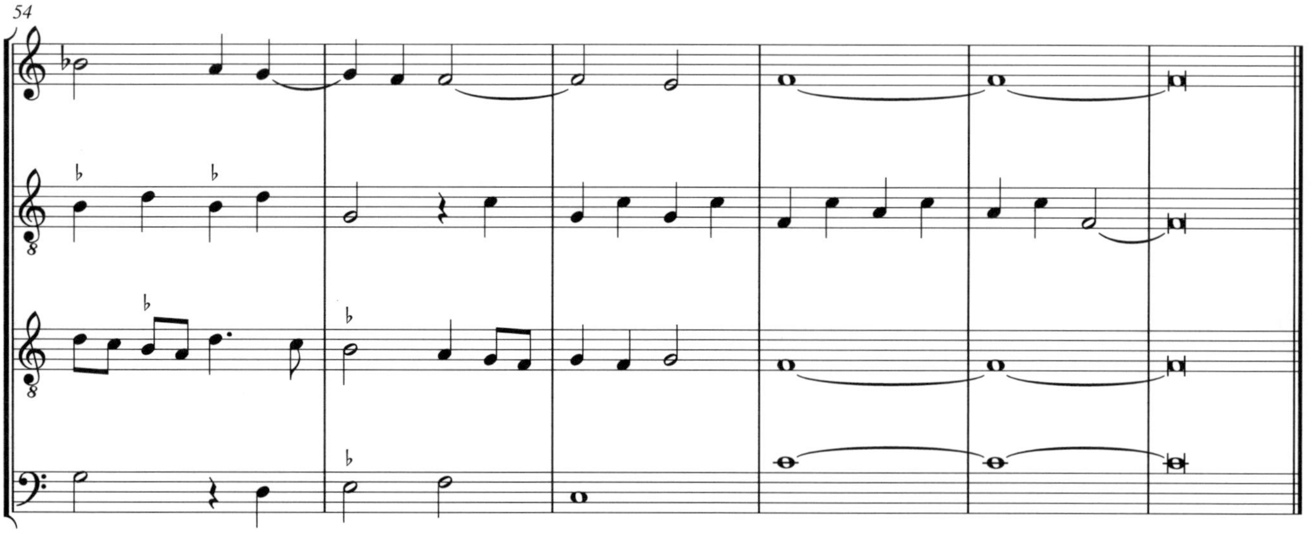
54

13. Fortuna disperata zibaldone

Florence 164–67, no. 39 — anonymous

44

I- ni- qua et ma- la- det-
-gia- na gri- - - gia.
-de- rin- di- na, la din- de- rin- di- na, la din- de- rin- di- na.
-stro m'ha ve do- ne. Ven- gho da

-ta, i- ni- qua et ma- la-
Ghie- rem, ghie- rem, ghie- rem. Bal- la- te cia- sche-
La vi- ta del- la sga- le- ra. Dal
Ro- ma dal- lo giub- bi- le- o.

-de- - cta, Che, di
-ri- - em. Le- van- tens,
pa- pa san- cto et som- mi con- fes- sa- to. Le- van-
D'u- na fa- ga- na gri- ga.

tal don- na _____ e- let- ta,
Don- na Jo- an- na. Le- van- tens, af- far _____ lo pan-
-tens, Don- na Jon- na. Noi sia- mo a
La tor- to- rel-

e- let- ta, La
Far din- de- rin- di- na. Se l'or- so non ri- tor-
mal par- ti- to. Chi se lo vuol sa- per, si
-la. Che man- ge- ra la spo- sa? U- na fa-

fe- mha _____ de- ne- ga- ta,
-na, Dam- me- ne un
se lo sap- pi- a, Et ma- ra- gnan. Suo- na lo cor- no, lo
-gia- na gri- ga. Dam- me- ne un po- co di

[de- ne- ga- ta,] la

po- co di quel- la maz- za cro- cha. Dam- me- ne un po- co

cor- no ca- po cac- cia. Chi gua- sta l'al- trui co-

quel- la maz- za croc- cha. En chi l'a- ves. En ch'il sa-

-fe- mha de- ne- ga- ta.

et non me ne dar trop- pa.

-se fa vil- la- ni- a.

-pes. U- na chuc- chia ra- sa.

14. Fortuna desperata

Canti C, fols. 68v–69

Jean Pinarol

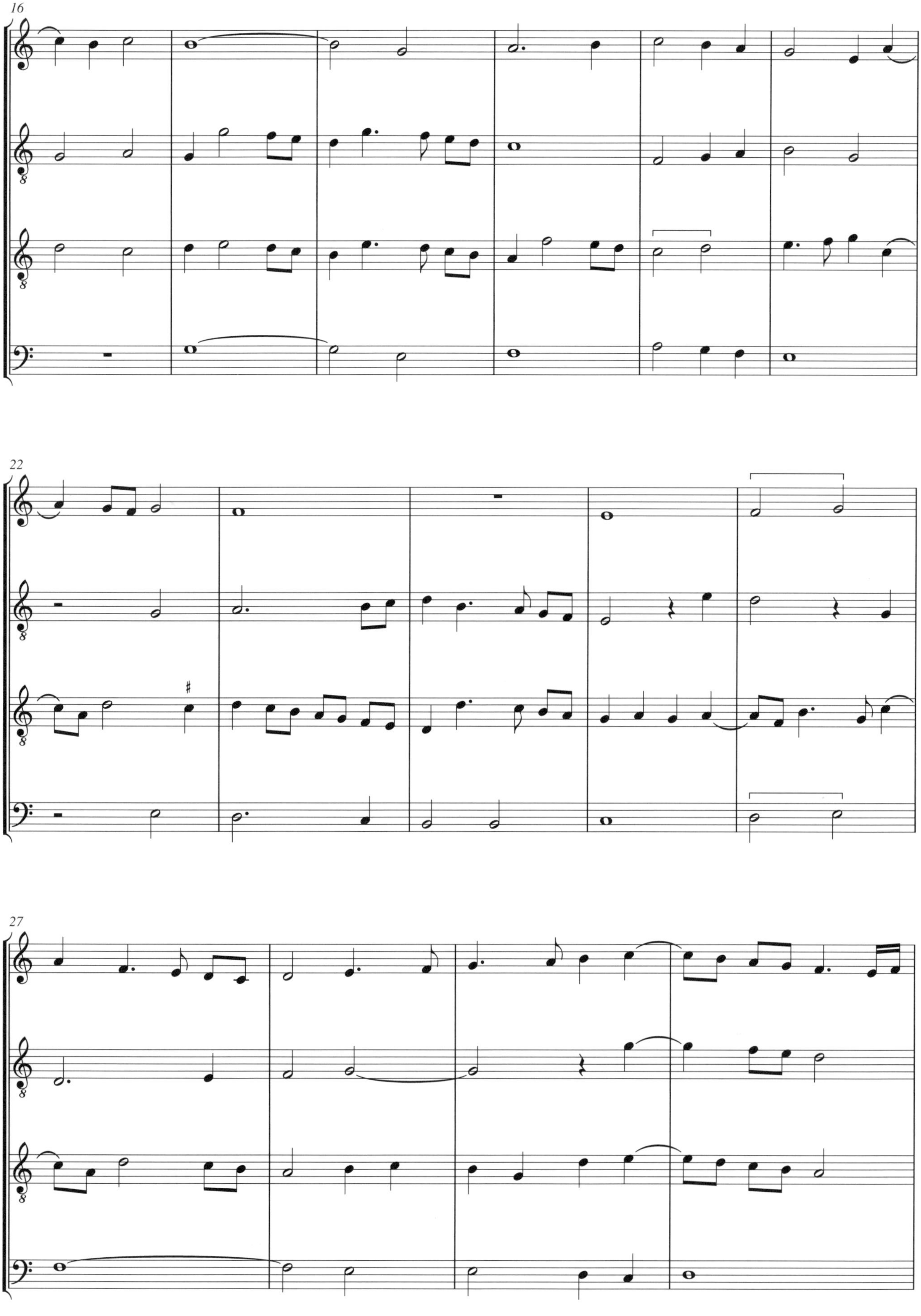
16
22
27

49

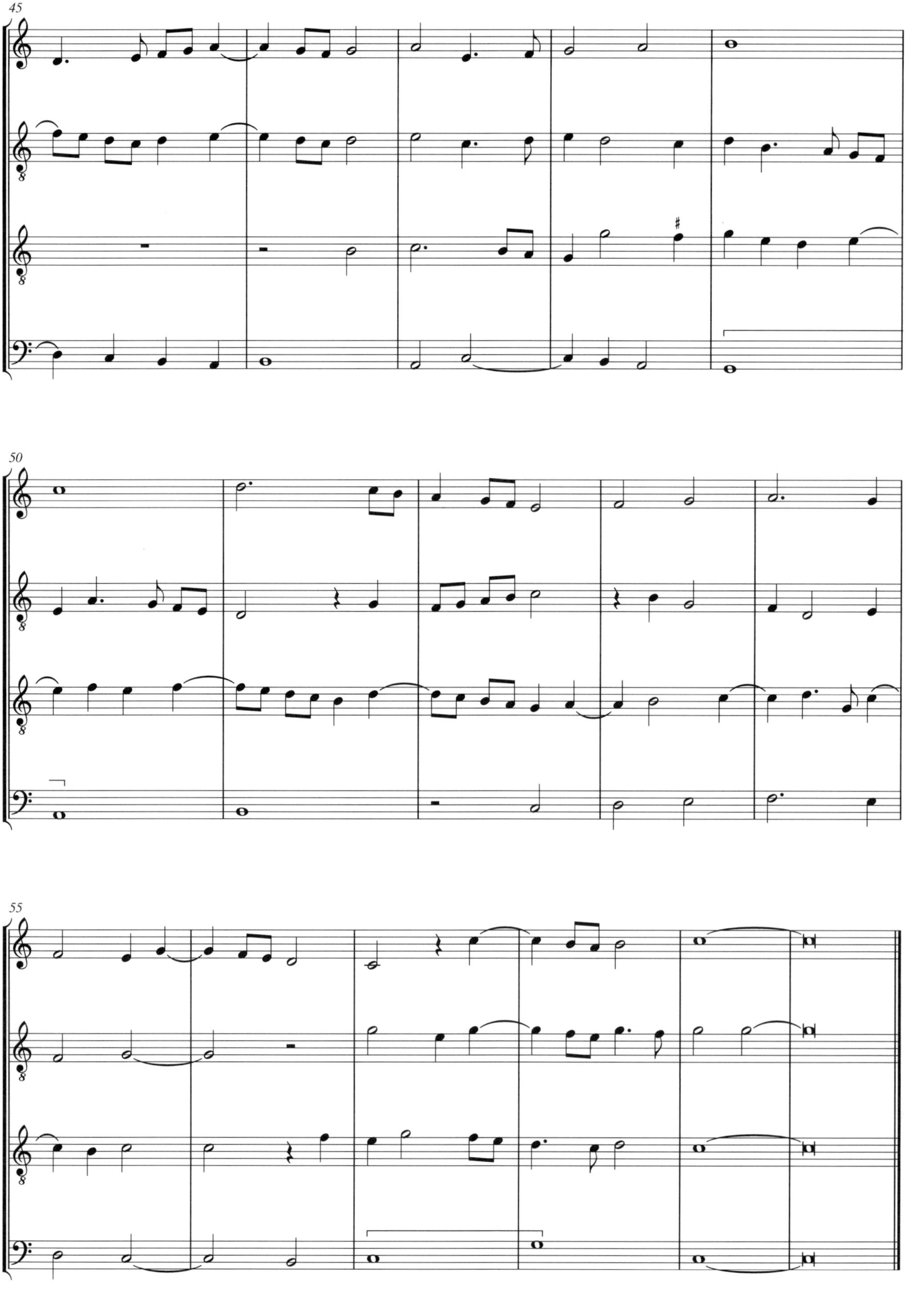
45
50
55

Settings Using the Tenor
15. Fortuna desperata

C.G. XIII.27, fols. 91v–92 (98v–99)

Heinrich Isaac

Fortuna desperata

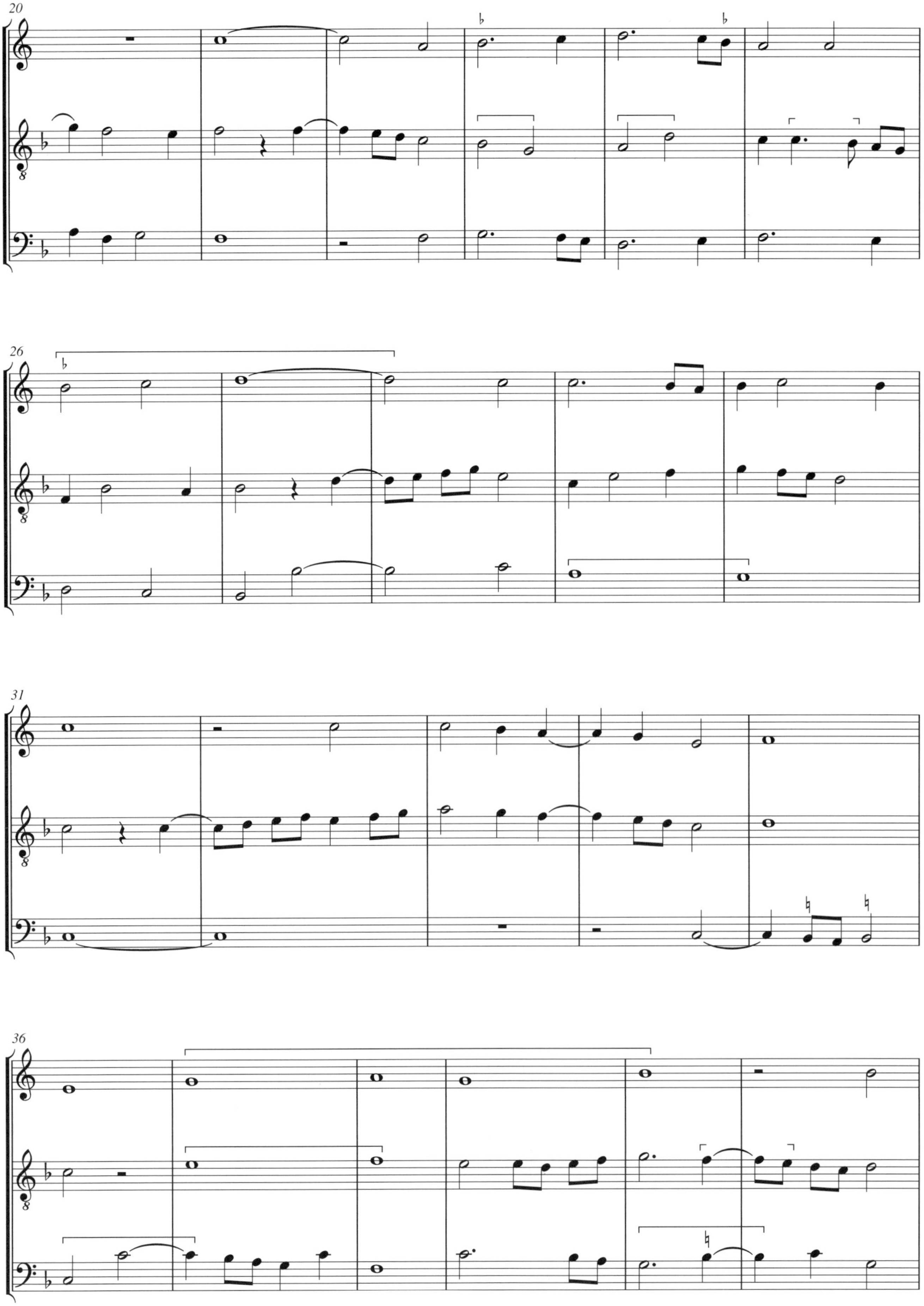
20
26
31
36

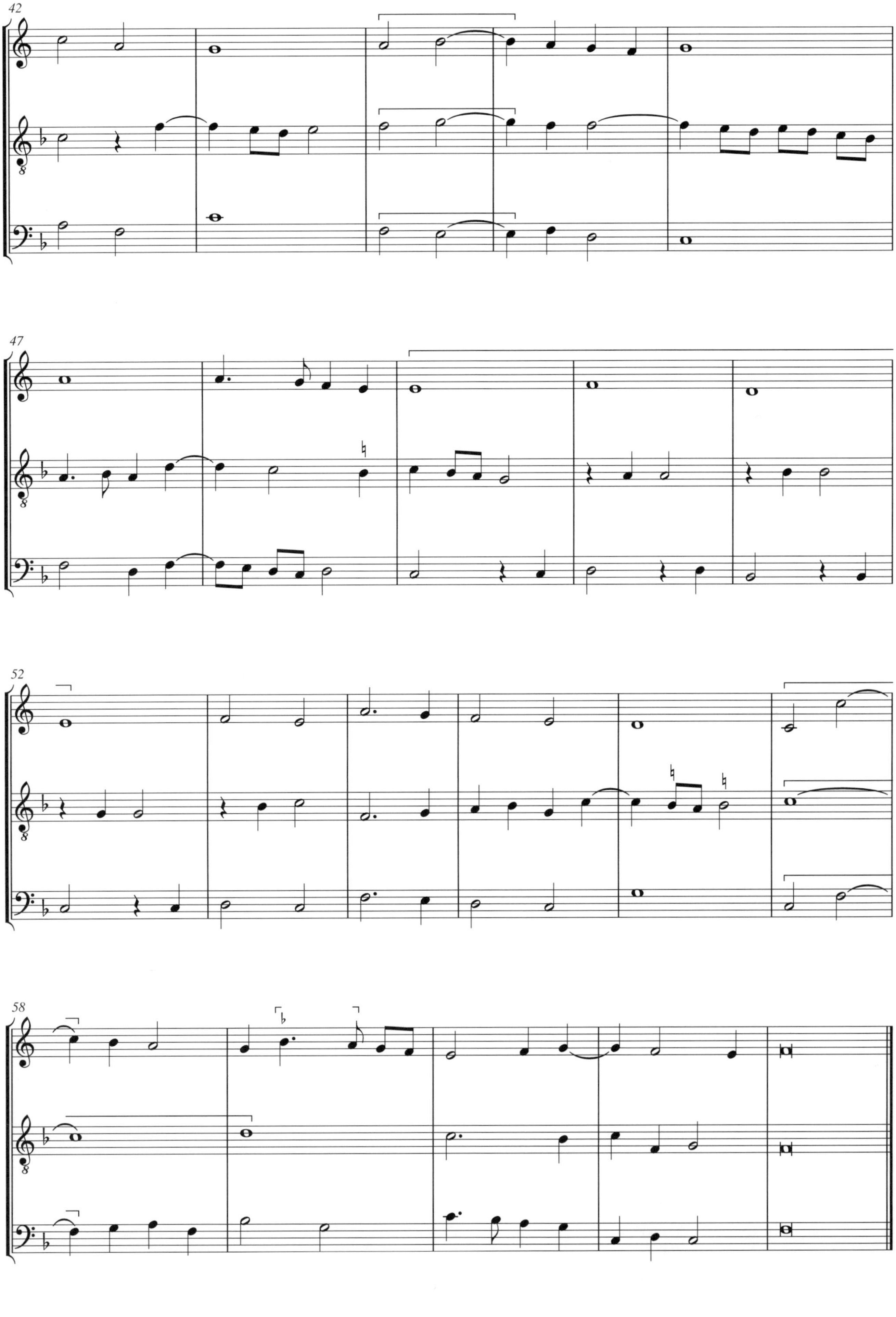
42
47
52
58

16. Sanctus

Bologna Q17, fols. 54v–55

Heinrich Isaac

55

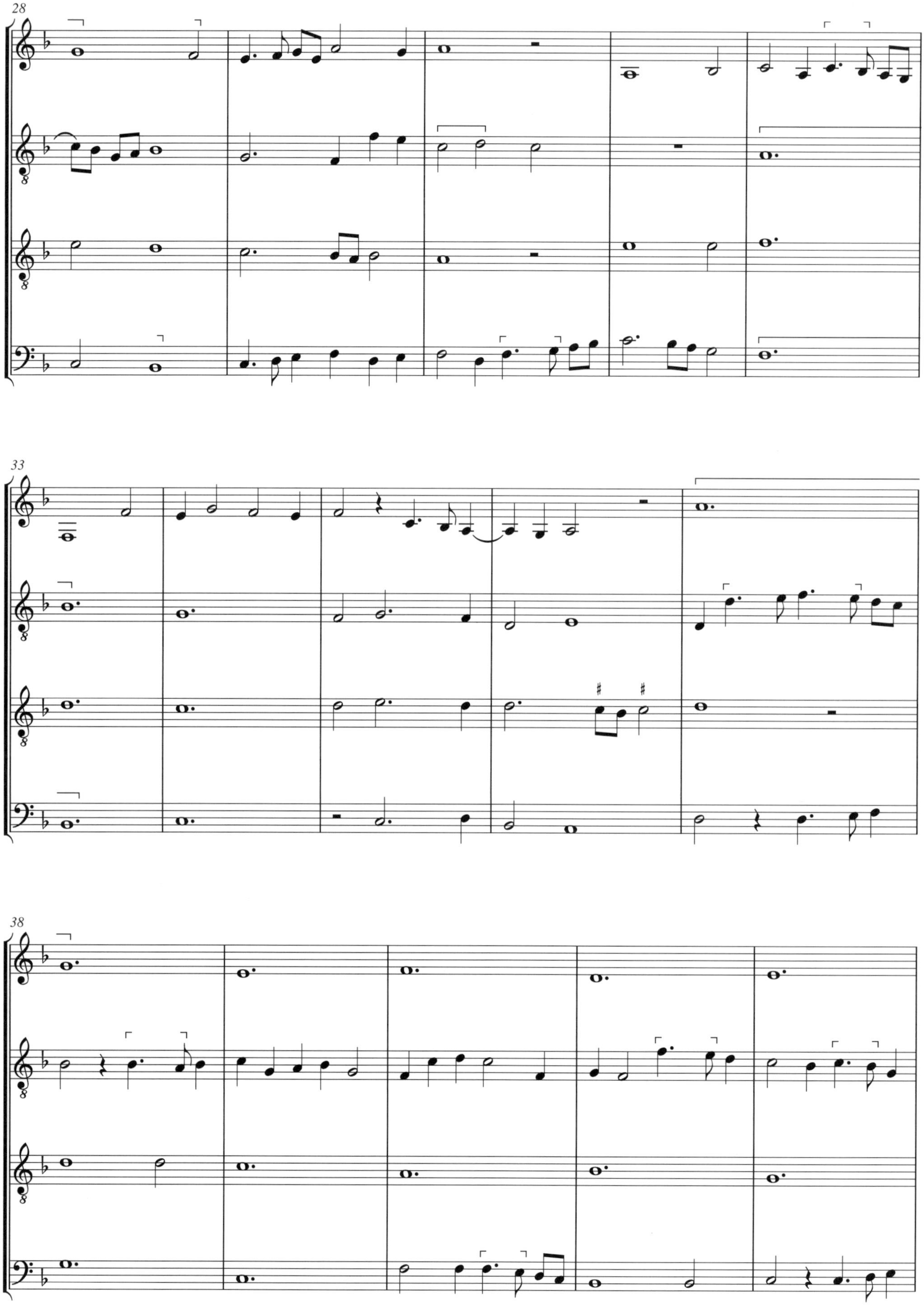
28
33
38

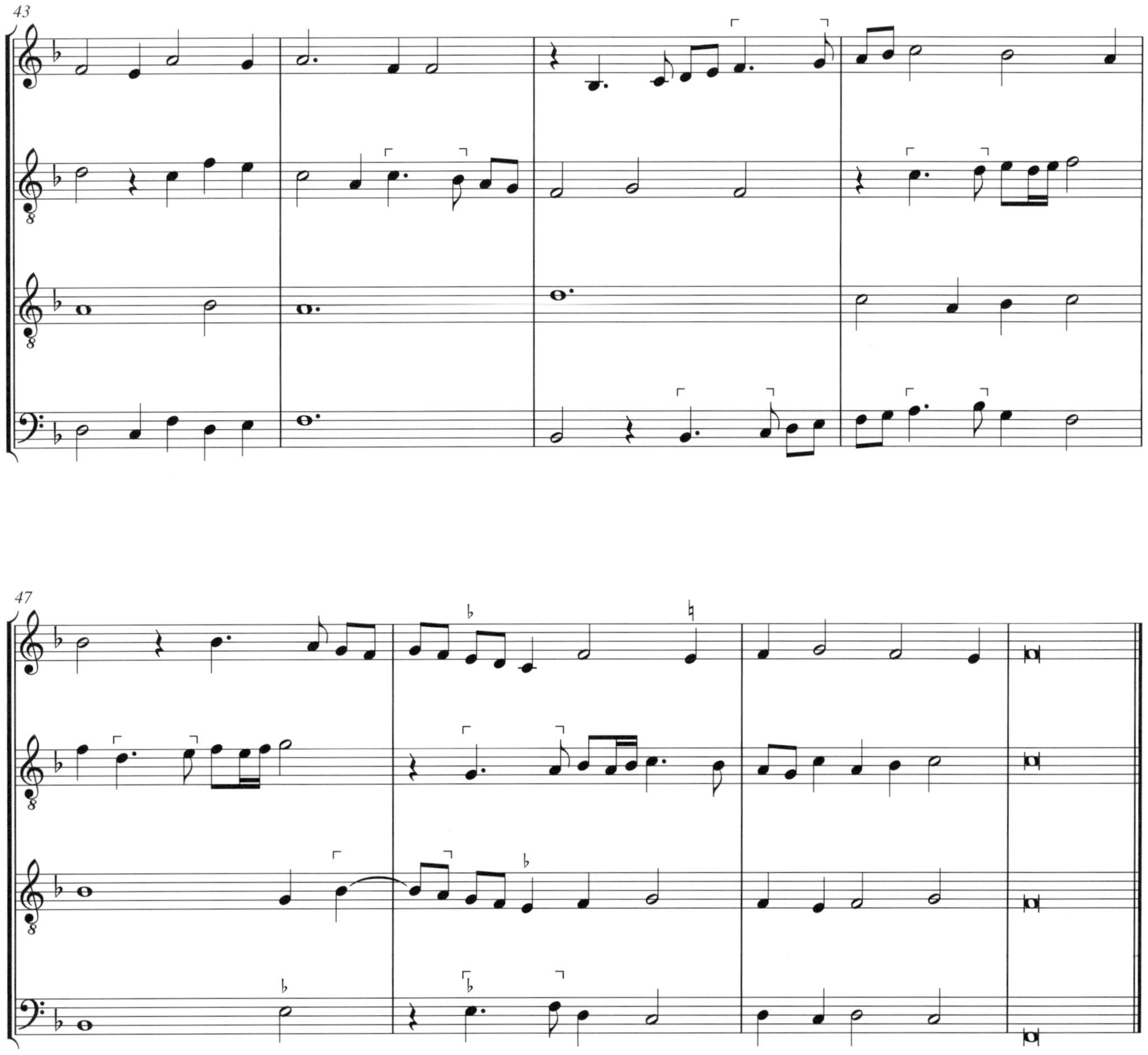
43
47

17. Fortuna desperata

St. Gall 462, fols. 5v–6 (pp. 18–19)   anonymous

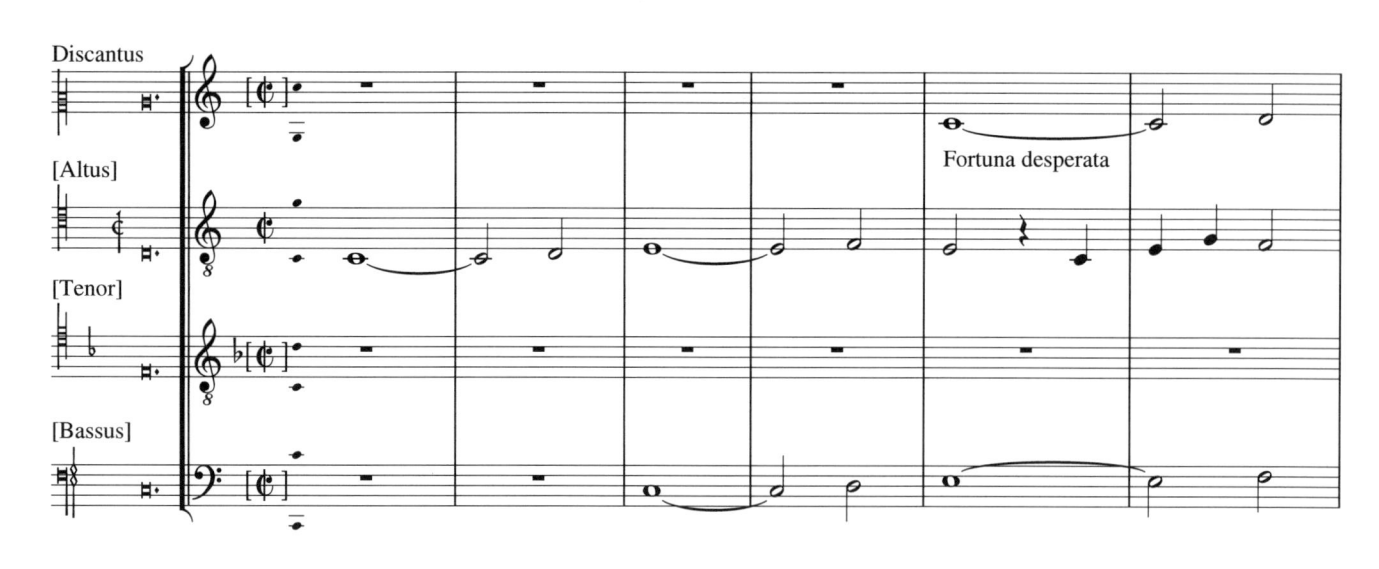

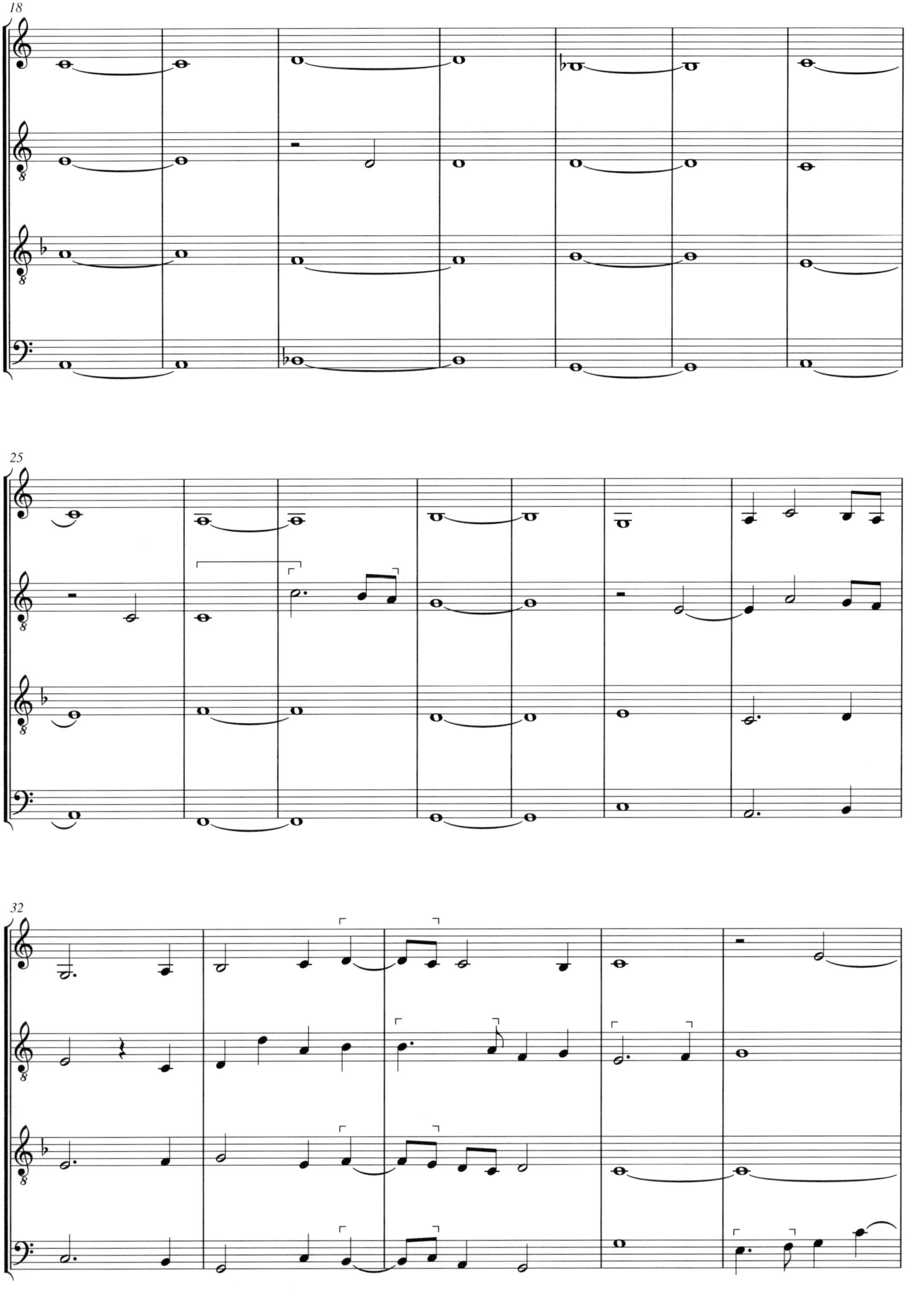
18
25
32

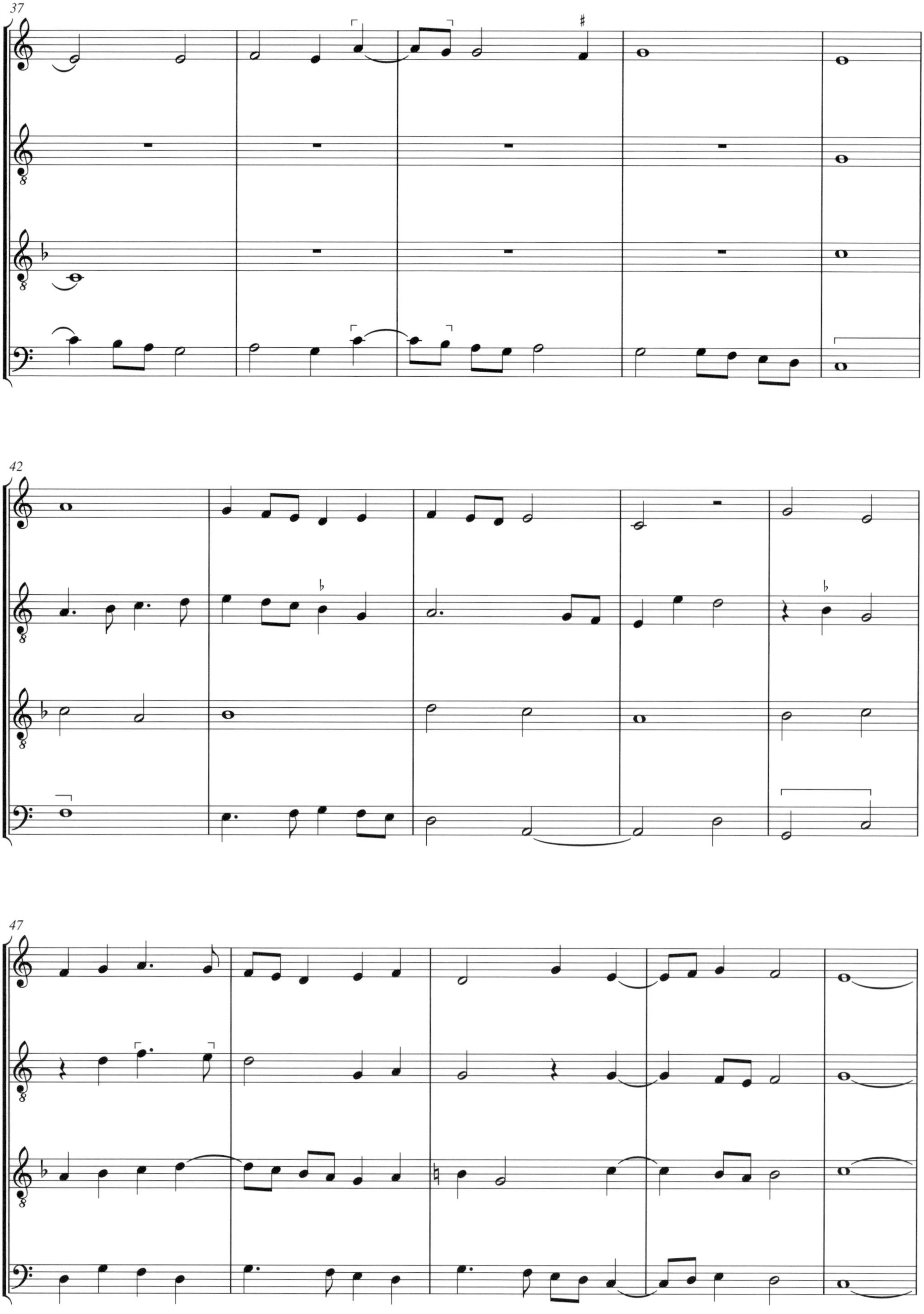
37
42
47

61

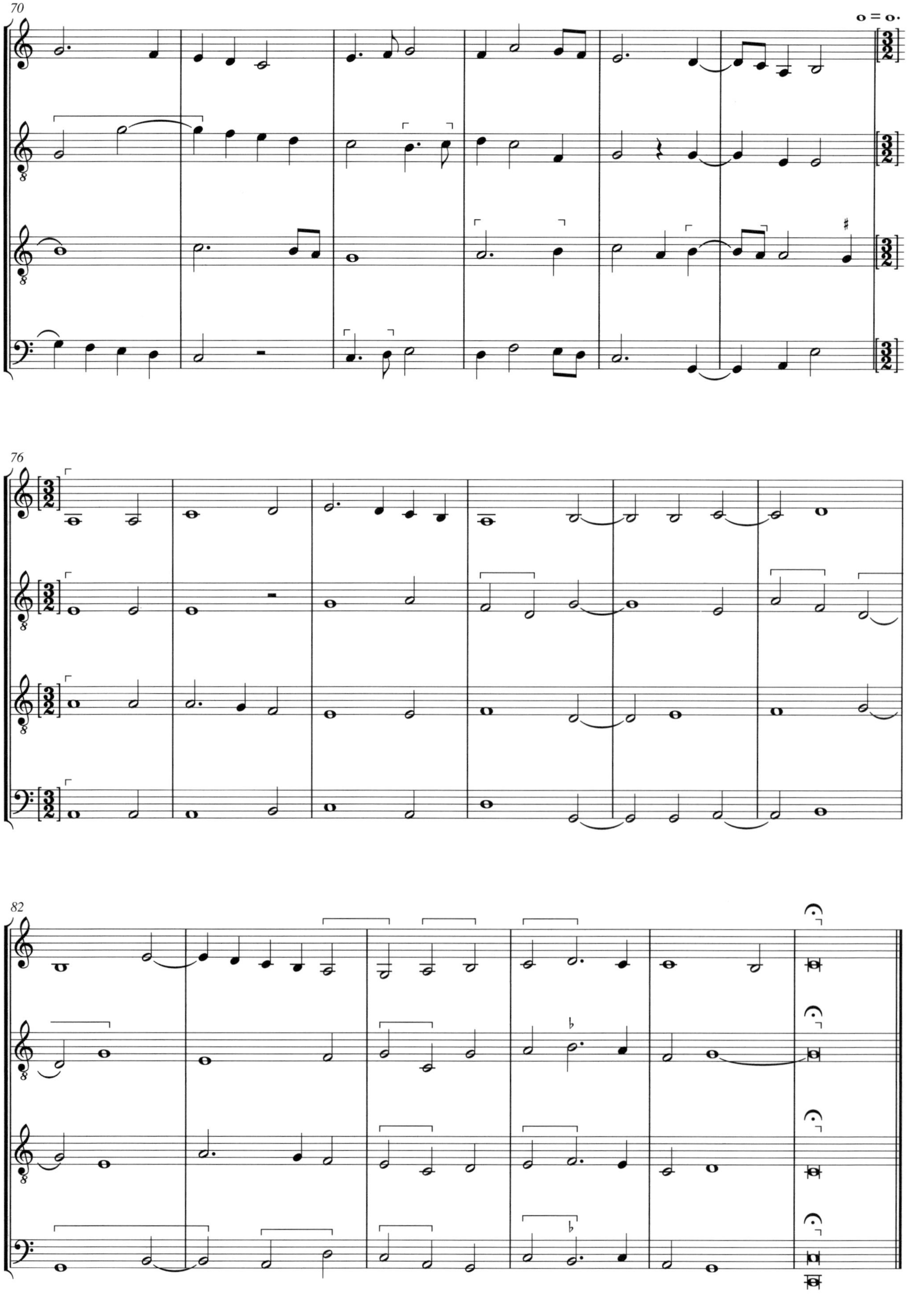
70
76
82

18. Esurientes implevit bonis

Wrocław 428, fols. 164(a)v–164(b)

anonymous

15
im- ple- - vit
tes im- ple- - - -
-vit bo- - nis
- - tes im- ple-
20
bo- - nis
- vit bo- - - -
- - - - vit bo-
25
et di- - -
-nis et di- vi- -
et di- - -
- - nis et di-

31
- - vi- tes di-
-tes di- - mi- -
- - - vi- tes di-
-vi- - tes di- mi- -
37
-mi- sit in- - a-
- sit in- - - a- - -
-mi- - sit
- - sit in- a- -
42
-nes,
- - - - -
in- a-
- - - - -

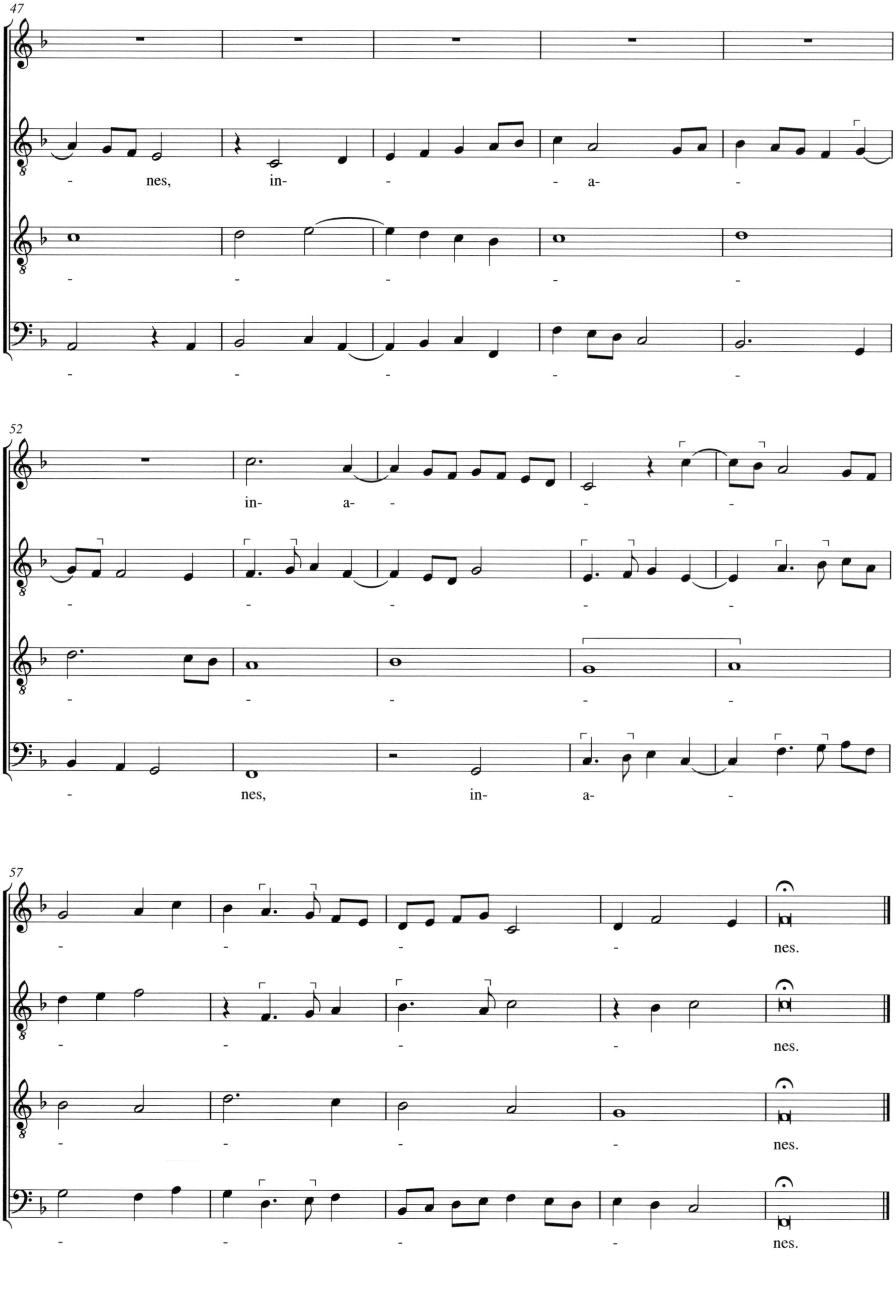
47
nes, in- a-
52
in- a-
nes, in- a-
57
nes.
nes.
nes.
nes.

19. O crux ave / Fortuna

Regensburg C120, pp. 162–63

anonymous

68

69

do- na ve- ni- am.]

20. Ich stund an einem Morgen / Fortuna

Ludwig Senfl

72

ei- nem Ort Da het ich mich ver--bor-gen.

[Ich höert kleg- li-

73

74

21. Es taget vor dem Walde / Fortuna

1534[17], no. 30

Ludwig Senfl

16
Die Ha- sen lau- fen bal-
bal- de; Stand ûf, Kät- ter- lîn! Hol- der
21
-de; Stand ûf, Kät- ter- lîn! Hol- der Buehl,
Buehl, stand ûf, Kät- ter- lîn! Hol- der Buehl,
27
hei- a- hô, Du bist
stand ûf, Kät- ter- lîn! Hol- der Buehl,

33
mîn,
hei- a- hô, Du bist
38
sô ich bin dîn;
mîn, sô ich bin dîn;
Stand ûf, Kät- ter-
44
Stand ûf, Kät- ter- lîn,
-lîn!

49
stand ûf, Kät- ter- lîn!
Es ta- get vor dem Wal- de;
Stand ûf, Kät- ter-
55
Es ta- get vor dem
-lîn! Die Ha- sen lau- fen bal- de;
60
Wal- de; Stand ûf, Kät- ter- lîn! Die Ha- sen lau- - fen bal- de.]
Stand ûf, Kät- ter- lîn, Kät- ter- lîn!]

22. Herr durch dein Blut (Pange lingua) / Fortuna

1534[17], no. 100

Ludwig Senfl

19
- - men. Thu- e durch dein
-o- - si Cor- - - po-
25
Güt, Dich er- bar- - men Un-
-ris my- ste- ri- um San-
31
-ser Sün- den und Ge-
-gui- nis- que pre- ti-

81

-chen. Mach uns mei- den,
Fru- ctus ven- tris

Durch dein Lei- den, Al Boß-
ge- ne- ro- si, Rex ef-

-heit und Mis- se- that.
-fu- dit gen- ti- um.]

23. Virgo prudentissima / Fortuna

Vienna 18810

Ludwig Senfl

15
quo pro- gre- de- ris
quo pro- - gre- - - -
progre- - de- ris, pro- gre- de- ris
pro- gre- - - de- ris
20
qua- si au- ro- ra,
- - - de- ris qua-
qua- - si au- ro- - ra,
qua- - - si au- ro- -
25
au- ro- - - ra, au-
-si au- ro- - ra
au- ro- - - - ra,
-ra,
au- ro- -

29
-ro- ra val- - - de ru-
val- - de ru- -
au- ro- ra val- de ru- ti- - -
- ra val- - de ru- - ti-
34
- - ti- lans? Fi- li- a Sy-
-ti- - lans? Fi- li- a Sy- -
-lans? Fi- li- a Sy-
-lans? Fi- - li- a Sy-
39
- on, to- - ta for-
- on,
- on, to- - - ta for- mo-
- on, to- ta for- - mo-

44
- mo- sa, et sua- - vis es, et
to- - ta for- mo- sa et sua-
-sa, to- ta for- mo- sa et sua- -
-sa, for- mo- sa et sua- - vis es,
49
sua- - vis es, pul-
- vis es, pul- chra ut
-vis es, pul-
pul- chra
54
- chra ut lu- na, e- le- cta
lu- - - -
- - chra ut lu- na, e-
ut lu- - - -

59
es, e- le- cta es, e- le- cta es, e-
-na, e- le- cta
-le- cta es, e- le- cta es, e- le- cta es, e- le-
-na, e- le- cta es, e- le- cta es, e- le-
64
-le- cta es ut sol.
ut sol.
-cta ut sol.
-cta ut sol, ut sol.

24. Helena desiderio plena / Fortuna

Vienna 18810

Ludwig Senfl

dicens, "Tu, Domine, ostende lignum in quo salus nostra fuit suspensa." Helena,

Fortuna Helena desiderio plena

34
de- si- de- ri- o ple- - na,
-na, de- - si- de- ri-
-na, de- si- de- - ri- o ple- - - na, de-
de- si- de- ri- o ple- - na, ple-
39
de- si- de- ri- o ple- na,
-o ple- na, ple- -
- si- de- ri- o ple- na, o- - - ra-
- na, ple- - - - na,
44
o- ra- bat cum la- chri- mis, cum la chri-
-na, o- ra-
- - bat cum la- chri- mis,
o- ra- bat cum la- chri- mis, cum la- chri-

48
-mis, di- - - - - cens,
- bat cum la- - chri-
cum la- chri- mis, di- - -
-mis, cum la- - chri- mis, di- cens, "Tu,
53
"Tu, Do- - mi- ne, tu, Do- mi- ne, o-
-mis, "Tu, Do- mi- ne,
- - cens, "Tu, Do- mi- ne,
Do- mi- ne, tu, Do- mi- ne, tu, Do- mi- ne,
58
-sten- - - de lig-
o- sten- de lig-
o- sten- - de lig- - num in quo
o- sten- de lig-

63
- num in quo sa- - - lus
-num in
sa- lus, in quo sa-
- num in quo sa-
68
no- stra, no- - stra, in quo sa-
quo sa- lus
-lus, in quo sa- - lus no- -
- lus, sa- - lus no- - stra,
73
-lus no- - - - -
no- - stra,
- stra, no- - stra fu- it su-
no- - - stra fu- -

93

25. Nasci, pati, mori / Fortuna

Vienna 18810

Ludwig Senfl

17
na- - sci,
na- - sci, pa- - ti,
-ri, na- - sci, pa- ti, mo- -
-sci, pa- - - ti, mo-
22
pa- - - ti, mo- ri, na-
mo- - - ri, na- - - sci,
- - ri, na- - sci, pa-
- ri, na- sci, pa- - ti, mo- - ri,
28
- - sci, na- - -
pa- ti, mo- - - ri, na- sci, pa-
-ti, mo- - - - ri, mo-
na- sci, pa- ti, mo- ri, na-

33
-sci, pa- - -
- ti, mo- - ri,
- - - ri, na-
- sci, pa- - ti, mo- - -
38
- - ti, mo- - - ri,
na- - - - sci, pa- ti,
- sci, pa- - ti, mo- - ri, mo-
-ri, na- - sci, pa- - -
44
na- - sci, pa- - ti, na-
mo- ri, mo- - - ri, na-
- ri, mo- - ri, na-
-ti, mo- - ri, na-

49
-sci, pa- ti, mo- ri, na-
-sci, pa- - ti, mo- -
-sci, pa- ti, mo- - -
-sci, pa- ti, mo- ri, na- -
53
- sci, pa- ti, mo- - ri.
- ri, na- sci, pa- - -
-ri, mo- - ri, na- - sci, pa-
- sci, pa- ti, mo- ri, na-
58
-ti, mo- - - ri.
- ti, mo- - - - ri.
- sci, pa- ti, mo- ri.

26. Fortuna ad voces musicales

1534[17], no. 31

Ludwig Senfl

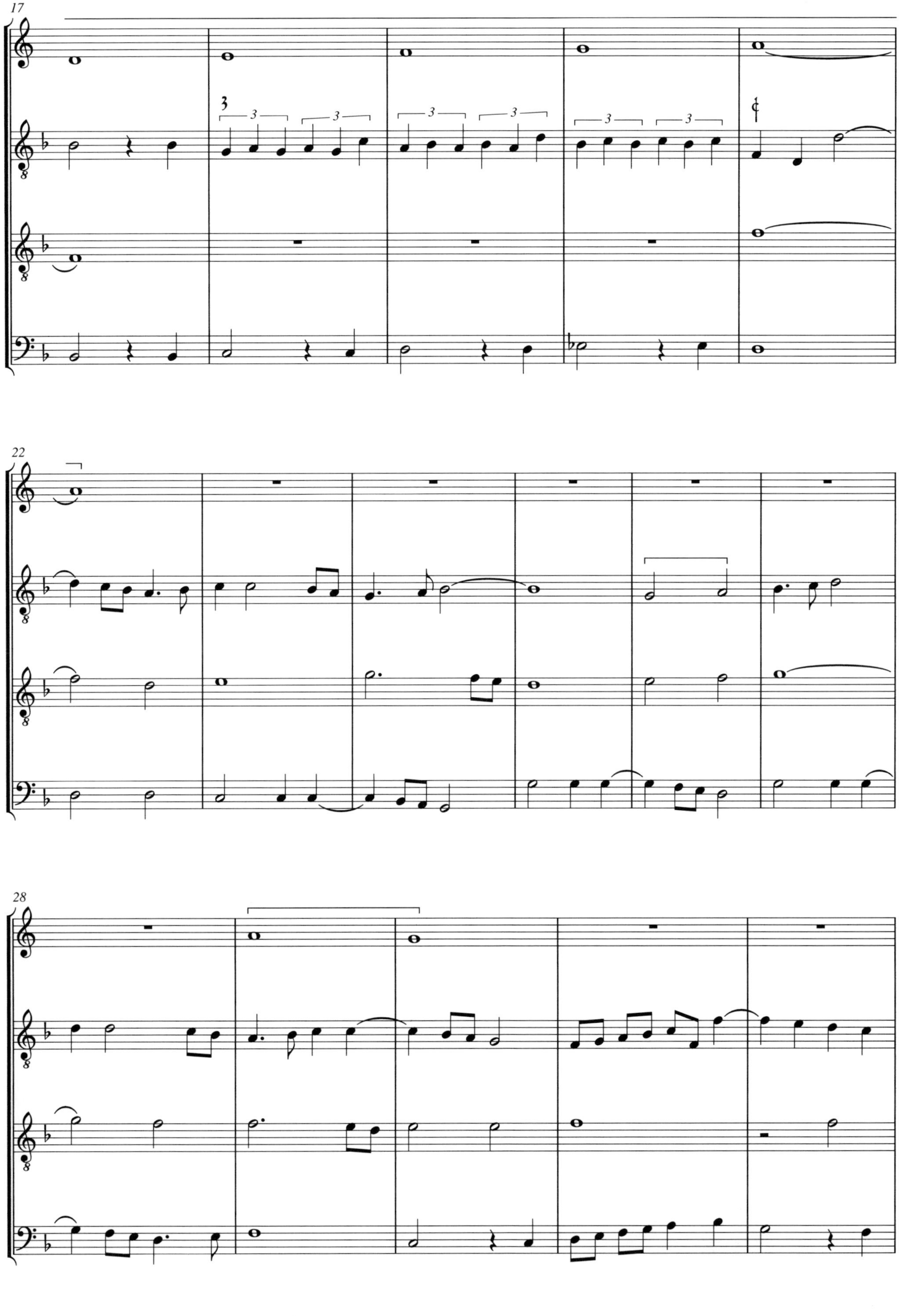
17
3
3
3
3
3
3
3
22
28

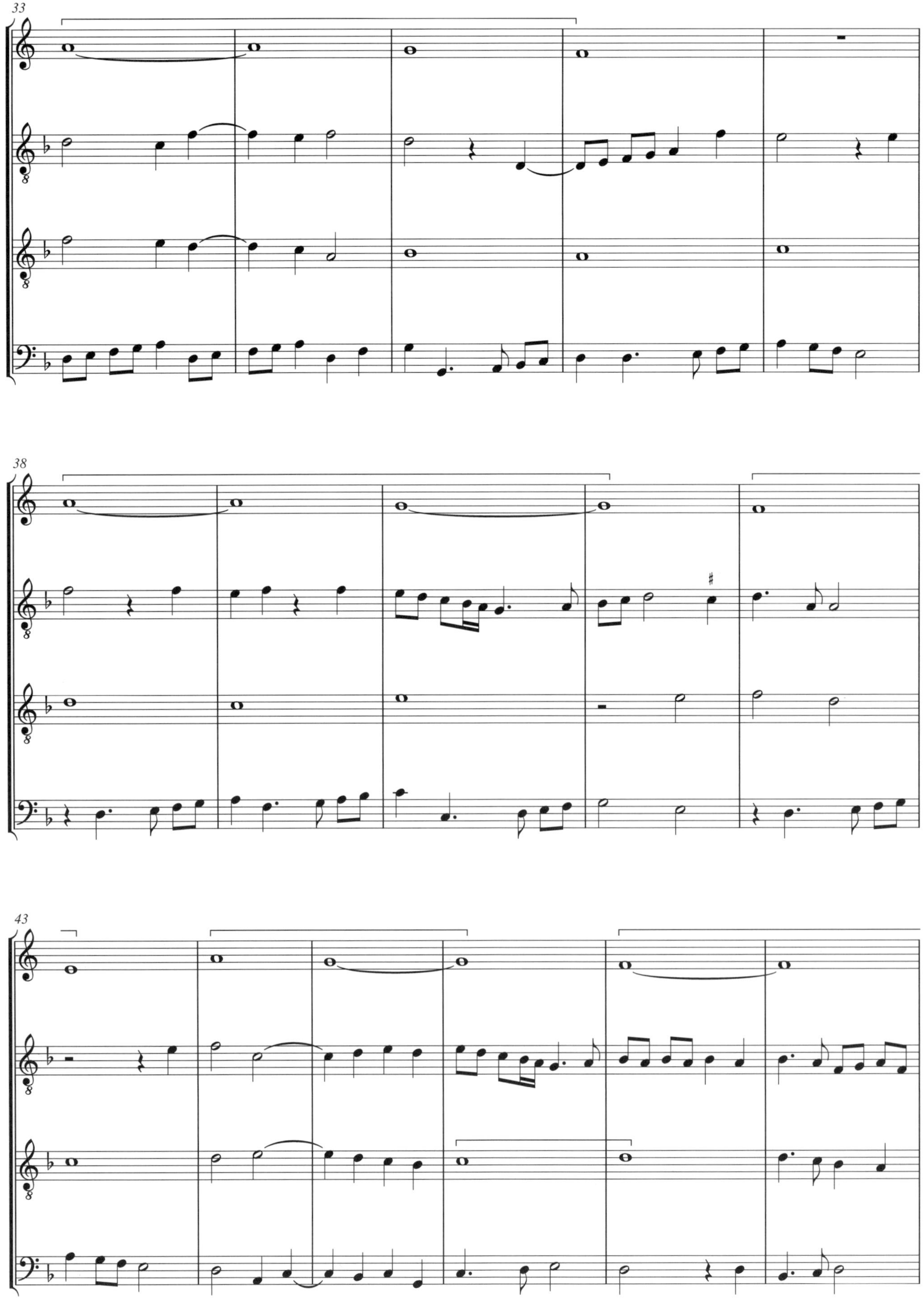
33
38
43

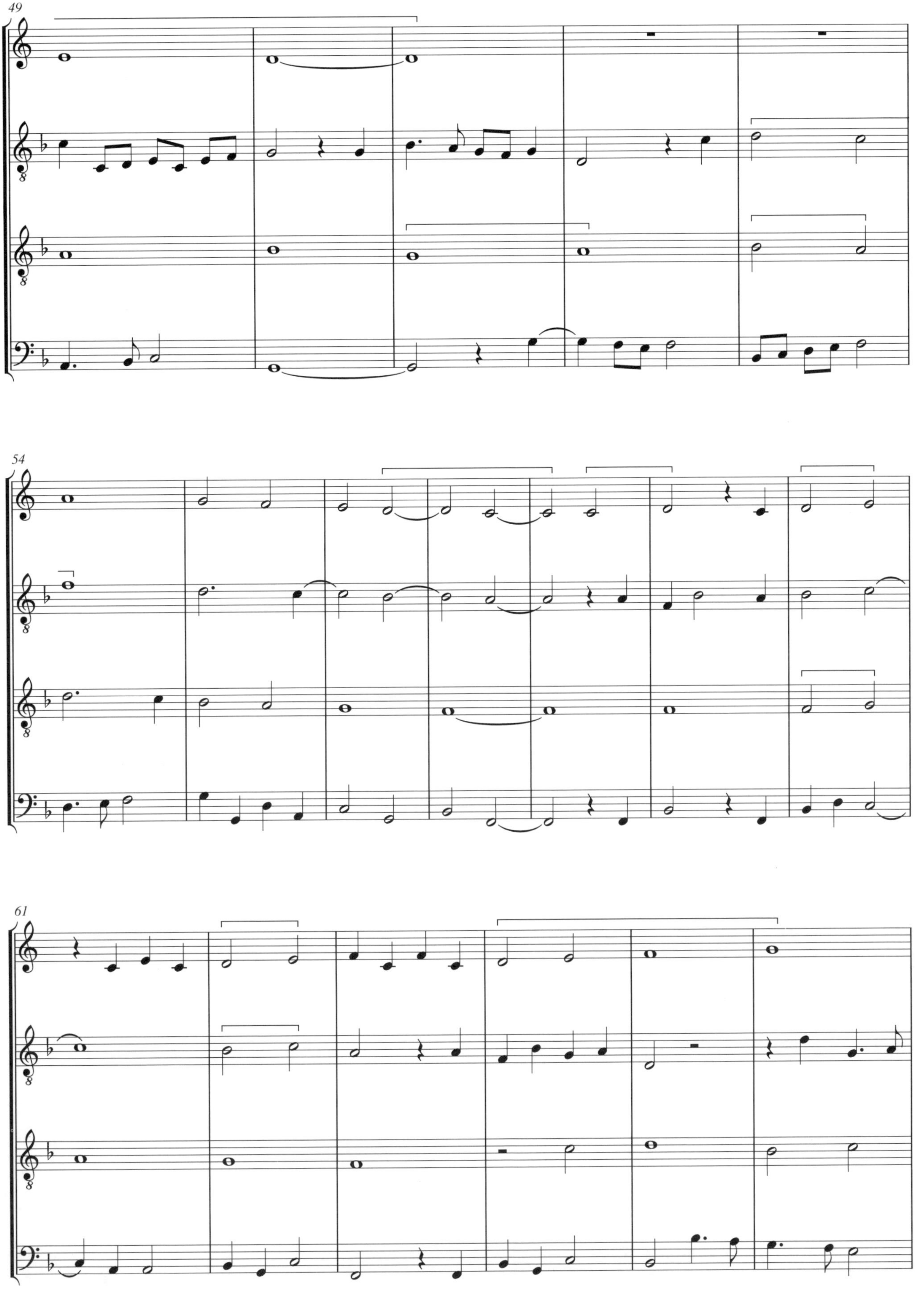
49
54
61

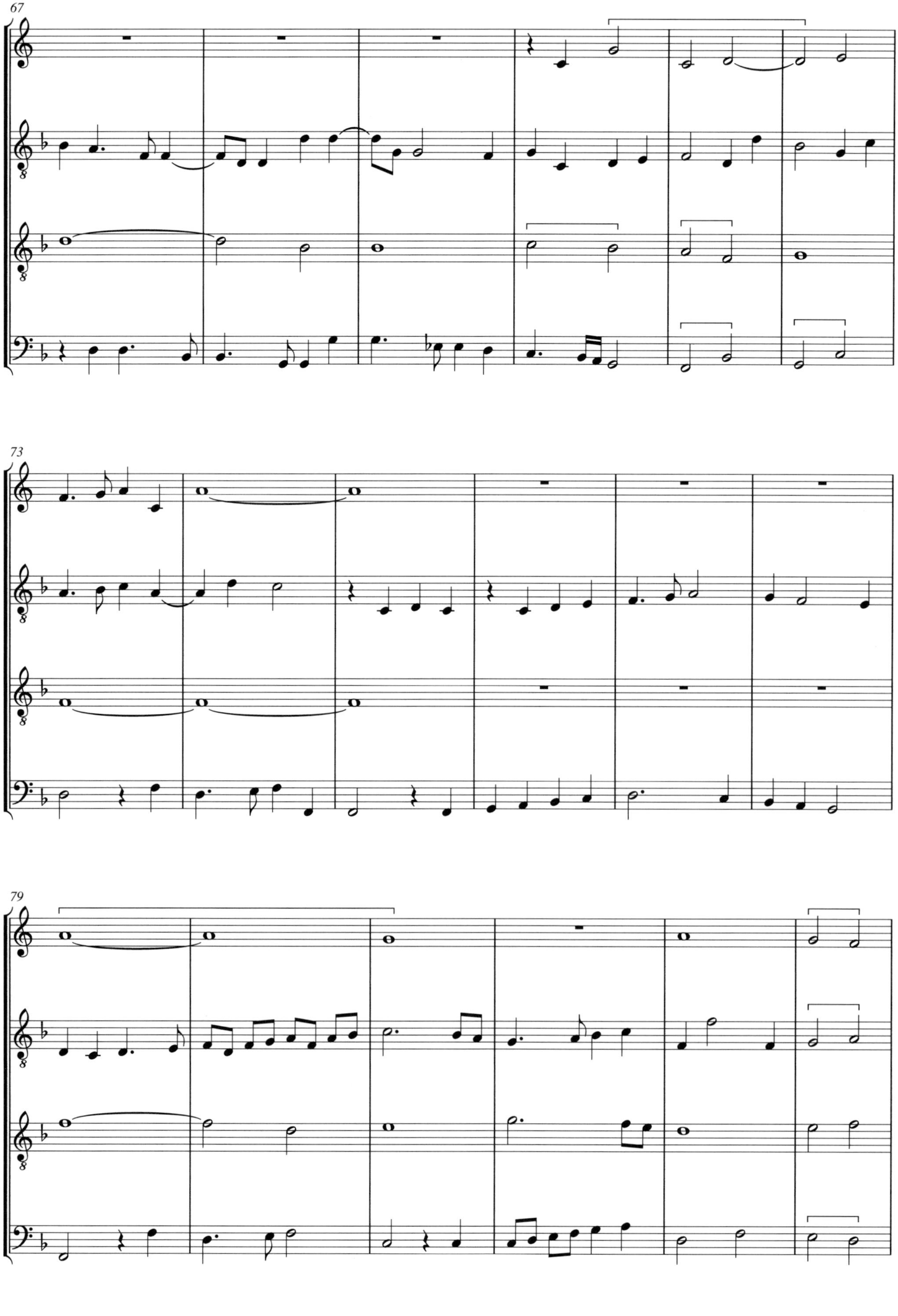
67
73
79

103

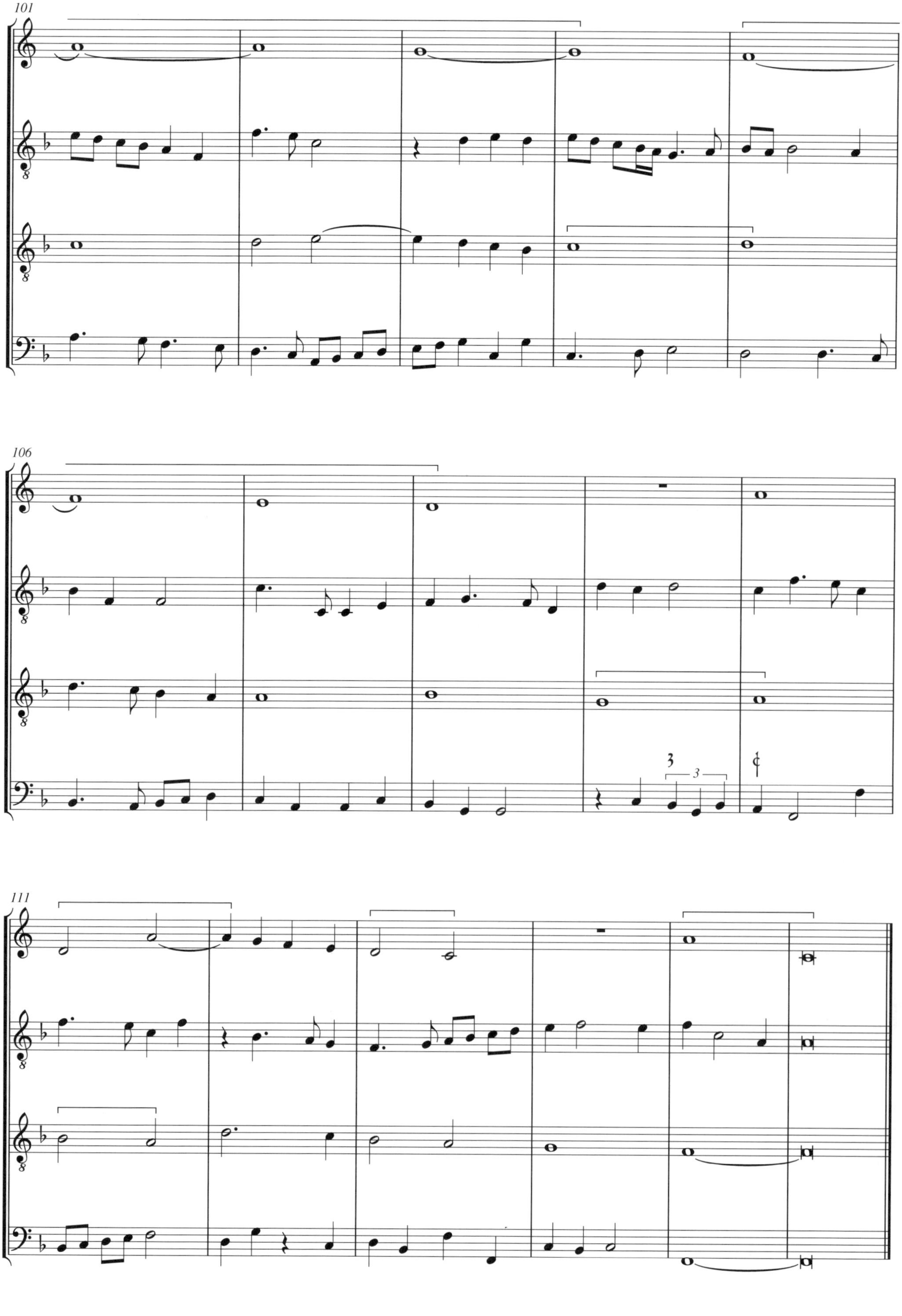
101
106
3
3
111

27. Passibus ambiguis

1553 Faber, pp. 140–51

Matthias Greiter

*See the critical commentary for an explanation of signature and ficta accidentals in FD27.

⟨for- tu- na,⟩ ⟨for- tu-
vo- lu-

-na⟩ vo- lu- bi- lis,
- bi- lis

vo- lu- bi- lis er-

er-

- - - rat

- - rat

Pars altera

Et manet

Et manet

Et manet

109

nul - - lo

cer- ta -

- ta te- nax-

111

Settings Using the Tenor in Mi
28. Fortuna desperata

Zwickau 78/3, no. 10 [Heinrich Isaac]

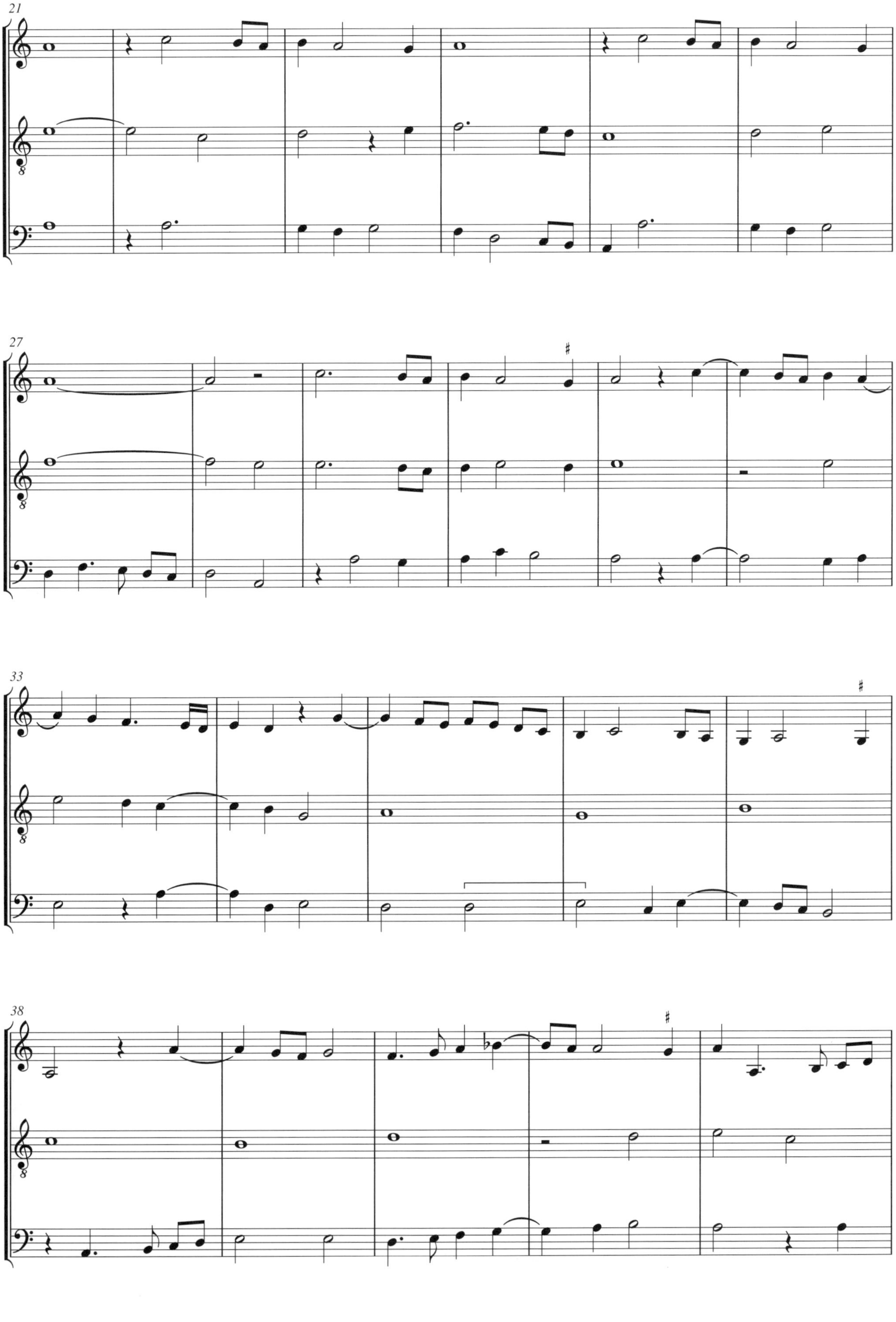
21
27
33
38

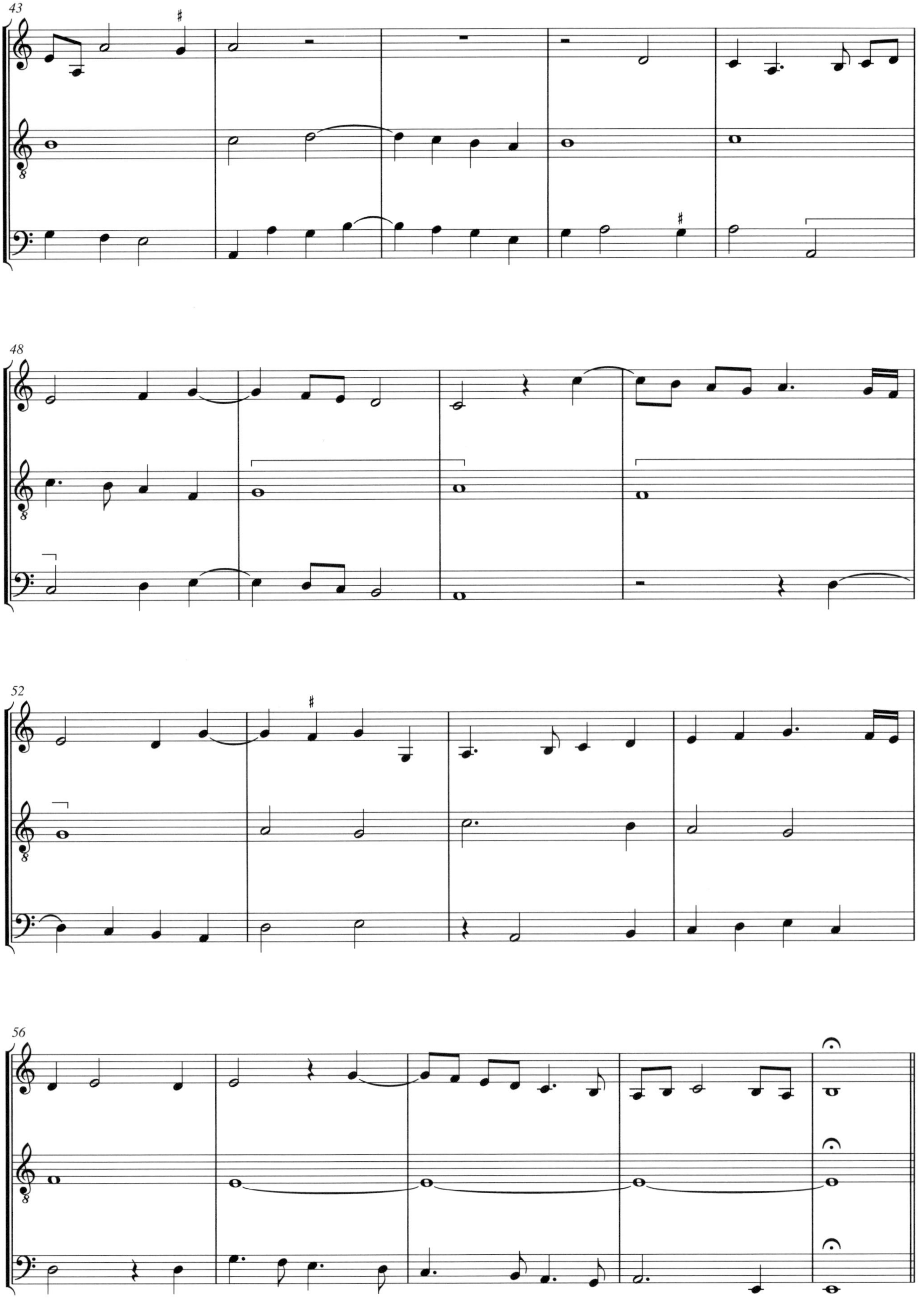
43
48
52
56

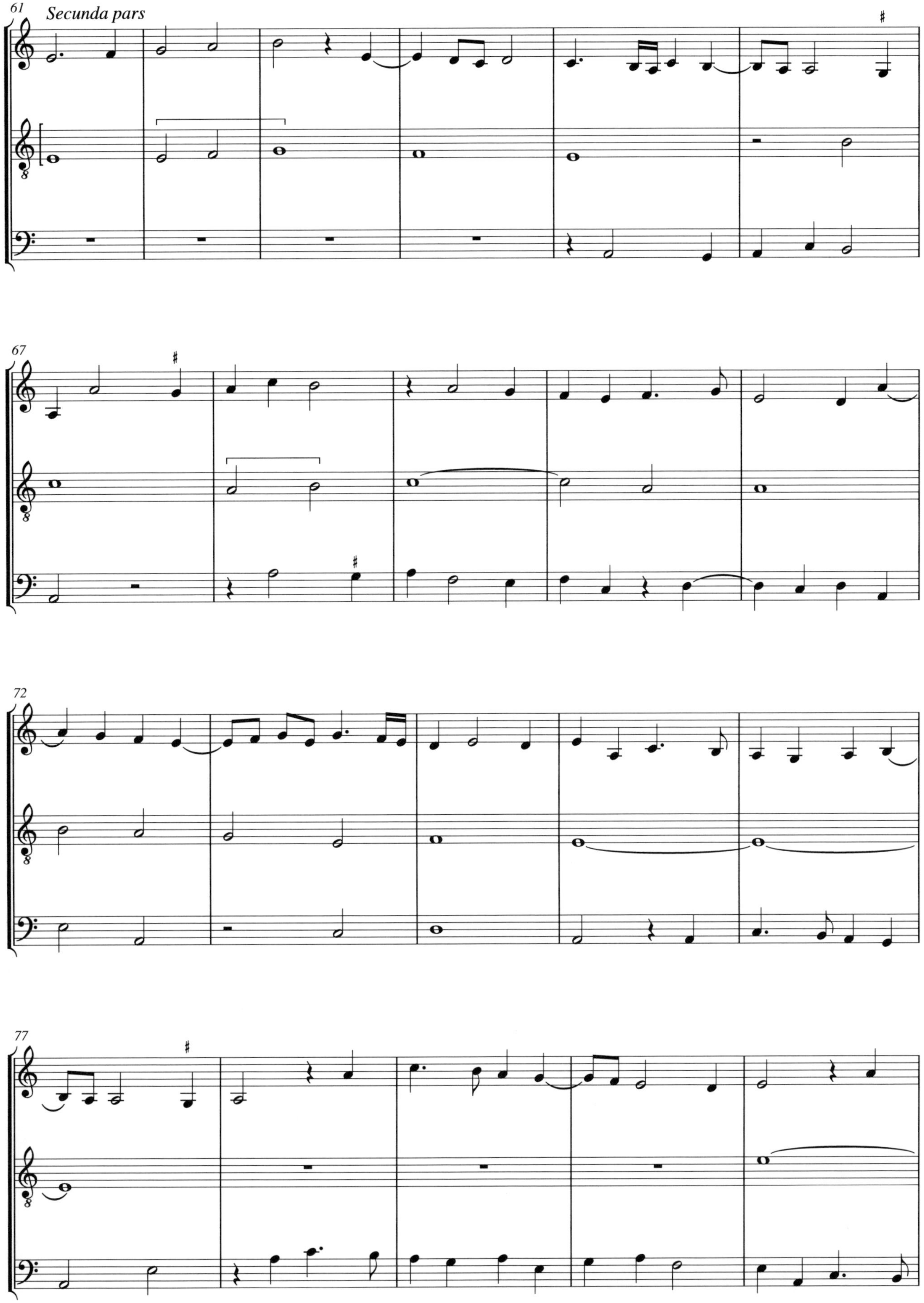
61
Secunda pars
67
72
77

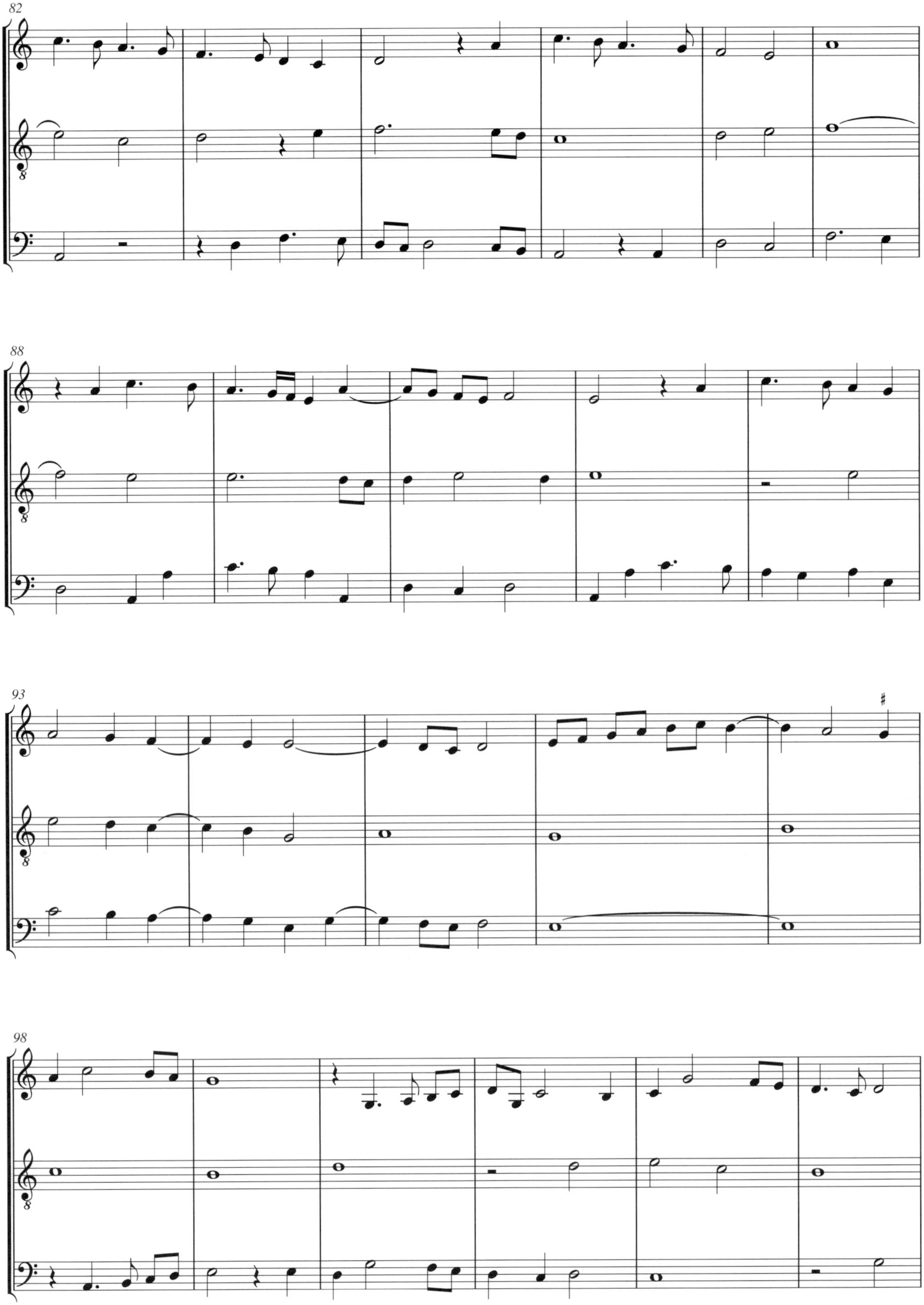
82
88
93
98

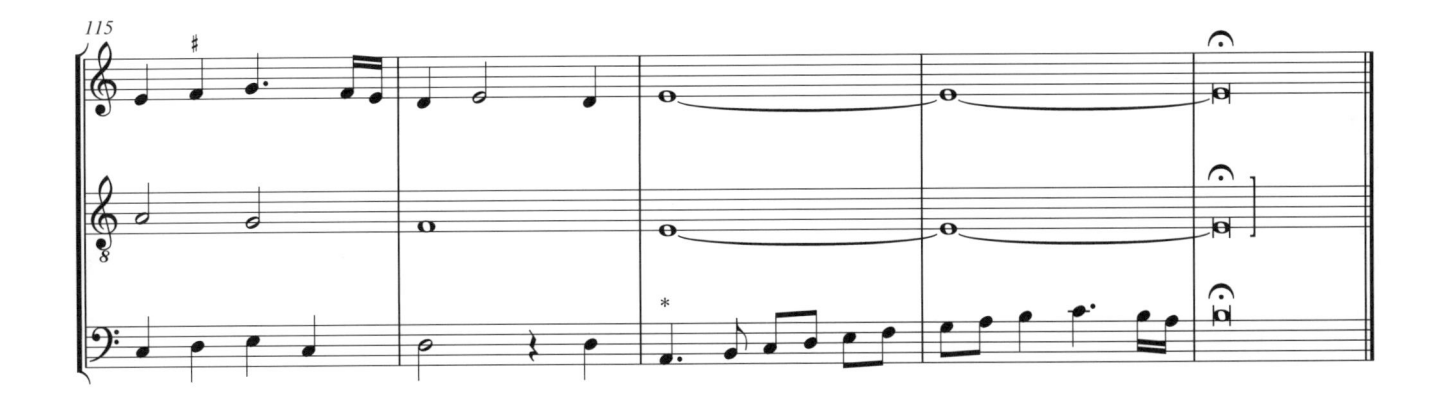

*See the critical commentary for an alternative bassus conclusion.

29. Fortuna desperata

Regensburg C120, pp. 284–85

anonymous

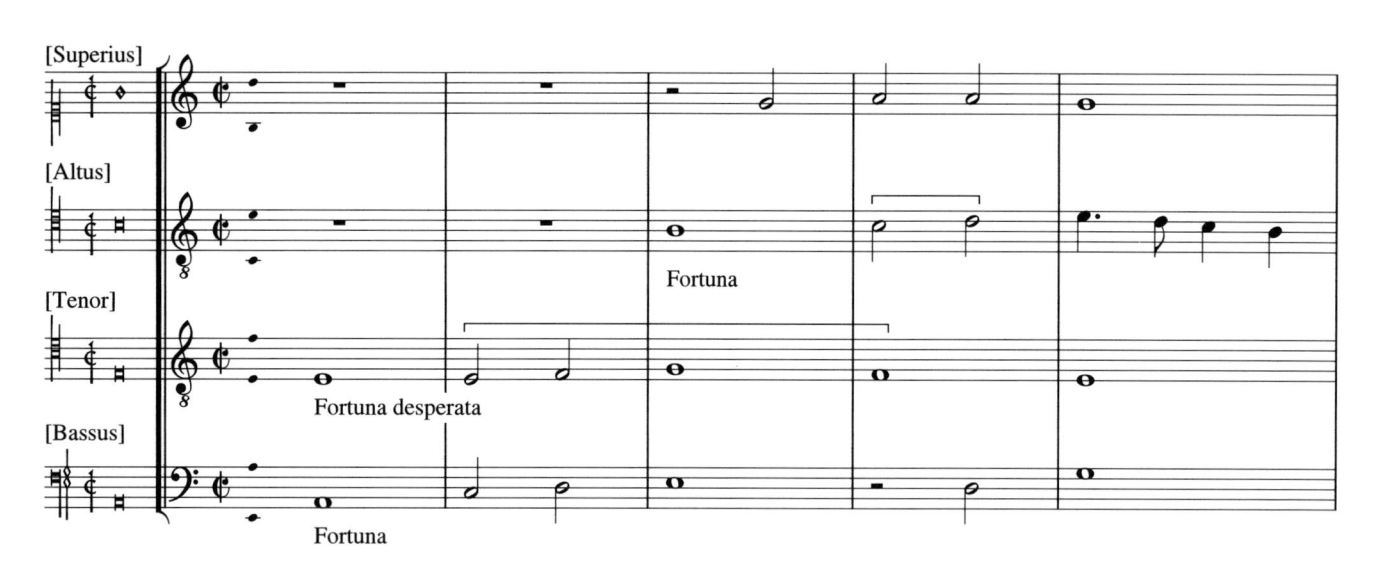

119

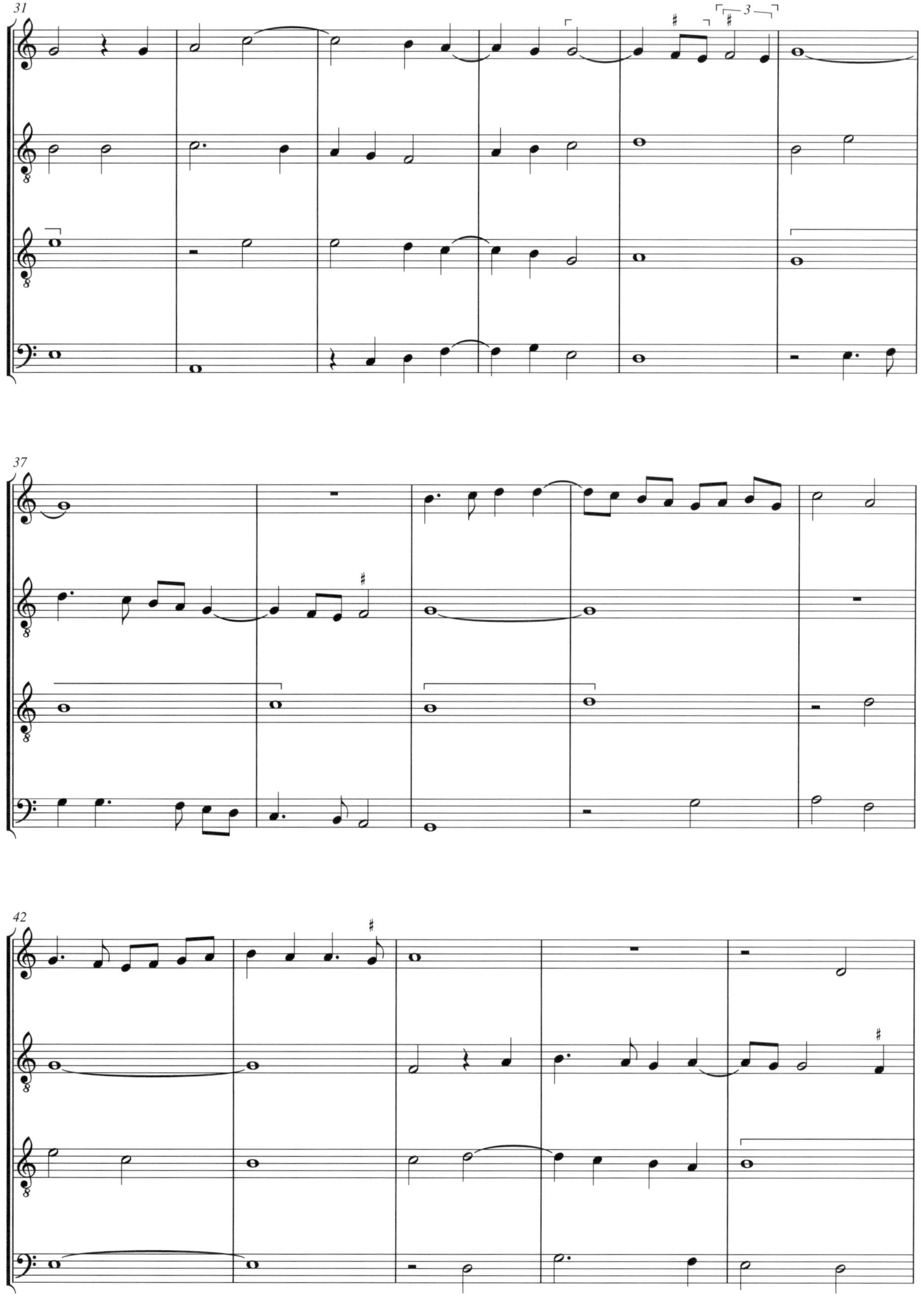
31
37
42
3

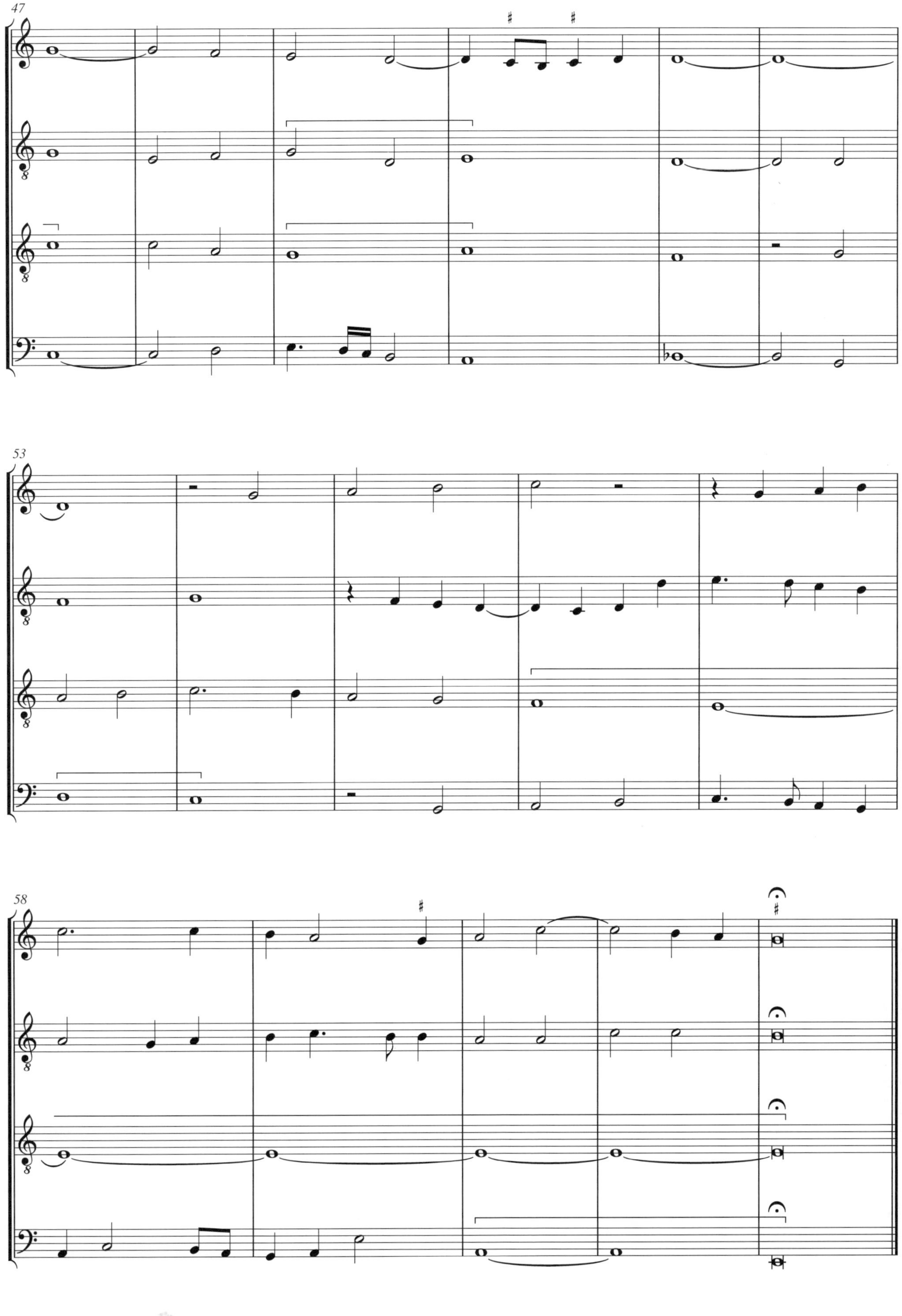
47
53
58

30. Ave mater matris Dei / Fortuna disperata

Bologna Q19, fols. 106v–107

Jacquet of Mantua

15
quam sal- - vi fi- unt re- - i.
[per quam sal- - vi fi- unt re-
- unt re- i, fi- unt re- -
quam sal- - vi fi- - unt re-
20
A- ve pro- le fe- cun- da- ta, [fe- cun- da- ta,] An- na
-i.] A- ve pro- le fe- - cun- da- ta, fe- cun- da-
-i. A- ve pro- le fe- - cun- da-
- i. A- ve pro- le fe- cun- da- ta, An-
25
De- o de- di- ca- ta, de- di- ca- ta,
-ta, An- na De- o de- di- ca- ta, An- na De-
-ta, An- na De- o de- di- ca- ta,
-na De- o de- di- ca- ta, An- na De- o de-

30
[de- - di- ca- - ta,] An- - na De- o de-
-o de- di- ca- ta, [de- di- ca- -
An- na De- o de- di- ca- - ta.
-di- ca- ta. Pro fi- de- li ple- be
35
- di- ca- ta. Pro fi-
-ta.] Pro fi- - de- li ple- be to- ta,
Pro fi- de- - li
to- ta, pro fi- de-
40
- de- li ple- be to- ta, [ple-
ple- be to- ta, [ple- - be to-
ple- - be to- - - ta, [ple-
- li ple- be to- -

45
- be to- ta,] A- - pud Chri-stum sis de- vo-
- ta,] A- pud Chri- stum sis de- vo-
- be to- ta,] A- pud Chri- stum sis
- - ta, A- pud
50
-ta, a- - pud Chri- stum sis de- vo- ta sis [de-
-ta, a- pud Chri- stum sis de- vo- ta. Al- le- lu-
de- vo- ta, a- pud Chri- stum sis de-
Chri- stum sis de- vo- - ta, a-
55
-vo- ta.] Al- le- lu- ia, al- le- lu- ia.
-ia, al- le- lu- - ia.
-vo- ta. Al- le- lu- ia, al- le- lu- ia.
-pud Chri-stum sis de- vo- ta. Al- le- lu- - ia, al- - le- lu- ia.

31. Consideres mes incessantes plaintes / Fortuna desperata

Vienna 18746
anonymous

Superius Cantus
fols. 22–22v

Contratenor: altus
fols. 24–24v

Tenores ad longum
fol. 20v

Secundus Tenor vel vagans
fols. 23–23v

Bassus
fols. 21v–22

Consideres

Consideres

Consideres mes incessantes plaintes.   Fortuna desperata

Consideres mes incessantes

Consideres mes incessantes plaintes

127

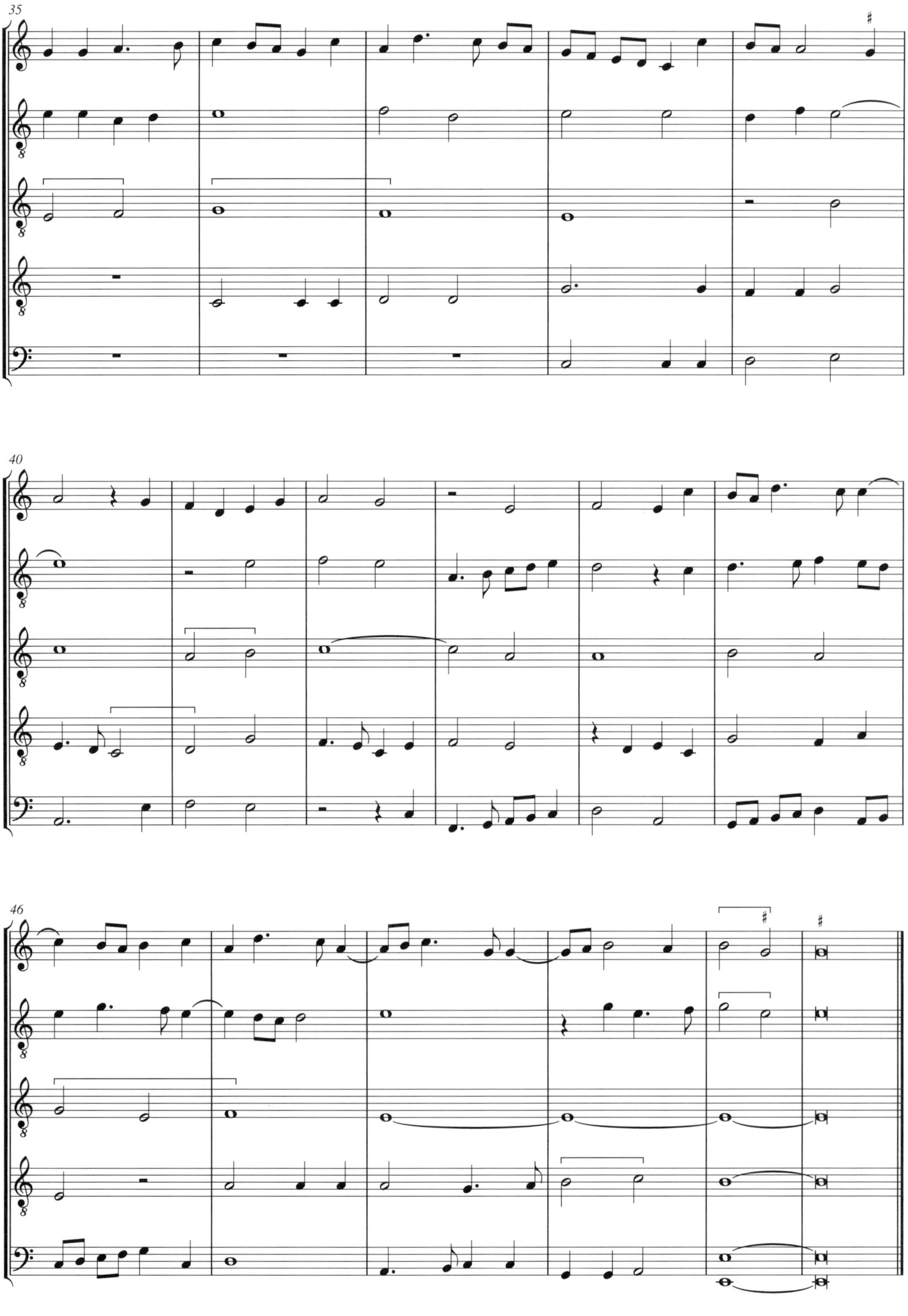
35
40
46

32. Anima mea liquefacta est / Amica mea

1554[9]

Cabilliau

15
-ctus lo- cu- tus est. Quae- si- vi et non in- ve- ni il- lum; vo-
Quae- si- vi, ⟨quae- si- vi⟩ et non in- ve- ni il- lum; vo-
-mi- - ca me-
Quae- si- vi et non in- ve- ni il- - lum; vo- ca-
lo- cu- tus est. Quae- si- vi et non in- ve- ni il-
20
-ca- vi et non re- spon- dit mi- - hi.
-ca- vi et non re- spon- dit mi- - - hi.
- - - a,
-vi et non re- spon- dit mi- hi. Ad- iu- ro
-lum; vo- ca- vi et non re- spon- dit mi- hi.
25
Ad- iu- ro vos, fi- li- e Ie- ru- - sa-
Ad- iu- ro vos, fi- li- e Ie- ru- sa-
⟨a- mi- ca me-
vos, fi- li- e Ie- ru- sa- lem, ad- iu- ro
Ad- iu- ro

131

45
qui- a a- mo- re, qui- a [a- mo- re lan-
qui- a a- mo- re lan- gue- o, ⟨qui- a a- mo- re
⟨a- mi- ca me- a.⟩
-mo- re lan- gue- o,] qui- a a- mo- re, qui-
-mo- re,⟩ qui- a [a- mo- re lan- gue- o,] qui- a
50
- gue- o.]
lan- gue- o,⟩ qui- a [a- mo- re lan- gue- o.]
-a [a- mo- re] lan- - gue- o, ⟨lan- gue- o.⟩
a- mo- re, ⟨qui- a a- mo- re⟩ lan- gue- o.

33. Fortuna

1534[17], no. 121

Wilhelm Breitengraser

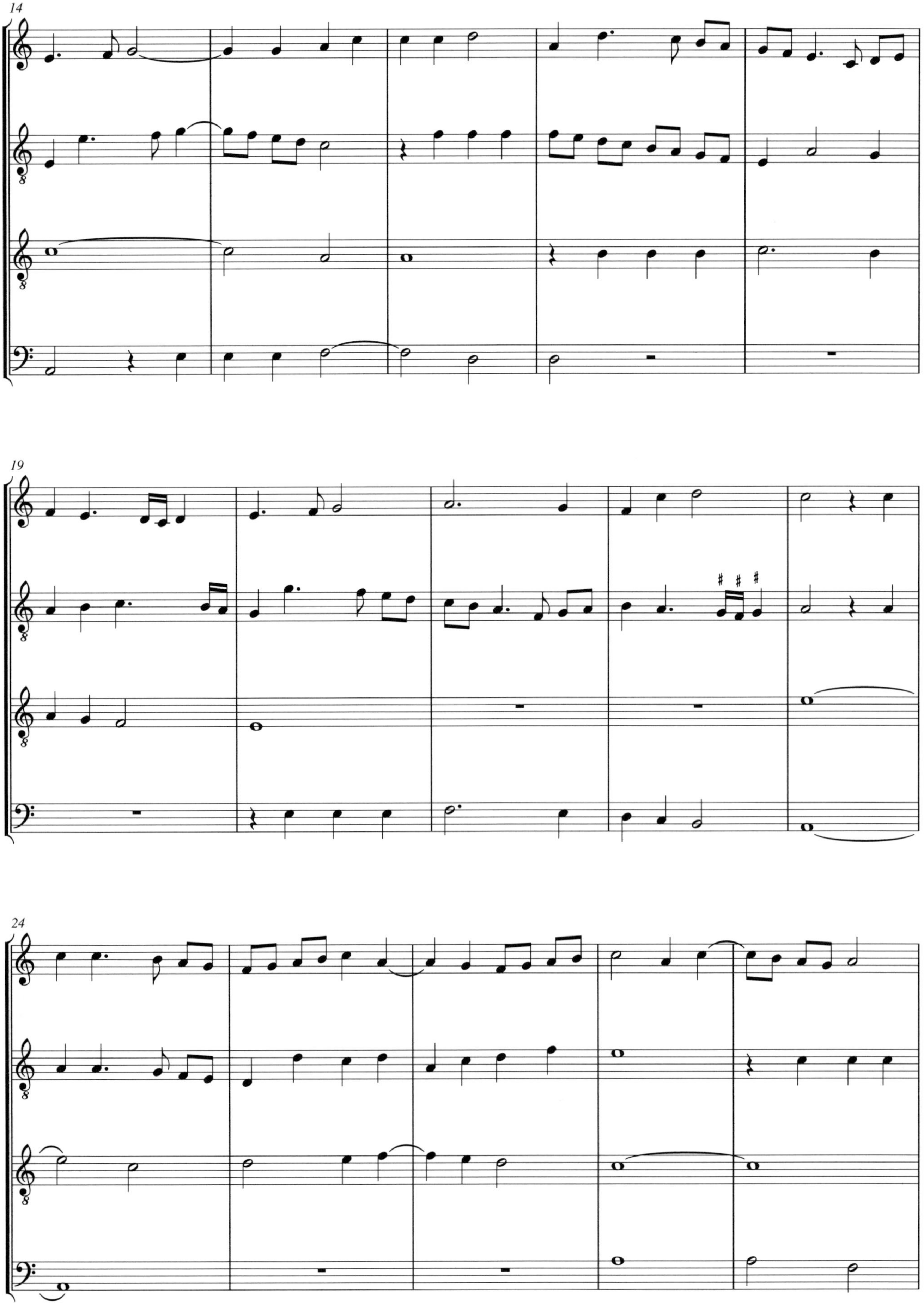
14
19
24

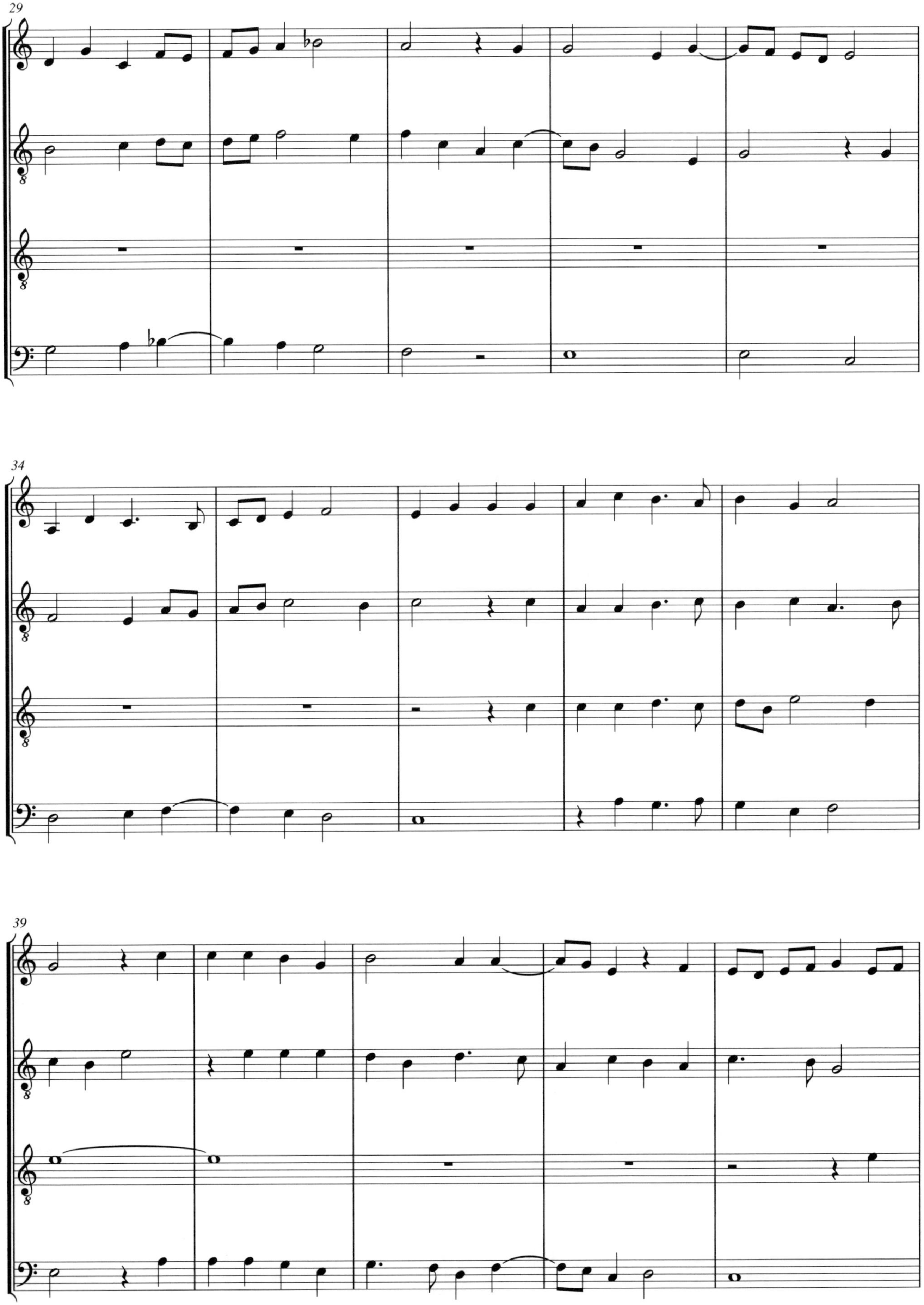
29
34
39

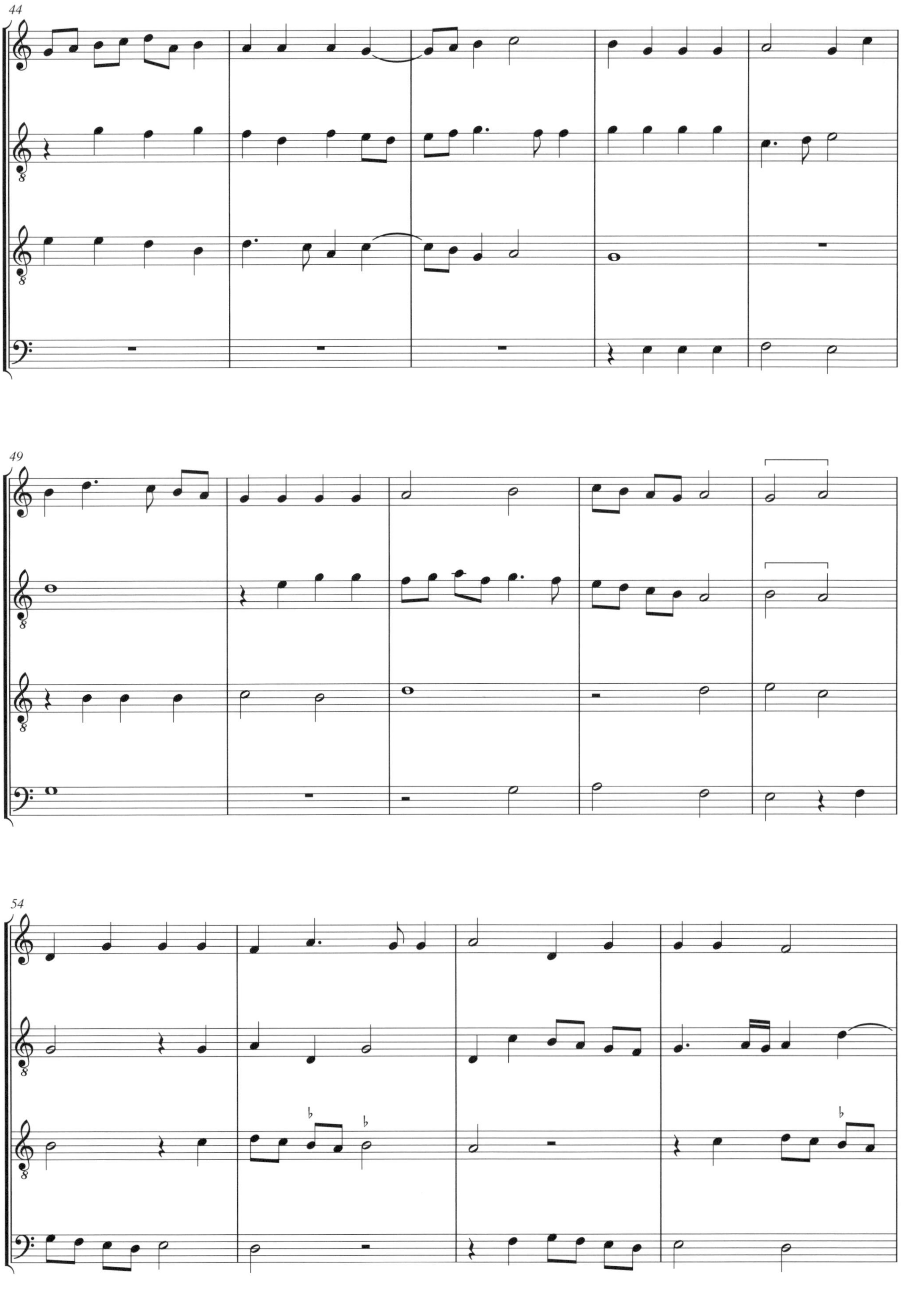
44
49
54

137

Settings with Voices Missing
34. Fortuna desperata quae te dementia coepit?

St. Gall 463, fol. 13v (no. 29)

anonymous

Discantus

Tenor
Vienna 18810, fol. 43v

-le- mur con- tra- ri- is [fa- - - - tis.] O so- ci- i (ne- que e- nim su- -mus ig- na- ri an- te ma- lo- rum, Sed

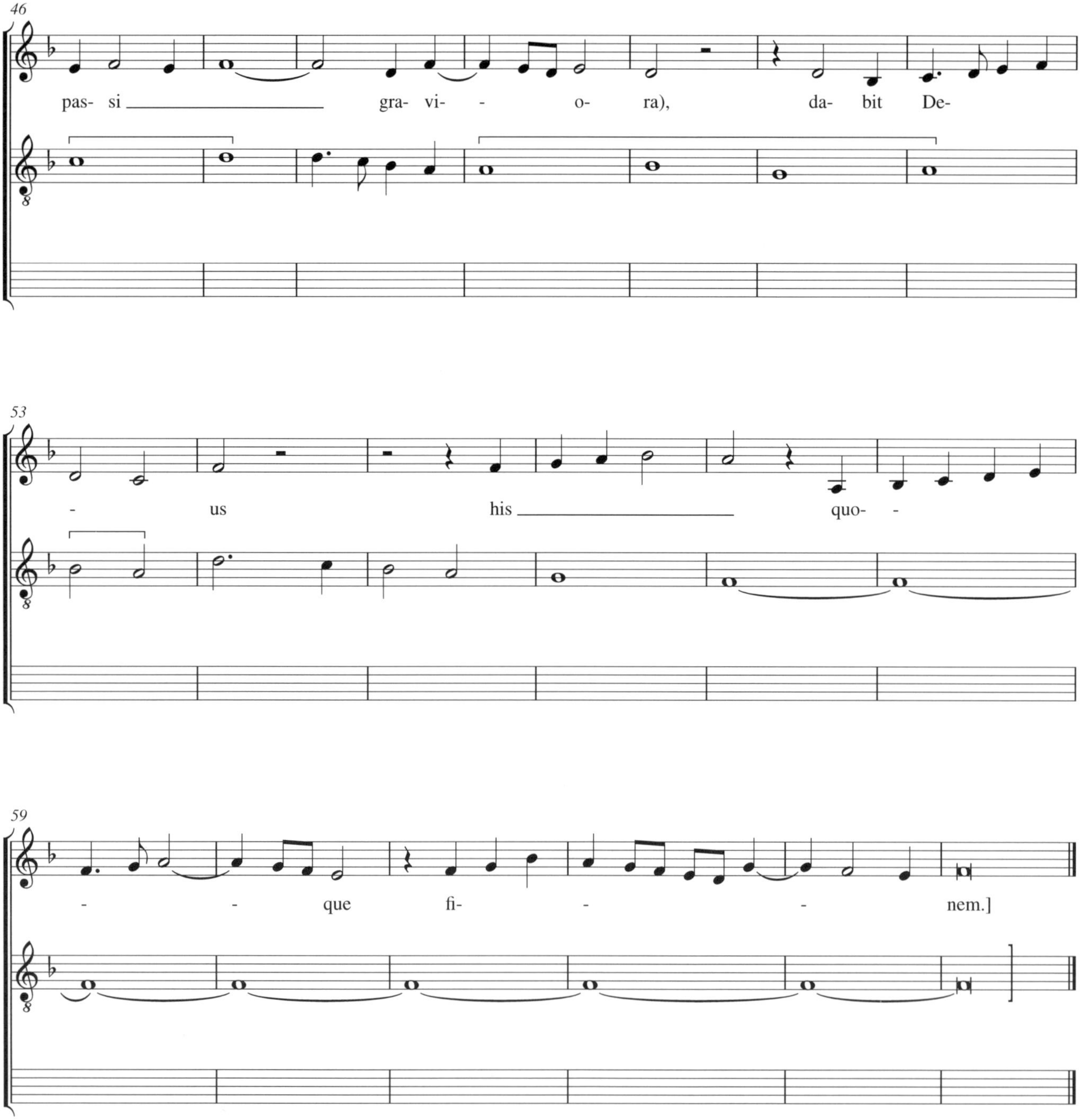
46
pas- si gra- vi- - o- ra), da- bit De-
53
- us his quo- -
59
- - que fi- - - nem.]

35. Fortuna

Munich 328–31

anonymous

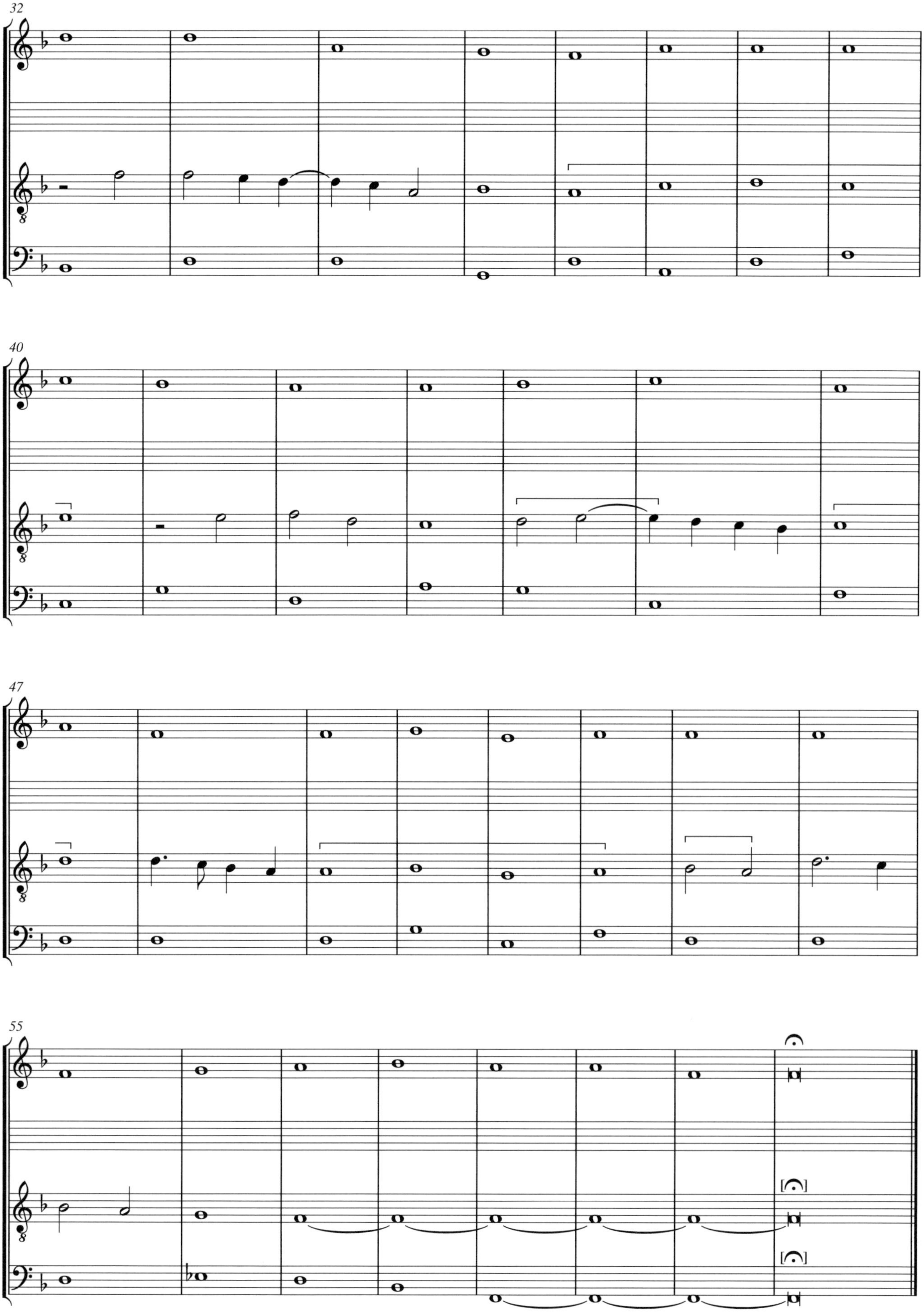
32
40
47
55

36. Fortuna desperata quae te dementia vertit?

Robertus Fabri

-ti- a ver- tit? So- le-

-mur con- tra- ri- is, [con- tra- ri- is] fa-

-tis. [O so- ci- -i (ne- que e- nim su- mus ig- na-

-ri an- te ma- lo- rum,

Sed pas- si gra- vi- o-

147

Critical Report

List of Sources

Unless otherwise noted, manuscript sigla, dating, and provenance are based upon information included in Charles Hamm and Herbert Kellman, eds., *The Census-Catalogue of Manuscript Sources of Polyphonic Music, 1400–1550*, 5 vols., Renaissance Manuscript Studies, no. 1 (Neuhausen-Stuttgart: Hänssler, 1979–88). Information on sources for the Josquin and Obrecht masses is from Josquin CW and Obrecht CW, respectively. Print sources include reference numbers, when available, for *Recueils imprimés XVIe–XVIIe siècles*, ed. François Lesure, series B/1 of *Répertoire international des sources musicales* [RISM] (München-Duisburg: G. Henle, 1960). Bibliographic information for facsimile editions is also provided. FD numbers refer to the numbers assigned to the pieces in this edition.

Augsburg 142a Augsburg, Staats- und Stadtbibliothek, MS 2° 142a (*olim* Cim. 43).
1505–14; Augsburg
FD6

Barcelona 5 Barcelona, Biblioteca de L'Orfeó Català, MS 5 (shelf mark: 12-VI-12).
late 15th century; place of origin unknown
Josquin mass

Basel F.IX.22 Basel, Öffentliche Bibliothek der Universität, MS F.IX.22.
1513 (prima pars) and 1515 (secunda pars); Basel and/or Freiburg[1]
FD28

Basel F.X.10 Basel, Öffentliche Bibliothek der Universität, MS F.X.10.
ca. 1500–1510; Basel
FD2?

Berlin 40021 Berlin, Staatsbibliothek Preussischer Kulturbesitz, MS Mus. 40021 (*olim* Z 21).
mass paper 1489–93; Germany
Obrecht mass

Berlin 40026 Berlin, Staatliches Institut für Musikforschung Preussischer Kulturbesitz, Mus. MS 40026 (*olim* Z 26)
ca. 1520–24;[2] Pforzheim
FD1, FD2, FD28, Luscinius intabulation, Buchner intabulation

Bologna A38 Bologna, Archivio Musicale della Fabbriceria di San Petronio, MS A.XXXVIII (*olim* CC).
ca. 1525; Bologna
Anonymous mass I

Bologna Q16 Bologna, Civico Museo Bibliografico Musicale, MS Q16 (*olim* 109).
1490s; probably Naples or Rome
FD3

Bologna Q17 Bologna, Civico Museo Bibliografico Musicale, MS Q17 (*olim* 148).
post-1497 and possibly post-1500;[3] northern Italy, probably Florence or vicinity
FD16

Bologna Q18 Bologna, Civico Museo Bibliografico Musicale, MS Q18 (*olim* 143).
ca. 1502–6; Bologna
FD12

Bologna Q19 Bologna, Civico Museo Bibliografico Musicale, MS Q19.
ca. 1518; northern Italy
FD30

Canti C *Canti C. N° cento cinquanta*. Venice: Petrucci, 1504 n.s. (*Canti C: Numero cento cinquanta*, Monuments of Music and Music Literature in Facsimile, 1st ser., music, vol. 25 [New York: Broude Bros., 1978].)
RISM 1504[3]
FD2, FD14

Cape Town Grey Cape Town, South African Public Library, MS Grey 3.b.12.

	pre-1506; northern Italy FD2
Casanatense 2856	Rome, Biblioteca Casanatense, MS 2856 (*olim* O.V. 208). ca. 1479–81; Ferrara FD9
C.G. XIII.27	Vatican City, Biblioteca Apostolica Vaticana, MS Cappella Giulia XIII 27. 1492–94; Florence FD2/7, FD15
Cortona/Paris	Cortona, Biblioteca Comunale, MSS 95–96 (superius and altus partbooks); Paris, Bibliothèque Nationale, Département des Manuscrits, Nouvelles Acquisitions Françaises, MS 1817 (tenor partbook). ca. 1519–23;[4] Florence FD13
C.S. 41	Vatican City, Biblioteca Apostolica Vaticana, MS Cappella Sistina 41. ca. 1492–95; Rome Josquin mass
Florence 107	Florence, Biblioteca Nazionale Centrale, MS Magliabechi XIX. 107bis. 1510–13; Florence Obrecht mass excerpts: Christe, Pleni, Benedictus, Agnus II
Florence 121	Florence, Biblioteca Nazionale Centrale, MS Magliabechi XIX. 121. ca. 1510; Florence FD1, FD15
Florence 164–67	Florence, Biblioteca Nazionale Centrale, MSS Magliabechi XIX. 164–167. (*Florence, Biblioteca nazionale centrale, MSS Magl. XIX, 164–167*, with an introduction by Howard Mayer Brown, Renaissance Music in Facsimile, vol. 5 [New York: Garland, 1987].) ca. 1520;[5] Florence FD13
Florence 196	Florence, Biblioteca Riccardiana, Edizioni rare 196. after 24 June 1514[6] Lauda text "Poi ch'io t'ebbi nel core"
Florence 337	Florence, Biblioteca Nazionale Centrale, MS Banco Rari 337 (*olim* Palatino 1178). ca. 1520; probably Florence FD13
Florence 2439	Florence, Biblioteca del Conservatorio di Musica Luigi Cherubini, MS Basevi 2439. (*Basevi Codex: Florence, Biblioteca del Conservatorio, MS 2439*, with an introduction by Honey Meconi, Facsimile Editions of Prints and Manuscripts [Peer, Belgium: Alamire, 1990].) ca. 1505–8; Habsburg-Burgundian court scriptorium Obrecht mass excerpts: Kyrie II, Sanctus, Osanna
Florence Pan. 27	Florence, Biblioteca Nazionale Centrale, MS Panciatichi 27. early 16th century; northern Italy, probably Mantua FD4
Frankfurt 20	Frankfurt am Main, Stadt- und Universitätsbibliothek, Fragm. lat. VII 20. ca. 1500; Frankfurt?[7] FD1?
Herdringen 9821	Herdringen, Schloss Fürstenberg, Bibliothek, MS 9821 (*olim* Paderborn, Erzbischöfliche Akademische Bibliothek). ca. 1545–50? probably Germany Anonymous mass II
Iesus. Laude facte	*Iesus. Laude facte & composte da piu persone spirituali*. . . . Florence, 1486 n.s. Lauda text "PO chi tebbi nel core"
Laude facte	*Laude facte & composte da piu persone spirituali*. . . . Florence? 1496? Lauda text "PO chi tebbi nel core"
Leipzig 1494	Leipzig, Universitätsbibliothek, MS 1494. ca. 1490–1504; possibly Leipzig FD2 (twice)
London 16439	London, British Library, Reference Division, Department of Manuscripts, MS Additional 16439. between autumn 1487 and 25 March 1488? Florence[8] original *Fortuna disperata* text
London 31922	London, British Library, Reference Division, Department of Manuscripts, MS Additional 31922. ca. 1510–20; probably London FD5
London 35087	London, British Library, Reference Division, Department of Manuscripts, MS Additional 35087. (*Chansonnier of Hieronymus Lauweryn van Watervliet: London, British Library Ms. Add. 35087*, with an

	introduction by William McMurtry, Facsimile Editions of Prints and Manuscripts [Peer, Belgium: Alamire, 1989].) pre-1509; Bruges? FD1	Paris 676	Paris, Bibliothèque Nationale, Département de la Musique, Fonds du Conservatoire, MS Rés. Vm⁷ 676. (*Manuscrit italien de frottele (1502): Fac-similé du ms. de la Bibliothèque nationale, Paris, Rés. Vm⁷ 676*, with an introduction by François Lesure [Geneva: Minkoff Reprint, 1979].) 1502;[13] Ferrara or Mantua FD2
Modena M.1.2	Modena, Biblioteca Estense e Universitaria, MS α.M.1.2 (Lat. 457; *olim* VI.H.1). ca. 1505; Ferrara Josquin mass, Obrecht mass		
Modena IV	Modena, Duomo, Biblioteca e Archivio Capitolare, MS Mus. IV. ca. 1520–30; probably Modena *J'ay pris amours* setting	Paris 4379	Paris, Bibliothèque Nationale, Département des Manuscrits, Nouvelles Acquisitions Françaises, MS 4379. (*Facsimile Reproduction of the Manuscripts Sevilla 5-I-43 and Paris n.a. fr. 4369 (pt. 1)*, with an introduction by Dragan Plamenac, Publications of Medieval Musical Manuscripts, no. 8 [Brooklyn: Institute of Medieval Music, 1962].) ca. 1470–85; probably Naples, possibly Rome FD1/2
Montserrat 765	Montserrat, Biblioteca del Monestir, MS 765. ca. 1540; Brussels[9] Appenzeller Requiem		
Munich 328–31	Munich, Universitätsbibliothek der Ludwig-Maximilians-Universität, MSS 8° 328–331 (*olim* Cim. 44c). by 1527; probably Augsburg[10] FD29, FD35		
Munich 718	Munich, Universitätsbibliothek der Ludwig-Maximilians-Universität, MS 4° 718. 1523–24; Ingolstadt?[11] FD1	Perugia 431	Perugia, Biblioteca Comunale Augusta, MS 431 (G.20). 1480–90, probably ca. 1485; Naples or vicinity FD1, FD2
		Pesaro 1144	Pesaro, Biblioteca Oliveriana, MS 1144 (*olim* 1193). pre-1500? Venice?[14] FD1? (twice)
Munich 1516	Munich, Bayerische Staatsbibliothek, Musiksammlung, Musica MS 1516. ca. 1540; probably Augsburg FD14		
Munich 3154	Munich, Bayerische Staatsbibliothek, Musiksammlung, Musica MS 3154. 1506/7; probably Innsbruck, possibly Augsburg Josquin mass	Regensburg C120	Regensburg, Bischöfliche Zentralbibliothek, MS C 120 (*olim* D XII). First part: ca. 1518–19; court of Maximilian I, Innsbruck?[15] Second part: ca. 1520–21; southern Germany, possibly Augsburg[16] FD19, FD29
Opera nova	*Opera nova de Laude facta*. Venice: Giorgio de Rusconi, 1512. Lauda text "PO chi thebbi nel core"	Rome 2856	See Casanatense 2856.
Paris 27	Paris, Bibliothèque Nationale, Département de la Musique, Rés. Vmd. 27. (*Tablature de luth italienne: Cent dix pièces pour luth seul et accompagnement pour luth d'oeuvres vocales: Fac-similé du ms. de la Bibliothèque nationale, Paris, Rés. Vmd. ms. 27. ca. 1505*, with an introduction by François Lesure [Geneva: Minkoff Reprint, 1981].) ca. 1505; Venice?[12] FD1	Segovia	Segovia, Archivo Capitular de la Catedral, MS s.s. (*Cancionero de la Catedral de Segovia: Ed. facsimilar de códice de la Santa Iglesia Catedral de Segovia*, with an introduction by Ramón Perales de la Cal [Segovia: Caja de Ahorros y Monte de Piedad, 1977].) northern repertoire probably pre-1497;[17] Spain FD1, FD8, FD9, FD10, Obrecht mass
		St. Gall 462	Saint Gall, Stiftsbibliothek, MS 462. 1510, with additions to 1530; Paris,

	with additions in Glarus FD2, FD17
St. Gall 463	Saint Gall, Stiftsbibliothek, MS 463. ca. 1540 or slightly later; Glarus or vicinity FD2, FD34, FD36
St. Gall 464	Saint Gall, Stiftsbibliothek, MS 464. ca. 1510–20; possibly Basel FD36
St. Gall 530	Saint Gall, Stiftsbibliothek, MS 530. ca. 1512–21;[18] Konstanz FD29, Obrecht mass excerpt: Benedictus
Stuttgart 26	Stuttgart, Württembergische Landesbibliothek, MS HB XVII/26. ca. 1560; Bavaria Josquin mass excerpt: Kyrie I
Tarazona 3	Tarazona, Archivo Capitular de la Catedral, MS 3. early 16th century; probably Seville Periquin mass
TVC	*Trium vocum carmina a diversis musicis composita.* Nuremberg: Formschneider, 1538. RISM 1538[9] FD28, Josquin mass excerpt: Pleni, Obrecht mass excerpt: Pleni
Uppsala 76b	Uppsala, Universitetsbiblioteket, MS Vokalmusik i Handskrift 76b. (*Uppsala, Universitetsbiblioteket, Vokalmusik I handskrift 76b*, with an introduction by Thomas G. MacCracken, Renaissance Music in Facsimile, vol. 20 [New York: Garland, 1986].) ca. 1515–35; France, possibly Troyes or vicinity Josquin mass
Vatican C.G. XIII.27	See C.G. XIII.27.
Vatican C.S. 41	See C.S. 41.
Vatican 11953	Vatican City, Biblioteca Apostolica Vaticana, MS Vaticani Latini 11953. ca. 1515–16; court of Maximilian I[19] FD19
Vienna 11778	Vienna, Österreichische Nationalbibliothek, Handschriften- und Inkunabelsammlung, MS 11778 (*olim* Theol. 37; VIII. A. 3). 1521–34 and probably ca. 1521–25; Habsburg-Burgundian court scriptorium Josquin mass
Vienna 18746	Vienna, Österreichische Nationalbibliothek, Musiksammlung, MS Mus. 18746 (*olim* A.N.35.H.14). 1523; Habsburg-Burgundian court scriptorium FD31
Vienna 18810	Vienna, Österreichische Nationalbibliothek, Musiksammlung, MS Mus. 18810 (*olim* A.N.35.E.126). (*Collection of German, French, and Instrumental Pieces: Wien, Österreichische Nationalbibliothek MS 18 810*, with an introduction by Matthias Schneider [Peer, Belgium: Alamire, 1987].) by 1533;[20] Augsburg or Munich FD11, FD20, FD23, FD24, FD25
Wolfenbüttel 78	Wolfenbüttel, Herzog August Bibliothek, MS 78 Quodlibetica 4°. ca. 1505; probably southern Germany FD1
Wrocław 428	Wrocław (Breslau), Biblioteka Uniwersytecka, Oddział Rękopisów, MS I-F-428. ca. 1510–30, perhaps ca. 1516; possibly Frankfurt an der Oder or vicinity FD18
Zwickau 78/2	Zwickau, Ratsschulbibliothek, MS LXXVIII, 2. 1531; probably Zwickau FD2
Zwickau 78/3	Zwickau, Ratsschulbibliothek, MS LXXVIII, 3. ca. 1535–45; probably Zwickau FD28
1502 Petrucci	*Misse Josquin.* Venice: O. Petrucci, 1502. (*Missarum Liber Agricole, Ghiselin, de la Rue, Josquin* [Rome: Vivarelli e Gullà, 1973].) Josquin mass
1503 Petrucci	*Misse Obreht.* Venice: O. Petrucci, 1503. Obrecht mass
1504[3]	See Canti C.
1507[6]	*Intabolatura de lauto. Libro secondo* [Francesco Spinacino]. Venice: Petrucci, 1507. (Francesco Spinacino, *Intabolatura de lauto: Libro primo [-secundo]*, with an introduction by François Lesure [Geneva: Minkoff Reprint, 1978].) FD1

1510 Obrecht	*Concentus harmonici quattuor missarum ... Jacobi Obrecht....* Basel: G. Mewes, [ca. 1510]. Obrecht mass
1516 Petrucci	*Liber primus Missarum Josquin.* Venice: O. Petrucci, 1516. (*Missarum Liber Agricole, Ghiselin, de la Rue, Josquin* [Rome: Vivarelli e Gullà, 1973].) Josquin mass
1526 Giunta	*Liber primus Missarum Josquin.* Rome: J. Giunta, G. G. Pasoti, and V. Dorico, 1526. Josquin mass
1531[5]	*Treze Motetz musicaulx avec ung prelude, le tout reduict en la tabulature des orgues....* Paris: Pierre Attaingnant, 1531. FD1
1534[17]	*Der erst Teil. Hundert und ainundzweintzig newe Lieder....* Nuremberg: Formschneider, 1534. FD20, FD21, FD22, FD26, FD33
1537 Heyden	Heyden, Sebald. *Musicae, id est Artis canendi, libri duo.* Nuremberg: Johann Petreius, 1537. FD26
1538[9]	See TVC.
1539[1]	*Liber quindecim missarum, à praestantissimis musicis compositarum....* Nuremberg: J. Petreius, 1539. Josquin mass
1539[2]	*Missae tredecim quatuor vocum a praestantiss. artificib. compositae.* Nuremberg: H. Grapheus, 1539. Josquin mass
1540 Heyden	Heyden, Sebald. *De arte canendi, ac vero signorum in cantibus usu, libri duo.* Nuremberg: Johann Petreius, 1540. (Sebald Heyden, *De arte canendi*, Monuments of Music and Music Literature in Facsimile, 2d ser., music literature, vol. 139 [New York: Broude Bros., 1969].) FD26
1540 Vaena	Vaena, Gonçalo de. *Arte novamente inventudo pera aprender a tanger.* Lisbon: G. Galharde, 1540.[21] Josquin mass: Benedictus only
1547 Glarean	Glarean, Heinrich. *Dodecachordon.* Basel: Heinrich Petri, 1547. (Heinrich Glarean, *Dodecachordon: A Facsimile of the 1547 Basel Edition*, Monuments of Music and Music Literature, 2d ser., music literature, vol. 65 [New York: Broude Bros., 1967].) RISM 1547[1] FD 26; Josquin mass excerpt: Agnus
1552[35]	Pisador, Diego. *Libro de musica de vihuela....* Salamanca: D. Pisador, 1552. Josquin mass excerpts: Benedictus and Pleni
1553 Faber	Faber, Gregor. *Musices practicae erotematum libri II.* Basel: Heinrich Petri, 1553. FD26, FD27
1554[9]	*Liber nonus ecclesiasticarum cantionum....* Antwerp: T. Susato, 1554. FD32
1554 Zanger	Zanger, Johannes. *Practicae musicae praecepta....* Leipzig: G. Hantzsch, 1554. Josquin mass excerpt: Christe
1563 Wilphlingseder	Wilphlingseder, Ambrosius. *Erotemata musices practicae, continentia praecipuas eius artis praeceptiones....* Nuremberg: C. Heussler, 1563. Josquin mass excerpt: Agnus I

Sigla for Works Cited

Modern Editions

Agricola	Agricola, Alexander. *Opera omnia.* Edited by Edward R. Lerner. Corpus mensurabilis musicae, vol. 22. N.p.: American Institute of Musicology, 1961–70.
AH	*Analecta hymnica medii aevi.* Edited by Guido Maria Dreves and Clemens Blume. 55 vols. Leipzig: O.R. Reisland, 1886–1922. Reprint edition, New York and London: Johnson Reprint, 1961.
Atlas	Atlas, Allan W. *The Cappella Giulia Chansonnier: Rome, Biblioteca Apostolica Vaticana, C.G.XIII.27.* 2 vols. Musicological Studies, vol. 27. Brooklyn, N.Y.: Institute of Mediaeval Music, 1975.
Baker	Baker, Norma Klein. "An Unnumbered Manuscript of Polyphony in

	the Archives of the Cathedral of Segovia: Its Provenance and History." Ph.D. diss., University of Maryland, 1978.
Berg-Kotterba	*Die Orgeltabulatur des Leonhard Kleber.* 2 vols. Edited by Karin Berg-Kotterba. Das Erbe deutscher Musik, vols. 91–92. Frankfurt: Henry Litolff, 1987.
Bernoulli	Bernoulli, Eduard. *Aus Liederbüchern der Humanistenzeit: Eine bibliographische und notentypographische Studie.* Leipzig: Breitkopf & Härtel, 1910.
Brooks	Brooks, Catherine V. "Antoine Busnois as a Composer of Chansons." 3 vols. Ph.D. diss., New York University, 1951.
Buchner	Buchner, Hans. *Sämtliche Orgelwerke.* 2 vols. Edited by Jost Harro Schmidt. Das Erbe deutscher Musik, vols. 54–55. Frankfurt: Henry Litolff, 1974.
Cattin	*Italian Laude and Latin Unica in MS Capetown, Grey 3.b.12.* Edited by Giulio Cattin. Corpus mensurabilis musicae, vol. 76. American Institute of Musicology; Neuhausen-Stuttgart: Hänssler, 1977.
Formschneyder	Formschneyder, Hieronymus. *Trium vocum carmina: Nürnberg, 1538.* 2 vols. Edited by Helmut Mönkemeyer. Monumenta musicae ad usum practicum, vols. 1–2. Celle: Moeck, 1985.
Geering-Trümpy	*Das Liederbuch des Johannes Heer von Glarus: Ein Musikheft aus der Zeit des Humanismus (Codex 462 der Stiftsbibliothek St. Gallen).* Edited by Arnold Geering and Hans Trümpy. Schweizerische Musikdenkmäler, vol. 5. Basel: Bärenreiter, 1967.
Gerber	*Der Mensuralkodex des Nikolaus Apel (Ms. 1494 der Universitätsbibliothek Leipzig).* 3 vols. Edited by Rudolf Gerber. Das Erbe deutscher Musik, vols. 32–34. Kassel: Bärenreiter, 1956–75.
Glarean	Glarean, Heinrich. *Dodecachordon.* 2 vols. Translation, transcription, and commentary by Clement A. Miller. Musicological Studies and Documents, vol. 6. N.p.: American Institute of Musicology, 1965.
Hernon	Hernon, Michael A. "Perugia MS 431 (G20): A Study of the Secular Italian Pieces." Ph.D. diss., George Peabody College for Teachers, 1972.
Heyden	Heyden, Sebald. *De arte canendi.* Translation and transcription by Clement A. Miller. Musicological Studies and Documents, vol. 26. N.p.: American Institute of Musicology, 1972.
Isaac	Isaac, Heinrich. *Weltliche Werke.* Edited by Johannes Wolf. Denkmäler der Tonkunst in Österreich, vol. 28. Vienna: Artaria, 1907. Reprint edition, Graz: Akademische Druck- und Verlagsanstalt, 1959.
Ivanoff	*Eine zentrale Quelle der frühen italienischen Lautenpraxis: Edition der Handschrift Pesaro, Biblioteca Oliveriana, Ms. 1144.* Edited by Vladimir Ivanoff. Münchner Editionen zur Musikgeschichte, vol. 7. Tutzing: Hans Schneider, 1988.
Jonas	*Das Augsburger Liederbuch: Die Musikhandschrift 2° Codex 142 a der Staats- und Stadtbibliothek Augsburg.* 2 vols. Edited by Luise Jonas. Berliner Musikwissenschaftliche Arbeiten, vol. 21. Munich: Musikverlag Emil Katzbichler, 1983.
Josquin CW	Josquin des Prez. *The Collected Works of Josquin des Prez.* New Josquin Edition. Utrecht: Vereniging voor Nederlandse Muziekgeschiedenis, 1987–.
Josquin Masses	Josquin des Prez. *Werken.* Edited by Albert Smijers. *Missen,* Deel I. Vereniging voor Nederlandse Muziekgeschiedenis; Amsterdam: G. Almsbach; Leipzig: Fr. Kistner and C. F. W. Siegal, 1929–31.
Josquin Secular	Josquin des Prez. *Werken.* Edited by Albert Smijers. *Wereldlijke Werken,* Deel II, Bundel IV. Edited by Myroslav Antonowycz and Willem Elders. Amsterdam: Vereniging voor Nederlandse Muziekgeschiedenis, 1965.
Josquin SSP	Josquin des Prez. *Sixteen Secular Pieces for Three Voices or Instruments.* Edited by Bernard Thomas. The Art of the Netherlanders 1470–1530, vol. 7. London: London Pro Musica Edition, 1994.

Loach	Loach, Donald Glenn. "Aegidius Tschudi's Songbook (St. Gall MS 463): A Humanistic Document from the Circle of Heinrich Glarean." 2 vols. Ph.D. diss., University of California at Berkeley, 1969.
LU	*The Liber Usualis with an Introduction and Rubrics in English*. Edited by the Benedictines of Solesmes. Tournai and New York: Desclee, 1963.
Martini	Martini, Johannes. *Secular Pieces*. Edited by Edward G. Evans, Jr. Recent Researches in the Music of the Middle Ages and Early Renaissance, vol. 1. Madison: A-R Editions, 1975.
Marx	*Tabulaturen des XVI. Jahrhunderts*. Vol. 1, *Die Tabulaturen aus dem Besitz des Basler Humanisten Bonifacius Amerbach*. Edited by Hans Joachim Marx. Schweizerische Musikdenkmäler, vol. 6. Basel: Bärenreiter, 1967.
Marx-Warburton	*Tabulaturen des XVI. Jahrhunderts*. Vol. 3, *St. Galler Orgelbuch: Die Orgeltabulatur des Fridolin Sicher: St. Gallen, Codex 530*. Edited by Hans Joachim Marx in collaboration with Thomas Warburton. Schweizerische Musikdenkmäler, vol. 3. Winterthur, Switzerland: Amadeus, 1992.
McMurtry	McMurtry, William M. "The British Museum Manuscript Additional 35087: A Transcription of the French, Italian, and Latin Compositions with Concordance and Commentary." Ph.D. diss., North Texas State University, 1967.
Moerk	Moerk, Alice Anne. "The Seville Chansonnier: An Edition of Sevilla 5-I-43 & Paris n.a.fr. 4379 (Pt. 1)." 2 vols. Ph.D. diss., West Virginia University, 1971.
Moser	*Frühmeister der deutschen Orgelkunst*. Edited by Hans Joachim Moser. Veröffentlichungen der Staatlichen Akademie für Kirchen- und Schulmusik Berlin, vol. 1. Wiesbaden: Breitkopf & Härtel, 1930.
Obrecht CW	Obrecht, Jacob. *Collected Works*. New Obrecht Edition. Edited by Chris Maas. Utrecht: Vereniging voor Nederlandse Muziekgeschiedenis, 1983–.
Obrecht Masses	Obrecht, Jacob. *Werken*. Edited by Johannes Wolf. *Missen*, Deel I. Vereeniging voor Noord-Nederlands Muziekgeschiedenis; Amsterdam: G. Alsbach; Leipzig: Breitkopf & Härtel, 1908.
Obrecht OO	Obrecht, Jacob. *Opera omnia*. Vol. 1, *Missae*. Edited by Albert Smijers. Vereniging voor Nederlandse Muziekgeschiedenis; Amsterdam: G. Alsbach, 1954.
Rokseth	*Treize motets et un prélude pour orgue, parus chez Pierre Attaingnant en 1531*. Edited by Yvonne Rokseth. Publications de la Société Française de Musicologie, ser. 1, vol. 5. Paris: E. Droz, 1930.
Schmidt	Schmidt, Henry Louis, III. "The First Printed Lute Books: Francesco Spinacino's *Intabulatura de Lauto, Libro primo and Libro secondo* (Venice: Petrucci, 1507)." 2 vols. Ph.D. diss., University of North Carolina at Chapel Hill, 1969.
Self	*The Si Placet Repertoire of 1480–1530*. Edited by Stephen Self. Recent Researches in the Music of the Renaissance, vol. 106. Madison: A-R Editions, 1996.
Senfl SW4	Senfl, Ludwig. *Sämtliche Werke*. Vol. 4. Edited by Arnold Geering and Wilhelm Altwegg. Basel: Hug, 1940. Also published as Das Erbe deutscher Musik, vol. 15. Wolfenbüttel and Berlin: George Kallmeyer, 1940. Reprint, Wolfenbüttel and Zürich: Möseler, 1962.
Senfl SW6	Senfl, Ludwig. *Sämtliche Werke*. Vol. 6. Edited by Arnold Geering and Wilhelm Altwegg. Wolfenbüttel and Zürich: Möseler, 1961.
Sherr Selections	*Selections from Bologna, Civico Museo Bibliografico Musicale, MS Q 19: "Rusconi Codex."* 2 vols. Edited by Richard Sherr. Sixteenth-Century Motet, vols. 6–7. New York and London: Garland, 1989.

Sherr Susato	*Liber nonus ecclesiasticarum cantionum quinque vocum . . . (Antwerp: Susato, 1554); Liber decimus ecclesiasticarum cantionum quinque vocum . . . (Antwerp: Susato, 1555).* Edited by Richard Sherr. The Susato Motet Anthologies. Sixteenth-Century Motet, vol. 17. New York: Garland, 1996.
Stevens	*Music at the Court of Henry VIII.* Edited by John Stevens. Musica Britannica, vol. 18. Royal Musical Association; London: Stainer & Bell, 1962. 2d, rev. ed., 1973.
Weiss	Weiss, Susan Forscher. "The Manuscript Bologna, Civico Museo Bibliografico Musicale, Codex Q 18 (olim 143): A Bolognese Instrumental Collection of the Early Cinquecento." Ph.D. diss., University of Maryland, 1985.
Whisler	Whisler, Bruce Allen. "Munich, Mus. MS. 1516: A Critical Edition." 2 vols. Ph.D. diss., University of Rochester, 1974.
Wolff	Wolff, Arthur S. "The Chansonnier Biblioteca Casanatense 2856: Its History, Purpose, and Music." 2 vols. Ph.D. diss., North Texas State University, 1970.

Secondary Literature

Cumming	Cumming, Julie E. "The Goddess Fortuna Revisited." *Current Musicology* 30 (1980): 7–23. (See esp. pp. 21–23.)
Loeffler	Loeffler, Alfred. "Fortuna desperata: A Contribution to the Study of Musical Symbolism in the Renaissance." *Student Musicologists at Minnesota* 3 (1968–69): 1–30. (See esp. pp. 23–30.)
Meconi	Meconi, Honey. "Art-Song Reworkings: An Overview." *Journal of the Royal Musical Association* 119 (1994): 1–42. (See esp. pp. 31–33.)
Picker	Picker, Martin. "Henricus Isaac and *Fortuna desperata*." In *Antoine Busnoys: Method, Meaning, and Context in Late Medieval Music.* Edited by Paula Higgins, 431–45. Oxford: Clarendon Press, 1999. (See esp. pp. 443–45.)

Editorial Method

The transcription of each work is normally based on a single source. When more than one source is available, the choice of source to be used is based on a variety of factors identified in the critical commentary. These factors include the age of the source, its completeness, the accuracy of its readings, and its proximity to the composer. Except in the case of obvious errors, variant readings are not drawn from concordant sources, but differences in pitch and rhythm are listed in the critical commentary. Differences in coloration and ligatures in concordant sources are not noted. Editorial additions are marked by square brackets. Casual dissonances in the music have normally not been editorially altered.

The voices are normally scored in the order superius-altus-tenor-bassus, even though this sometimes places a higher-ranging tenor above a lower-ranging altus. Additional voices are placed by range. For manuscripts that lack voice designations, part order in the edition is determined by the traditional distribution in the sources. Titles are normally taken from vocal incipits, and the numbering of the pieces is editorial.

The original clef, signature accidentals, mensuration sign, and first notated pitch or ligature in each voice part are shown in the incipit at the beginning of each work; initial rests have not been indicated. Ordering and placement of these elements have been standardized, as have clef shapes. The range of each voice is shown after the modern clef, key signature, and meter signature, showing the range of pitches as they appear in the modern clef. The original designation of each part as it appears in the primary source is given above the incipit. Any differences of clef, signature accidentals, mensuration sign, and voice designation found in the concordant sources are given in the critical commentary.

Without regard to the designation of the voice part, the clefs used in the transcription have been determined as follows: (1) parts originally in any G clef or C1 or C2 clefs are transcribed in treble clef; (2) parts originally in C3, C4, or C5 clefs are transcribed in transposed treble clef with the exception of the discantus of FD34, where C3 is transcribed in treble clef; and (3) parts originally in any F clef are transcribed in bass clef.

The original note values have been reduced by half in the transcription, i.e., breves are transcribed as whole notes in imperfect tempus. Final longs have been regularized. Ligatures are marked by a solid bracket above the notes included; coloration by an open bracket or brackets, in the case of a series interpreted as minor color. Notes that continue across a barline in the transcription are divided into appropriate values and connected with a tie.

Key signatures have been used only in those voice parts that carry signature accidentals in the primary source. Unless otherwise noted (see esp. FD27), accidentals within the staff are present in the primary source, but specific accidentals that duplicate signature accidentals have been removed and reported in the critical commentary. Those accidentals placed above the staff are editorial suggestions as to what contemporary performers may have done.

Texts are normally taken from the best musical source, and text repetitions indicated by an *ij* sign are expanded in angle brackets. Punctuation, capitalization, and archaic conventions of typography, such as the use of *i* or *j* and *u* or *v* have been tacitly modernized, and abbreviations are silently expanded. The original texts as well as added and contrafact texts and their translations are given in the critical commentary. Word divisions follow modern practices and normally permit either Italian or German pronunciation of Latin; in FD24, 34, and 36, word breaks were arranged specifically for this purpose. Texts are otherwise as they appear in the sources unless noted in the critical commentary.

Critical Commentary

Each entry in the critical commentary begins with the number and title of the setting as they appear in the edition and the composer (if known), along with the number of voices utilized and an explanation of the relationship of each piece to the original version. Information concerning the sources for each work includes its location, attribution, and incipits and/or texting in the primary source as well as in any concordant sources and intabulations (the sources in each group are given in approximate chronological order). References to the numbering of the piece according to the lists of Meconi, Picker, Cumming, and Loeffler, as well as a listing of any modern editions and the source on which that edition was based, are also given. Sources for the texts and translations are given following the translation.

Notes to the transcription are given in temporal order according to voice part and report all textual and musical differences between the primary and concordant sources and the transcription that are not otherwise covered by the editorial method described above; sources are given in approximate chronological order. Variant readings from intabulations normally include accidentals only. Unique variants for the original superius, tenor, and bassus voices are listed as such. For these voices, I also use the term "error" to indicate a unique variant that will not work within the context of the piece (e.g., when a scribe writes a breve rest instead of a semibreve rest).

The following abbreviations are used in the commentary: M(m). = measure(s); br = breve; sbr = semibreve; min = minim; smin = semiminim; S = superius; A = altus; T = tenor; B = bassus; Q = quintus; V = vagans. Texting sigla are as follows: t = fully texted; i = incipit only; x = no text; m = part is missing. Pitches are indicated according to the system in which c′ = middle C. Measure indications refer either to the entire measure or to a specified note within it, ignoring any ties across barlines; thus, "M. 5 to m. 6, note 2" refers to all of measure 5 and the first two notes of measure 6.

1. *Fortuna desperata (uncertain)*

a 3
The original composition.

Sources

Primary source. **Paris 4379,** fols. 40v–41 (n11v–n12); anonymous; t–i–i;[22] T and B = fortuna desperata.

Concordant sources. **Perugia 431,** fols. 83v–84 (original foliation 93v–94); anonymous; i–i–x; S = FOrtuna desperata, T = fortuna desperata (written at the bottom of the page); this version is crossed out in the manuscript. **Segovia,** fol. 174; Anthonius busnoys; t–i–i; T and B = fortuna desperata. **Frankfurt 20,** fol. 1; anonymous; i–t–m; S = fortuna desperata, T = contrafact text "O panis vite." **Wolfenbüttel 78,** fol. 2v; anonymous; x–x–x. **London 35087,** fols. 11v–12; anonymous; t–t–t. **Florence 121,** fols. 25v–26; anonymous; i–x–x; S = FOrtuna desperata.

Intabulations. **Pesaro 1144,** pp. 25–27; anonymous; lute tablature; title = Fortuna; very free intabulation of S? **Pesaro 1144,** pp. 31–35; anonymous; lute tablature; title = tuna disp;[23] free intabulation. **Paris 27,** fols. 52–53; anonymous; lute tablature; title = Fortuna desperata; intabulation of S, lower voices extremely free. **1507[6],** fols. 38v–41; Francesco Spinacino; intabulation for two lutes;[24] title = Fortuna desperata; extremely free S over fairly strict T and B; all transposed up a fourth. **Berlin 40026,** fols. 63v–64v; H[ans] B[uchner]; keyboard tablature; title = Fortuna in ut; florid intabulation transposed down a fourth. **Munich 718,** fols. 119, 129v–130, 141; anonymous; viol tablature; title in index = Forduna (in section for each voice part); title with each voice part = Fortuna (title at head of S; at end of piece for T and B). **1531[5],** fols. 83v–86; anonymous; keyboard tablature; title = Fortuna.

References

Inventory numbers. Meconi 1; Picker 1; Cumming A I; Loeffler A, E1, E2.

Modern editions. Berg-Kotterba, 1:98–100 (Berlin 40026). Brooks, 3:201–3 (Segovia). Hernon, 356–58

(Perugia 431). Isaac, 190 (Paris 4379, with si placet voice). Ivanoff, 2–6 (first Pesaro 1144 entry) and 16–26 (second Pesaro 1144 entry). Lewis Jones, "The Thibault Lute Manuscript: An Introduction," *The Lute* 22 (1982): 81 (tablature edition, Paris 27). Josquin Secular, 53:25–27 (London 35087). Josquin Masses, 13:105 (London 35087). McMurtry, 232–35 (London 35087). Honey Meconi, "Poliziano, *Primavera,* and Perugia 431: New Light on *Fortuna desperata,*" in *Antoine Busnoys: Method, Meaning, and Context in Late Medieval Music,* edited by Paula Higgins (Oxford: Clarendon Press, 1999), 471–72 (Paris 4379). Moser, 60–61 (Berlin 40026). Obrecht CW, 4:XXX–XXXII (primarily Segovia). Obrecht OO, 3:170–71 (London 35087). Obrecht Masses, 136–37 (Paris 4379, with si placet voice). Joshua Rifkin, "Busnoys and Italy," in *Antoine Busnoys,* 556–57 (Paris 4379). Rokseth, 55 (London 35087 and 1531[5]). Schmidt, 1:49–56, in comparison with model; 2:270–75, intabulation only (1507[6]). Self, 29–33 (Paris 4379, with si placet voice). Reinhard Strohm, *The Rise of European Music 1380–1500* (Cambridge: Cambridge University Press, 1993), 621–22 (London 35087).

Texts and Translations

Fortuna desperata

Fortuna desperata,
Iniqua e maledecta,
Che, de tal dona electa,
La fama ai denegrata.[25]
    Fortuna desperata.[26]

O morte dispiatata,
Inimica e crudele,
Che, d'alto più che stelle,
Tu l'hai cusì abassata.
    F.d.[27]

Meschina e despietata,
Ben piangere posso may,
Et desiro finire
Li mei guay.

      *

Hopeless fortune,
Unjust and cursed,
Who has defamed the reputation
Of so distinguished a lady.
    Hopeless fortune.

O pitiless death,
Hostile and cruel,
Who has thus lowered one
Who was higher than the stars.
    Hopeless fortune.

Wretched and pitiless,
Well can I cry now,
And I desire to end
My woes.

Text source. Stanzas 1 and 2 from Paris 676, fols. 24v–25;[28] stanza 3 from Perugia 431, fols. 84v–85 (old foliation 94v–95).[29]

O panis vite

O panis vitae, veneranda refectio rite,
Ens, caro sincera, verbum patris, hostia vera,
Nosmet inhaerere tibi fac, Deus et homo vere,
Atque, tui, Jesu pie, nos ale corporis esu.

      *

O bread of life, rightly our venerable sustenance,
Supreme being, flesh untainted, word of the father, true host,
Make us cling to you, God and truly man,
And, faithful Jesus, nourish us by the eating of your body.

Text source. AH, 5:22.[30]

Comments

The earliest surviving source to contain *Fortuna desperata* is Paris 4379, which has the original three voices and to which the most famous si placet altus was added somewhat later. It is thus the earliest source for both the original three-voice version and the most widely disseminated si placet version, and it has been used for the edition of both FD1 and FD2. Only a few changes that do not reflect the Paris 4379 reading have been made in the edition of FD1. The first is the move to C instead of F in measure 13 of the superius; as discussed in the introduction, the C is surely the original reading. The second change involves the texting and the underlay. The version of the text used here comes from the best texted musical source, Paris 676; the text as it appears in Paris 4379 is used for FD2. Text underlay in the superius follows what was laid out in the introduction as a very likely underlay for the original version; the result makes excellent musical sense and is highly singable. It does not always conform to the ligatures of the edition, but the song circulated with so many changes in ligatures that strict adherence to the ligature patterns of a given source seems unnecessarily binding. Given the many variants of underlay in the texted versions, however, performers should feel free to alter this aspect of the edition.

Only one source, the much later London 35087, texts the tenor and bassus with the "Fortuna desperata" text. I have added text to the tenor line of FD1 editorially (although I have not followed London 35087) because the text fits smoothly and well and easily matches the underlay of the superius line. Because this is not true in the case of the bassus (contra), I have left this voice untexted.

The Frankfurt 20 fragment, recently identified by David Fallows, was found in the binding of a copy of Thomas Aquinas's *Summa theologica* (Pt. 2, Bk. 1) published in Venice by Theodorus de Ragazonibus on 31 March 1490. The musical fragments are clearly from Germanic territory, but it is impossible to ascertain precisely when they were bound into the book. The volume was previously owned by the Dominikanerkloster in Frankfurt, so the music may have come from that city as well. The source is unusual in having a contrafact text (one of several contrafacta applied to *Fortuna desperata*) in the tenor voice only, although the superius incipit leaves no doubt as to the work's identity. Given the fragmentary nature of what survives, it is possible that the manuscript originally contained a four-voice setting or possibly even a replacement contratenor setting, although I have treated it throughout the edition as if it were a source for FD1. Similar ambiguity holds for some of the intabulations, which were included here for the sake of simplicity.

The source Munich 718 requires some special explanation. Compiled by Jorg Weltzell, who was probably enrolled at the University of Ingolstadt, the manuscript consists of two sections, the first of which deals with mathematics. The second section is predominantly music for viols (one of the earliest surviving collections) with a small number of pieces for lute at the very end. The viol music is actually written in German lute tablature, and each voice is intabulated separately in the section of the manuscript devoted to that voice part (hence ensemble performance directly from the manuscript is impossible). Weltzell apparently worked from vocal originals and made few changes while intabulating. The version is striking for its lack of ornamentation; hence the decision to include Munich 718's reading in the "Notes to the Transcription" while excluding all other intabulations (except regarding accidentals). As seen in the transcription notes, the source still contains the largest number of unique variants, but most of these are directly attributable to the limitations of the tablature, which precluded the notation of rhythmic values longer than a breve (see for example Munich 718's treatment of the tenor dotted long in mm. 15–17). Other variants come from Weltzell's method of copying. He first wrote a phrase or more of pitches, marked the spot with a fermata, and then added (not always correctly) the rhythmic notation—hence the large number of fermatas and their lack of alignment among the different voices. Taking the idiosyncrasies of the source into account, what is striking about the reading is the relative stability of this very latest ensemble source of the original version.

For further discussion of the work and its transformation, see the introduction.

NOTES TO THE TRANSCRIPTION

Superius. Part name, D[iscantus] in Wolfenbüttel 78; Discantus in Munich 718. Clef, G3 in Wolfenbüttel 78; none in Munich 718. Signature accidentals, b' is flat in Frankfurt 20 (mm. 1–43 only). Mensuration, lacking in Wolfenbüttel 78. M. 1 to m. 2, note 1, f' dotted br in Segovia, Florence 121. M. 3, fermata in Munich 718 (unique variant). M. 5 to m. 6, note 1, a' dotted br in Florence 121. M. 6, a' br in Munich 718. M. 9 to m. 10, note 1, f' dotted sbr–e'–min–f' sbr in Segovia; f' br–f' sbr in Munich 718. M. 13, note 1, f' sbr in Paris 4379, Perugia 431, Segovia, Frankfurt 20, Wolfenbüttel 78, Paris 27. M. 13, note 2, f' sbr in Munich 718 (unique variant). M. 14, e' br in Munich 718 (unique variant). M. 17 to m. 18, note 1, c" sbr–c" br in Perugia 431 (unique variant); c" dotted br in Segovia, Florence 121. M. 19, b' sbr–b' sbr in Perugia 431 (unique variant); b' dotted sbr–c" min in Frankfurt 20. M. 20, note 2, c" min–b' min in Frankfurt 20, Segovia, Florence 121. M. 22, rest, br rest in Perugia 431 (error). M. 23, g' sbr–g' min–f' min in Munich 718 (unique variant). M. 24, e' br in Segovia, Florence 121, Munich 718. M. 26, note 2, a' dotted sbr in Perugia 431 (error). M. 27, specific flat in Paris 4379, Perugia 431, Segovia,[31] Florence 121, Munich 718; flat in signature in Frankfurt 20; no flat in Wolfenbüttel 78, London 35087. M. 27 to m. 28, note 1, b♭' br–b♭' sbr in Perugia 431, Munich 718. M. 28, note 2 to m. 29, note 1, a' br in Munich 718. M. 29, note 2, g' min–f' min in Florence 121, Munich 718. M. 31, a' sbr–a' min–b' min in Munich 718 (unique variant). M. 32, c" br in Munich 718. M. 32, note 2, sbr rest in Frankfurt 20 (unique variant). M. 34, note 3 to m. 35, note 1, a' dotted sbr–g' smin–f' smin in Segovia, Wolfenbüttel 78. M. 34, note 3 to m. 35, a' sbr–g' br in Munich 718 (unique variant). M. 38, a' sbr–a' min–g' smin–f' smin in Munich 718 (unique variant). M. 39, e' sbr–e' sbr in Segovia (unique variant). M. 44, note 2 to m. 45, note 1, g' sbr–g' min in Munich 718 (unique variant). M. 47, d' br in Munich 718. M. 48, f' sbr–f' min–e' smin–d' smin in Munich 718 (unique variant). M. 49, fermata in Frankfurt 20 (unique variant). M. 50, fermata in Frankfurt 20 (unique variant). M. 51, fermata in Frankfurt 20 (unique variant). M. 54, note 1, specific flat in Paris 4379, London 35087, Munich 718; no flat in Perugia 431, Segovia, Frankfurt 20, Wolfenbüttel 78, Florence 121. M. 54, b♭' sbr–b♭' min–a' min in Munich 718 (unique variant). Mm. 55–56, g' min–f' min–f' sbr–e' br in Munich 718 (unique variant). M. 55, note 2 to m. 56, f' br–e' sbr in Wolfenbüttel 78; f' dotted sbr–e' smin–d' smin–e' sbr in London 35087. M. 56, note 2, d' smin–e' smin in Frankfurt 20, Florence 121. M. 57, fermata in Frankfurt 20, Wolfenbüttel 78, Munich 718.

Tenor. Part name, missing in Perugia 431, Segovia, London 35087; T[enor] in Wolfenbüttel 78; Tenor in Frankfurt 20, Florence 121, Munich 718. Clef, C3 in Perugia 431, Segovia, Frankfurt 20, Wolfenbüttel 78, London 35087, Florence 121. Signature accidentals, b is flat in Wolfenbüttel 78 for staves 1 and 3 only (mm. 1–17 and 41–57); none in Perugia 431, Frankfurt 20. Mensuration, lacking in Frankfurt 20, Wolfenbüttel 78. M. 4, omitted in Perugia 431 (error). M. 5, fermata in Munich 718 (unique variant). M. 7, d′ br in Segovia, Florence 121, Munich 718. M. 9 to m. 10, note 1, d′ br in Perugia 431 (dot lacking; error); d′ br–d′ sbr in Munich 718. Mm. 15–17, f br–f br–f br with fermata in m. 17 in Munich 718 (unique variant). M. 17, omitted in Perugia 431. M. 21 to m. 22, note 1, f′ dotted br in Frankfurt 20, Segovia, London 35087, Florence 121; f br–f sbr in Munich 718 (unique variant). M. 23, e′ sbr–e′ sbr in Perugia 431; e′ dotted sbr–f′ min in Frankfurt 20. M. 26, note 2, f′ min in Munich 718 (error). M. 27 to m. 28, note 1, g′ br–g′ sbr in London 35087, Munich 718. M. 28, note 1, omitted in Perugia 431 (error). M. 31, fermata in Munich 718 (unique variant). M. 33, note 3 to m. 34, note 1, d′ min in Munich 718. M. 35, signature flat and specific flat in Paris 4379; signature flat in Segovia, London 35087, Florence 121; no flat in Perugia 431, Frankfurt 20, Wolfenbüttel 78. Mm. 36–37, omitted in Perugia 431 (error); after this point Perugia 431 puts first the equivalent of mm. 49–57 followed by the equivalent of mm. 38–49; variants are listed below as if these sections were in the correct order. M. 38, c′ br in Perugia 431 (unique variant). M. 39, d′ br in Perugia 431 (unique variant). M. 40, fermata in Munich 718 (unique variant). M. 41, rest, min rest in Frankfurt 20 (error). M. 43, c′ sbr–c′ sbr in Munich 718 (unique variant). M. 44, note 2 to m. 45, note 1, e′ sbr–e′ min in Munich 718 (unique variant). Mm. 47–48, d′ sbr–d′ dotted sbr–c′ min–b min–a min in London 35087 (unique variant). M. 48, d′ min–c′ min–b sbr in Perugia 431; d′ dotted sbr–c′ smin–b smin in Segovia, Wolfenbüttel 78; d′ sbr–d′ min–c′ smin–b smin in Munich 718 (unique variant). M. 48, note 3, b min–a min in Frankfurt 20. M. 49, fermata in Frankfurt 20 (unique variant). M. 50, fermata in Frankfurt 20 (unique variant). M. 51, fermata in Frankfurt 20 (unique variant). M. 52, a sbr–a sbr in Frankfurt 20 (unique variant). M. 53, b dotted sbr–a min in Segovia (unique variant). M. 54, note 1, d′ sbr–d′ min in Munich 718 (unique variant). M. 55, note 2, a br in Munich 718 (error). M. 57, fermata in Frankfurt 20, Wolfenbüttel 78, Munich 718.

Bassus (Contra). Part is missing in Frankfurt 20. Part name, none in Perugia 431, Segovia, London 35087; Ba[ssus] in Wolfenbüttel 78; Contra in Florence 121; Bassus in Munich 718. Clef, F3 in Wolfenbüttel 78, London 35087. Signature accidentals, B and b are flat in London 35087; none in Perugia 431, Wolfenbüttel 78, Florence 121. Mensuration, lacking in Wolfenbüttel 78. M. 3, f long in Perugia 431 (error). M. 6, notes 1–2, a min–g min in Segovia. M. 8, see table 2 in the introduction for presence or absence of flat. M. 9 to m. 10, note 1, d long in Perugia 431 (error); d long–d sbr in Wolfenbüttel 78 (error); d br–d sbr in Munich 718 (unique variant). M. 10, note 2 to m. 11, g br–g sbr in Munich 718 (unique variant). M. 14, fermata in Munich 718 (unique variant). M. 15, note 1, c′ sbr–c′ min in Munich 718 (unique variant). M. 15, notes 2–3, b min in Perugia 431 (unique variant). M. 16, note 2, d′ min–c′ smin–b smin in Munich 718 (unique variant). M. 19, g sbr–g sbr in Segovia. M. 20, note 1, signature flat and specific flat in Paris 4379; specific flat in Florence 121, Munich 718; signature flat on b in Segovia, London 35087; no flat in Perugia 431, Wolfenbüttel 78. M. 20, b♭ dotted sbr–a smin–g smin in London 35087 (unique variant). Mm. 21–22, f br–f br in Munich 718 (unique variant). M. 23 to m. 24, note 1, c dotted br in Wolfenbüttel 78, Florence 121. M. 24, c br in Munich 718. M. 27 to m. 28, note 1, see table 2 in the introduction for presence or absence of flat. M. 27 to m. 28, note 1, e♭ br–e♭ sbr in Munich 718. Mm. 27–28, e dotted sbr–d sbr in Perugia 431 (error). M. 31, note 1, f sbr–f min in Munich 718 (unique variant). M. 33, note 1, specific flat in Florence 121, Munich 718; signature flat in Paris 4379, Segovia, London 35087; no flat in Perugia 431, Wolfenbüttel 78. M. 33, note 2 to m. 34, note 1, c′ sbr–g min in Munich 718 (unique variant). M. 34, extra f sbr added at end of measure in Perugia 431 (error). M. 35, see table 2 in the introduction for presence or absence of flat. M. 37, note 1, g min in Perugia 431 (unique variant). M. 37, notes 1–2, a dotted min–g smin in London 35087, Florence 121, Munich 718. M. 37, notes 3–4, f dotted min–e smin in London 35087 (unique variant). M. 38, d sbr–d sbr in London 35087 (unique variant); d sbr–a sbr in Perugia 431 (unique variant). M. 39, a br in Wolfenbüttel 78, Munich 718; omitted in Perugia 431 (error). M. 40, a br in Munich 718; omitted in Perugia 431 (error), Wolfenbüttel 78 (see note for m. 42). M. 41, notes 1–2, a dotted min–g smin in London 35087, Munich 718. M. 41, note 3, f min–e sbr in Wolfenbüttel 78 (the f min has been blackened in, possibly to show that it should be deleted); f min–e min in Munich 718. M. 42, d br with long underneath in Wolfenbüttel 78 (the br has been blackened in, possibly to indicate that it should be deleted; long at this point would compensate for the omission of m. 40) (unique variant); fermata in Munich 718 (unique variant). M. 44, note 2 to m. 45, note 1, c sbr–c sbr in Perugia 431 (unique variant). Mm. 47–48, d br–d br in Munich 718. M. 50, specific flat in Paris 4379, Segovia, Wolfenbüttel 78, Munich 718; signature flat in

London 35087; no flat in Perugia 431, Florence 121. M. 52, note 1, g sbr in Perugia 431 (unique variant); f is flatted in Wolfenbüttel 78. M. 54, note 1, g sbr–g min in Munich 718 (unique variant). M. 55, note 1, see table 2 in the introduction for presence or absence of flat. M. 57, f in London 35087, Florence 121, Munich 718; fermata in Wolfenbüttel 78, Munich 718.

2. *Fortuna desperata* (anonymous)

a 4

A si placet altus is added to the original composition.

Sources

Primary source. **Paris 4379,** fols. 40v–41 (n11v–n12); anonymous; t–i–i–i; A, T, and B = fortuna desperata. This is the earliest source. The altus has been added in a different hand.

Concordant sources. **Perugia 431,** fols. 84v–85 (old foliation 94v–95); anonymous; t–t–x–x; three stanzas of text are given: the text for stanzas 1 and 2 is laid nonstop through the superius and tenor lines, i.e., the text for the second stanza begins towards the end of the superius and continues through the tenor, after which the words "In ciascum parte e data fortuna desperata etc" (in each part is given fortuna desperata etc.) are written (see plate 2). **Leipzig 1494,** fol. 62; anonymous; x–x–t–x; T = contrafact text "Virginis alme parens"; titled "Fortuna" at the top of the page. **Leipzig 1494,** fol. 162v; anonymous; t–t–m–m; S and A = two strophes of the contrafact text "Ave stella fulgida."[32] **C.G. XIII.27,** fols. 56v–57 (63v–64); felice; i–x–x–x; S = fortuna desperata; see FD7 below. **Basel F.X.10,** fol. 8 (no. 17), bassus only;[33] anonymous; m–m–m–i; B = Fortüna. **Paris 676,** fols. 24v–25; anonymous; t–i–i–i; S = two stanzas of text; A, T, and B = fortuna desperata. **Canti C,** fols. 1024v–1027 [126v–127]; anonymous; i–i–i–i; S = Fortuna desperata, A, T, and B = fortuna. **Cape Town Grey,** fols. 79v–80 (old foliation 78v–79); anonymous; t–i–i–i; S = four stanzas of the contrafact text "Poi che t'hebi nel core"; A = Poi che che[34] thebi nel core, T = Poi che thebi nel core Jesu clemento, B = Poi che thebbi nel cor Jesu. **St. Gall 462,** fols. 6v–7 (pp. 20–21); anonymous; i–x–t–x; S = fortuna desperata; T = contrafact text "Fortuna desperata quae te dementia vertit." **Zwickau 78/2,** fols. 42–43, 41v–42v, 39v–40v, 42v–43v (no. 54); anonymous; x–x–x–x. **St. Gall 463,** fols. 53r, 112r (no. 144); anonymous; ½t–½t–m–m; S and A = "Fortuna desperata quae te dementia cepit. Solemur contrariis"; listed in index as "Fortuna desperata antiquum."

Intabulation. **Berlin 40026,** fols. 132–133v (no. 88); anonymous; keyboard tablature; titled "Fortuna Quatuor in fa."

References

Inventory numbers. Meconi 2a; Picker 2a; Cumming A II 1; Loeffler B1, B2, B3, B4, B5, E2.

Modern editions. Atlas, 2:38–42 (C.G. XIII.27; includes "Felice" replacement contratenor). Berg-Kotterba, 2:61–63 (Berlin 40026). Bernoulli, 36–37 (St. Gall 462). Brooks, 3:317–20 (Canti C). Cattin, 38–39 (Cape Town Grey). Geering-Trümpy, 17–18 (St. Gall 462). Gerber, 1:71 (Leipzig 1494, fol. 62). Hernon, 2:359–64 (Perugia 431). Isaac, 190 (Paris 4379). Josquin Masses, 13:106 (Canti C). Moerk, 2:311–13 (Paris 4379). Obrecht Masses, appendix: 136–37 (Paris 4379). Self, 29–33 (Paris 4379).

Texts and Translations

Fortuna desperata, see FD1.

Virginis alme parens

Virginis alme parens,
Fortunam vista praesta
Celi, que vitam
Corpore ratificas.

*

Mother of the bountiful virgin,
Present the treasure of the view
Of heaven, you who ratify
Life through the body.

Text source. Leipzig 1494, fol. 62.

Ave stella fulgida

Ave stella fulgida,
Speculum decoris,
Virga Iesse florida,
Vinculum amoris.

Gemma celi nitida,
Medela languoris,
Labe carens sordida,
Mater salvatoris.

*

Hail shining star,
Mirror of beauty,
Flowering rod of Jesse,
Chain of love.

Bright jewel of heaven,
Cure for weakness,
Free from filthy stain,
Mother of the savior.

Text source. Leipzig 1494, fol. 162v.

Poi che t'hebi nel core (Francesco d'Albizo)

Poi che t'hebi[35] nel core,
Jesu clemente e pio,
Crescie tanto il disio,
Che gli arde a tutte l'hore.

Non ti partire, Signorre,
Da mi che ti voglio
Che tuto il piacer mio
È star in questo ardorre.

Ardime de splendore,
Dolce e piatoso idio,
Ch'ogni cosa in oblio
Ho dato per tuo amor.

Ah quanto è grando error
Amar il mondo rio,
Che bene sancto e giulio
Si cambia per dolor.

*

Since I have had you in my heart,
Jesus indulgent and charitable,
The desire is growing so much
That it burns all the time.

Do not depart, Lord,
From me who craves for you
So that all my pleasure
Is to remain in this ardor.

Consume me with splendor,
Sweet and merciful God,
That I have forgotten everything
For the sake of your love.

Ah, how great an error
To love the world's sin,
That holy and happy well-being
Is exchanged for sorrow.

Text source. Cape Town Grey, fols. 79v–80.

Fortuna desperata quae te dementia coepit [vertit]

Fortuna desperata, quae te dementia cepit?[36]
Solemur contrariis[37] fatis.[38]
O socii[39] (neque enim sumus ignari ante malorum,
Sed passi graviora), dabit Deus his quoque finem.

*

Desperate fortune, what madness seizes you?
May we be comforted in our adverse fate.
O comrades (certainly we have not been ignorant of
   evil before,
Having suffered more serious things), God will end
   this as well.

Text source. St. Gall 462, fols. 6v–7.

Derivation. Line 1: Virgil, *Eclogae*, 2.69.[40] Line 2: Virgil, *Aeneid*, 1.239.[41] Lines 3–4: Virgil, *Aeneid*, 1.198–99.

COMMENTS

A si placet altus voice has been added to the original three voices. This version of *Fortuna desperata* was the most widely circulated of any, appearing in eleven ensemble sources (twice in one of them) and one intabulation (the Basel F.X.10 bassus is included here on the assumption that this is the likeliest version for it to have included, although it may have held FD3, 4, 5, or an unknown version instead). As discussed in the introduction, the version used here is that of what is probably the earliest surviving source. The text and its underlay are based on Paris 4379. In addition to using the original text, the work was also associated with two different sacred contrafacta in Leipzig 1494 (one of these, the somewhat cryptic and problematic text *Virginis alme parens,* contains a reference to *fortuna* within its text), a lauda text in the Cape Town Grey manuscript (the same text used for FD4), and a classical Latin compilation in St. Gall 462 and 463 (also used for other *Fortuna desperata* settings in St. Gall 463 and 464). In addition, a series of excerpts from Latin poetry (by Tibullus and the Bolognese humanist Philippus Beroaldus the elder) adorn the opening in St. Gall 462 where this work is found.[42] The work is classified modally as "Ionicus, idest quintus" in St. Gall 463, where it is also described as "antiquum."

NOTES TO THE TRANSCRIPTION

Superius. For C.G. XIII.27, see FD7. Part missing in Basel X.F.10. Part name, discantus in St. Gall 462, St. Gall 463, Zwickau 78/2. Signature accidentals, b′ is flat in Leipzig 1494 (fol. 162v), St. Gall 462 (first system only, m. 1 to m. 30, note 1), Zwickau 78/2, St. Gall 463. M. 1 to m. 2, note 1, f′ dotted br in Cape Town Grey. M. 5, a′ sbr–a′ sbr in Canti C (unique variant). M. 5 to m. 6, note 1, a′ dotted br in Cape Town Grey. M. 9 to m. 10, note 1, f′ br–f′ sbr in Leipzig 1494 (fol. 62); f′ br in Paris 676 (dot lacking; error); f′ dotted sbr–e′ min–f′ sbr in St. Gall 462, St. Gall 463. M. 13, note 1, c′ sbr in Leipzig 1494 (fol. 62), Paris 676, St. Gall 462, Zwickau 78/2, St. Gall 463. M. 13, note 2 to m. 14, note 1, f′ dotted sbr–e′ smin–d′ smin in St. Gall 462, St. Gall 463. M. 17 to m. 18, note 1, c″ dotted br in Perugia 431, Cape Town Grey. M. 19, b♭′ dotted sbr–c″ min in Zwickau 78/2. M. 20, note 2, c″ min–b♭′ min in St. Gall 462, St. Gall 463. M. 21, a′ sbr–a′ sbr in St. Gall 462 (unique variant). M. 24, e′ br in Leipzig 1494 (fol. 62); e′ dotted sbr–d′ smin–e′ smin in Canti C (unique variant). M. 27, specific flat and signature flat in Leipzig 1494 (fol. 162v); specific flat in Paris 4379, Paris 676, Canti C, Cape Town Grey; signature flat in St. Gall 462, Zwickau 78/2, St. Gall 463; no flat in Perugia 431, Leipzig 1494 (fol. 62). M. 27 to m. 28, note 1, b♭′ br–b♭′ sbr in Paris 676, St. Gall 462, St. Gall 463. M. 29, a′ dotted sbr–g′ smin–f′ smin in Zwickau 78/2. M. 29, note 2, g′ min–f′ min in Leipzig 1494 (fol. 62), St. Gall 463. M. 30, g′ dotted sbr–f′ smin–g′ smin in Canti C (unique variant); g′ sbr–g′ sbr in St. Gall 462, St. Gall 463. M. 32, note 2 to m. 33, note 1, d″ br in Cape Town Grey (unique variant). M. 34, note 3 to m. 35, note 1, a′ sbr–a′ sbr in Paris 676 (unique variant); a′ dotted sbr–g′ smin–f′ smin in St. Gall 462, Zwickau 78/2, St. Gall 463. M. 38, a′ sbr–g′ min–f′ min in Perugia 431. M. 42, note 2, extra f′ br follows f′ sbr in Leipzig 1494 (fol. 162v) (error). M. 47, d′ br in Leipzig 1494 (fol. 62); d′ dotted sbr–e′ min in Zwickau 78/2 (unique variant). M. 48, f′ dotted sbr–e′ smin–d′ smin in Leipzig 1494 (fol. 62), Zwickau 78/2. M. 53, g′ dotted sbr–a′ min in Zwickau 78/2 (unique variant). M. 54, note 1, specific flat in Paris 4379, Perugia 431, Paris 676, Canti C, Cape Town Grey; signature flat in Leipzig 1494 (fol. 162v), Zwickau 78/2, St. Gall 463; no flat in Leipzig 1494 (fol. 62), St. Gall 462. M. 55, note 2 to m. 56, f′ dotted sbr–e′ smin–d′ smin–e′ sbr in Leipzig 1494 (fol. 62), St. Gall 462, St. Gall 463; f′ br–e′ sbr in Zwickau 78/2. M. 57, fermata in Leipzig 1494 (fol. 62), Leipzig 1494 (fol. 162v), Cape Town Grey, St. Gall 462, Zwickau 78/2.

Altus. Part missing in Basel X.F.10. Part name, CONTRA ALTUS in Perugia 431; Altus in C.G. XIII.27, St. Gall 462, Zwickau 78/2, St. Gall 463; Contra in Paris 676, Canti C. Signature accidentals, b is flat in Perugia 431 (first system only, m. 1 to m. 17, note 1), Leipzig 1494 (fol. 162v) (first two staves only, mm. 1–43); none in Leipzig 1494 (fol. 62). Mensuration, lacking in Paris 676, Cape Town Grey. M. 6, notes 3–4, a dotted min–g smin in Leipzig 1494 (fol. 62). M. 8, g sbr–sbr rest in Canti C. M. 11, rest, br rest in Leipzig 1494 (fol. 162v). M. 12, rest and note 2, sbr rest in St. Gall 462, St. Gall 463. M. 13, c′ sbr–b sbr in St. Gall 462; d′ sbr–c′ sbr in St. Gall 463. M. 19, note 1, e′ min in St. Gall 462, St. Gall 463. M. 24, g br in Leipzig 1494 (fol. 62). M. 25, notes 1–2, f dotted min–g smin in Zwickau 78/2. M. 25, note 3 to m. 26, a dotted sbr–b♭ min–c′ min–d′ min in Leipzig 1494 (fol. 162v), St. Gall 462, St. Gall 463. M. 26, min rest–b min–c′ min–d′ min in Zwickau 78/2. M. 27, specific flat in Paris 4379, Perugia 431, Leipzig 1494 (fol. 62), Leipzig 1494 (fol. 162v), Paris 676, Canti C, Cape Town Grey, Zwickau 78/2; no flat in C.G. XIII.27, St. Gall 462, St. Gall 463. M. 31, note 2, e′ sbr in C.G. XIII.27. M. 35, specific flat in Canti C, Cape Town Grey, Zwickau 78/2; no flat in Paris 4379, Perugia 431, Leipzig 1494 (fol. 62), Leipzig 1494 (fol. 162v), C.G. XIII.27, Paris 676, St. Gall 462, St. Gall 463. M. 36, c′ dotted sbr–d′ min in Canti C. M. 38, f′ dotted sbr–g′ min in St. Gall 462, St. Gall 463. M. 38 to m. 39, note 1, f′ br–g′ br–a′ dotted br with minor color in Perugia 431. M. 40, note 2 to m. 41, note 1, c′ sbr in Perugia 431. M. 42, a br in St. Gall 462, St. Gall 463. M. 42 to m. 43, note 1, a br–a sbr in Leipzig 1494 (fol. 62), Paris 676, Canti C. M. 43, br rest in St. Gall 462, St. Gall 463. M. 44, note 1, extra min rest before b sbr in Leipzig 1494 (fol. 162v). M. 47, note 1, g′ sbr in Leipzig 1494 (fol. 62), Leipzig 1494 (fol. 162v), St. Gall 462. M. 53, d′ sbr–c′ sbr in Leipzig 1494 (fol. 62). M. 54, b dotted sbr–c′ min in Zwickau 78/2. M. 55 to m. 56, note 1, c′ sbr–c′ min–c′ sbr–c′ sbr in Canti C. M. 55, note 1 to m. 56, c′ dotted sbr–c′ dotted sbr in Perugia 431, Paris 676, Cape Town Grey; c′ sbr–c′ br in Zwickau 78/2. M. 57, c′ br–c′ long in Zwickau 78/2; a in Perugia 431, Paris 676, Cape Town Grey; c′ in Leipzig 1494 (fol. 62), C.G. XIII.27, Canti C, St. Gall 462, St. Gall 463; fermata in Leipzig 1494 (fol. 62), Leipzig 1494 (fol. 162v), St. Gall 462, Zwickau 78/2.

Tenor. Part missing in Leipzig 1494 (fol. 162v), Basel F.X.10, St. Gall 463; for C.G. XIII.27, see FD7. Part name, T in Perugia 431; none in Leipzig 1494 (fol. 62), Cape Town Grey; Tenor in Paris 676, Canti C, Zwickau 78/2; TENOR in St. Gall 462. Clef, C3 in Perugia 431, Leipzig 1494 (fol. 62), Canti C, Cape Town Grey, St. Gall 462, Zwickau 78/2. Signature accidentals, b and b′ are flat in Perugia 431 (first system, m. 1 to m. 23, note 1). Mensuration, lacking in Paris 676, Cape Town Grey. M. 7, d′ br in Leipzig 1494 (fol. 62), Zwickau 78/2. M. 9 to m. 10, note 1, d′ br–d′ sbr in Leipzig 1494 (fol. 62), St. Gall 462, Zwickau 78/2. Mm. 15–17, f long–br rest in Leipzig 1494 (fol. 62), Paris 676. M. 21 to m. 22, note 1, f′ dotted br in Paris 676, Canti C, Cape Town Grey. M. 23, e′ sbr–e′ sbr in Paris 676; e′ dotted sbr–f′ min in Zwickau 78/2. M. 24, g′ dotted sbr–f′ smin–e′ smin in Leipzig 1494 (fol. 62), Paris 676, Zwickau 78/2. M. 25, d′ sbr–d′ sbr in Paris 676. M. 27 to m. 28, note 1, g′ br–g′ sbr in Leipzig 1494 (fol. 62), Paris 676. M. 29, f′ dotted sbr–e′ smin–d′ smin in Perugia 431, Leipzig 1494 (fol. 62), Zwickau 78/2. M. 29, notes 2–3, d′ sbr in Paris 676. M. 30, e′ sbr–e′ sbr in St. Gall 462. M. 35, signature flat and specific flat in Paris 4379; b is long in Cape Town Grey (unique variant). M. 44, note 2, specific flat in Paris 676. M. 48, d′ dotted sbr–c′ smin–b smin in Perugia 431, Leipzig 1494 (fol. 62), Canti C, St. Gall 462, Zwickau 78/2; d′ min–c′ min–b min–a min in Paris 676. M. 52, sbr rest–a sbr in Paris 676. M. 56, g is long in Cape Town Grey (error). M. 57, fermata in Cape Town Grey, St. Gall 462, Zwickau 78/2.

Bassus (Contra). Part missing in Leipzig 1494 (fol. 162v), St. Gall 463. Part name, CONTRA BASSUS in Perugia 431; none in Leipzig 1494 (fol. 62), Cape Town Grey; Bassus in C.G. XIII.27, Paris 676, Canti C, St. Gall 462, Zwickau 78/2; Basus in Basel F.X.10. Clef, C5 in Cape Town Grey; F2 in Basel F.X.10, St. Gall 462; F3 in Leipzig 1494 (fol. 62), Canti C, Zwickau 78/2. Signature accidentals, b is flat in Perugia 431 (m. 1 to m. 37, note 2 only), St. Gall 462 (mm. 1–31 only); none in Leipzig 1494 (fol. 62), C.G. XIII.27, Canti C; B and b are flat in Zwickau 78/2. Mensuration, lacking in

Basel F.X.10, Paris 676, Cape Town Grey, St. Gall 462. M. 3, f dotted sbr–e smin–d smin in Leipzig 1494 (fol. 62) (unique variant). M. 4, c sbr–c sbr in Leipzig 1494 (fol. 62) (unique variant). M. 6, notes 1–2, a min–g min in Perugia 431, Basel F.X.10, St. Gall 462. M. 8, e♭ sbr–e♭ sbr in Zwickau 78/2. M. 9 to m. 10, note 1, d br in Paris 676 (dot lacking; error). M. 12, note 1, d sbr in Basel F.X.10 (unique variant). M. 16, d' dotted sbr–c' smin–b smin in Leipzig 1494 (fol. 62). M. 19, g sbr–g sbr in Basel F.X.10, St. Gall 462. M. 20, note 1, specific flat and signature flat in Paris 4379, Paris 676; specific flat in Canti C; signature flat in Perugia 431, Basel F.X.10, Cape Town Grey, St. Gall 462, Zwickau 78/2; no flat in Leipzig 1494 (fol. 62), C.G. XIII.27. M. 21, f br in Leipzig 1494 (fol. 62), Paris 676. M. 22, f dotted sbr–e smin–d smin in Leipzig 1494 (fol. 62) (unique variant); sbr rest–f sbr in Paris 676. M. 23 to m. 24, note 1, c dotted br in Canti C. Mm. 23–24, c long in Leipzig 1494 (fol. 62), Cape Town Grey. M. 24, c br in Zwickau 78/2. M. 26, note 2, d sbr in St. Gall 462 (unique variant). M. 27, see table 2 in the introduction for presence or absence of flat. M. 27 to m. 28, note 1, e dotted long in Leipzig 1494 (fol. 62) (error); e br–e sbr in Basel F.X.10. M. 33, note 1, signature flat and specific flat in Perugia 431; specific flat in Canti C; signature flat in Paris 4379, Basel F.X.10, Paris 676, Cape Town Grey, Zwickau 78/2; no flat in Leipzig 1494 (fol. 62), C.G. XIII.27, St. Gall 462. M. 35, g long in Leipzig 1494 (fol. 62) (unique variant); see table 2 in the introduction for presence or absence of flat. M. 37, notes 1–2, a dotted min–g smin in Leipzig 1494 (fol. 62), Paris 676. Mm. 39–40, a br–a br in Canti C. M. 41, notes 1–2, a dotted min–g smin in Leipzig 1494 (fol. 62), Canti C, Cape Town Grey; g min–f min in Basel F.X.10 (unique variant). M. 41, note 3, f min–e min in Leipzig 1494 (fol. 62). M. 45, note 2, min rest–d min in Zwickau 78/2 (unique variant). M. 47–48, d br–d br in Paris 676. M. 50, specific flat in Paris 4379, Perugia 431, C.G. XIII.27, Paris 676, Canti C, St. Gall 462; signature flat in Zwickau 78/2; no flat in Leipzig 1494 (fol. 62), Basel F.X.10, Cape Town Grey. M. 52, note 1, sbr rest in C.G. XIII.27, Paris 676. M. 52, note 2, a sbr in Paris 676. M. 53, note 2, e sbr in Basel F.X.10 (unique variant); a sbr in Paris 676 (unique variant). M. 54–57, pitches notated a third too high in Paris 676; variants listed below have transposed this passage down. M. 54, note 2, f min in Paris 676. M. 55, see table 2 in the introduction for presence or absence of flat. M. 55, f sbr–g sbr in C.G. XIII.27 (error). M. 55, note 2, f min–e smin–d smin in Leipzig 1494 (fol. 62) (unique variant). M. 56, e long in Leipzig 1494 (fol. 62) (unique variant). M. 57, simultaneous f and c' in Perugia 431; f in Canti C; F in Leipzig 1494 (fol. 62) (unique variant); a in Basel F.X.10 (unique variant); fermata in Cape Town Grey, St. Gall 462, Zwickau 78/2.

3. Fortuna desperata (anonymous)

a 4

A si placet altus is added to the original composition.

Source

Bologna Q16, fols. 117v–118;[43] anonymous; i–i–i–i; S = [F]ortuna desperata, A = [F]ortuna, T = [F]ortuna disperata, B = fortuna disperata; index = fortuta [*sic*] disperata.

References

Inventory numbers. Meconi 2b; Picker 2b; Cumming A II 3; Loeffler B6.

Modern editions. Brooks, 3:312–15. Self, 29–33 (altus only).

Comments

An original si placet altus, related in some ways to the other si placet altus voices, is added to the original three voices. This new line presents problems at the end of the song. The E–F–G dissonance in measure 51 suggests that this line is a semibreve off at this point; Brooks switches the semibreve rest from measure 46 to before measure 54, which eliminates this problem. Measure 56 also seems incorrect; it is possible that the line break that occurs halfway through measure 55 led to a scribal error, but the custos on the previous line directs the singer to A.

The work, a later addition to the manuscript, immediately follows *Fortune par ta cruaulte* and precedes *De tous biens plaine*. These works are all part of a small section of very widely distributed pieces (including *Nunca fue pena maior* and Agricola's *Si dedero*) added to the collection.

Notes to the Transcription

Superius. Mm. 14 and 56, unique variants.

Bassus. M. 50, specific flat.

4. Fortuna desperata / Poi che t'hebi nel core (anonymous)

a 4

A si placet altus is added to the original composition.

Source

Florence Pan. 27, fols. 22v–23;[44] anonymous; t–i–x–x; both folios are headed "Fortuna desperata" but the text with the song is the contrafactum "Poi che t'hebi nel core"; S = "Poi che te hebi nel core" text with a second stanza; A = Poÿ che te hebi nel core.

REFERENCES

Inventory numbers. Meconi 2c; Picker 2c; Cumming A II 4; Loeffler B7.

Modern editions. Cattin, XXVII (altus only). Self, 29–33 (altus only).

TEXT AND TRANSLATION

Poi che t'hebi nel core, see FD2.

COMMENTS

A new si placet altus voice, related in some ways to the other si placet altus parts, has been added to the original three voices. In the manuscript the work immediately follows an anonymous *Fortuna che te gioua de straciarme*. The piece is transmitted with two stanzas of a lauda text (stanzas 1 and 3 of the text as given under FD2) by Francesco d'Albizo that is also found in Cape Town Grey.

NOTES TO THE TRANSCRIPTION

The altus, tenor, and bassus all have the number 112 written at the end of their voice parts; this tally equals the number of semibreves in the voice without the final long. The superius has the number 111.[45]

Superius. The text is spelled for the most part as it appears in Cape Town Grey. I suggest breaking the ligature at measure 47 for purposes of underlay.

Altus. The signature flat is given in the source only from measure 1 to measure 34, note 2, but it has been retained throughout in the edition. The pitch b does not appear in the manuscript after measure 34. M. 54, c'.

Bassus. B and b are flatted in the signature in measures 1–36 only; the B in measure 50 is specifically flatted in the manuscript, so the flat has been retained in the signature of the edition throughout the voice part.

5. Fortune esperee (anonymous)

a 4

A si placet altus is added to the original composition.

SOURCE

London 31922, fols. 4v–5 (no. 2); anonymous; i–i–i–i; all voices have incipit "Fortune esperee."

REFERENCES

Inventory numbers. Meconi 2e; Picker 2d; Cumming A II 2; Loeffler B8.

Modern editions. An Anthology of Early Renaissance Music, ed. Noah Greenberg and Paul Maynard (New York: W. W. Norton, 1975), 212–13 (without altus voice). Brooks, 3:322–25. Josquin Masses, 13:107. Self, 29–33 (altus only). Stevens, 2.

COMMENTS

A si placet altus has been added to the original three voices; this new voice, while unique, is clearly related to the other si placet altus voices. The textual incipit that remains ("hoped-for fortune") suggests that a contrafact text was present at one point, although the aural similarity of "esperee" and "desperata" is striking. The piece is unique among *Fortuna desperata* settings in that it uses c mensuration in all voices. It is the first secular piece in its sole source, appearing after the opening *Benedictus* by Isaac—a possible gesture to the popularity of its model.

NOTES TO THE TRANSCRIPTION

Superius. Mm. 6–7, unique variant. M. 19, signature flat begins.

Tenor. M. 51, unique variant.

Bassus. M. 6, flat appears before e (see plate 5), but presumably refers to measure 8, where it has been placed in the edition. M. 18, unique variant. Mm. 28–29, unique variant. M. 44, flat given on e space (see plate 5), presumably in reference to upcoming e in measure 55, where it has been placed in the edition. M. 50, specific flat. M. 52, note 1, no sign of congruence. M. 52, note 2, sign of congruence.

6. Fortuna desperata (Alexander Agricola)

a 6

Three new si placet voices are added to the original composition.

SOURCE

Augsburg 142a, fols. 46v–47; Allexannderr A; i–x–x–x–i–x; the second "incipit" occurs after the end of the vagans voice, just above the bassus; S = fortuna, V = fortuna desperata.

REFERENCES

Inventory numbers. Meconi 2d; Picker 5; Cumming A II 5; Loeffler D15.

Modern editions. Agricola, 5:68–70. Jonas, 1:127–31.

COMMENTS

Agricola has added three new si placet voices (the contra altus, vagans, and bassus) to the original three voices of the song; an earlier example of a triple si placet setting is found in the *O rosa bella* family.[46] The contra altus opens like the most common si placet altus (see FD2) but then proceeds differently.

NOTES TO THE TRANSCRIPTION

Discantus (original superius part). M. 49, signature flat drops out, but is retained in the edition since m. 54, note 1, would be flatted by ficta.

Contra Altus. M. 35, note 2, sharp sign is written under the d', doubtless to flatten the preceding e'.

Tenor (original tenor part). The tenor part is written in the wrong clef, C4 instead of C3, throughout. M. 29, the signature flat drops out (the affected notes are m. 35, note 1; m. 45, note 4; m. 48, note 3; m. 50, note 1; m. 53, note 1; and m. 55, note 1); the signature flat has been retained in the edition since all affected notes would be flatted by ficta.

Baricanor (original bassus part). Mm. 15–16, unique variant. Mm. 40–41, unique variant.

Bassus. The signature flat is placed a third too low throughout.

7. *Fortuna desperata (Felice?)*

a 3

A new contratenor is added to the original superius and tenor.

SOURCE

C.G. XIII.27, fols. 56v–57 (63v–64); felice;[47] i–x–x; S = Fortuna desperata.

REFERENCES

Inventory numbers. Meconi 3a; Picker 4; Cumming A III 1; Loeffler D14.

Modern edition. Atlas, 2:38–42 (includes all five voices).

COMMENTS

The opening on which this piece is placed in the manuscript contains five musical voices. On the left side of the opening are the three voices of the original song; on the right side is the most popular of the si placet altus voices plus a bassus that appears nowhere else. This new bassus, a lively line employing triplets, is reminiscent of the other replacement contratenor, ascribed to Josquin, in FD8. Atlas presents all five voices in his edition and demonstrates how the two bassus lines are incompatible. Similarly, the new bassus cannot work in conjunction with the si placet altus (see, for example, mm. 42 and 50 in Atlas's edition). What we have then is a collection of voices from which three possible pieces can be derived: the original song, a si placet version (the original superius, tenor, and bassus plus the si placet altus), and a replacement contratenor setting (the original superius and tenor and the new bassus); the last has been edited here. Placing together a group of voices that can be combined in different ways occurs elsewhere in early music: in some medieval motets, in another piece in the same manuscript, and in other art-song reworkings such as the *O rosa bella* family.[48]

It is unclear how much Felice contributed to the five voices in the manuscript. Did he write the original work or contribute the best-known si placet voice (or both), or was he responsible only for the replacement contratenor? If he is the "Ser Felice di Giovanni Martini" noted in contemporary documents, as is widely believed, whatever contribution he made must have been before his death in 1478.[49] One wonders, too, about the "di Giovanni Martini" associated with his name. Does this indicate some connection between Felice and the composer of one of the earliest derivative settings of the work (FD9)?

NOTES TO THE TRANSCRIPTION

Superius. Mm. 5–6, unique variant.

Bassus. Mm. 22 and 54, the switch to o 2 results in a series of triplets, although they are not specifically marked as such in the manuscript.

8. *Fortuna disperata (Josquin des Prez?)*

a 3

A new contratenor is added to the original superius and tenor.

SOURCE

Segovia, fol. 182v; Josquin du pres; i–i–i; all incipits = fortuna disperata.

REFERENCES

Inventory numbers. Meconi 3b; Picker 3; Cumming A III 2; Loeffler D1.

Modern editions. Josquin CW, 27:16–17. Josquin Secular, 53:27–29. Josquin SSP, 26–27.

COMMENTS

A replacement contratenor bassus is added to the original superius and tenor. This new bassus voice is in a lower range than the original and is considerably livelier; it is similar in character to the one in FD7 and likewise uses triplets. The attribution to Josquin has not generally been accepted, not least because of the differences between this version of the original voices and the one he uses in his mass.[50] It is nonetheless a charming work.

Measures 47–48 in the tenor line present a particularly problematic reading. These measures are made of two components, a dotted semibreve D (a unique variant) and C and B minims. The latter pitches also present a unique reading, but one that generates jarring parallel seconds with the superius. Modern editors have previously dealt with this by turning measure 47 into a breve D and measure 48 into descending minims (D–C–B–A); this reading appears in Paris 676 and FD19. In Josquin CW the breve D is tied to the following minim D; the other two editions suggest this as a possibility by adding an editorial tie between the breve D and the minim D. This revised version, which changes pitch as well as rhythm, generates parallel motion between the superius and tenor; as already noted in the introduction, the amount of textural homogeneity between the two voices varied considerably from source to source.

Tying the breve D of measure 47 and the minim D of measure 48 is, however, a notational impossibility in the fifteenth century and I have consequently not followed this popular solution here. I have instead rhythmically altered the D–C–B of measure 48 to conform to the earlier and more common reading of dotted breve followed by two semiminims (found in Paris 4379, Perugia 431 [FD2], Leipzig 1494 [fol. 62], Canti C, Wolfenbüttel 78, St. Gall 462, FD18, the Munich 328–31 reading of FD29 [the Phrygian version of this line], Zwickau 78/2, and the other tenor reading in Segovia, in its version of FD1). I have maintained the flavor (and the uniqueness) of the manuscript reading for FD8 by keeping the tie to the D in measure 47. This reading would have been notationally complex but possible in the fifteenth century: a half-colored long followed by two colored minims. I wonder whether the scribe did not encounter something like this and then change it to the more easily read version in the manuscript. That version certainly works well enough if the tenor line is on its own, and if the scribe was thinking horizontally rather than vertically while he was copying—as he surely was— the clash with the superius would not have been apparent.

Notes to the Transcription

Superius. M. 32, signature flat drops out; it has been retained throughout the edition since ficta would generate flats for the remainder of the piece.

Tenor. Mm. 47–48, d' dotted br–c' min–b min (unique variant).

Bassus. Mm. 49–55, triplets not specifically indicated in the manuscript; the number 3 is placed at the beginning of this passage.

9. *Fortuna disperata (Johannes Martini)*

a 4

The original superius is in the superius.

Sources

Primary source. **Casanatense 2856,**[51] fols. 147v–149 (no. 102);[52] .Jo. martini; i–i–i–i; S, A, and T = Fortuna disperata, B = fortuna. This is the earlier source and was compiled in Ferrara while Martini, the probable composer, was in residence.

Concordant source. **Segovia,** fols. 115v–116; ysaac; i–i–i–i; all incipits = fortuna disperata.

References

Inventory numbers. Meconi 6a; Picker 12; Cumming B II 4; Loeffler D5/D6.

Modern editions. Martini, 19–21 (Casanatense 2856). Wolff, 2:399–404 (Casanatense 2856).

Comments

This work is one of the earliest surviving reworkings of *Fortuna desperata*. The superius of the original is placed, untransposed and with the original note values, in the superius of the new composition. The lower three voices are highly imitative and motivic, and two have very large ranges (a twelfth for the bassus and a thirteenth for the altus). Gombosi criticized the work as "dull, insignificant, and uninteresting,"[53] yet the fact that it was copied at least twice in the fifteenth century suggests a different contemporary assessment. Picker viewed the motivic repetition at different pitch levels in the bassus as a reflection of Fortune's mutability, and Lowinsky wondered whether the recurring rising motive was an intentional quotation of the inverted first phrase of *Fortuna d'un gran tempo*.[54]

The versions in the two manuscripts show some significant differences. In the crucial measure 13 of the superius, Segovia uses the F reading even though there are no parallel fifths to be avoided in this setting. Segovia also changes the unusual F–A third of the final sonority to the more accustomed F–C fifth, and there are other instances where Segovia presents a more conventional, though less accurately copied, version.

The ascription to Martini in Casanatense 2856 takes precedence over that to Isaac in Segovia. Aside from being the earlier source, Casanatense 2856 was compiled in Ferrara while Martini was resident there and is presumably accurate about assigning works to him.

Notes to the Transcription

Superius. M. 1 to m. 2, note 1, f' dotted br in Segovia. M. 13, note 1, f' in Segovia. M. 17 to m.

18, note 1, c″ dotted br in Segovia. M. 20, note 2, c″ min–b′ min in Segovia. M. 25, unique variant in Casanatense 2856; f′ br in Segovia. M. 27, no flat in Segovia. M. 34, note 3 to m. 35, note 1, a′ dotted sbr–g′ smin–f′ smin in Segovia. M. 43, e′ sbr–e′ sbr in Segovia (unique variant). M. 48, note 3, d′ min–c′ min in Segovia (Segovia's reading is that of the original). M. 54, no flat in Segovia. M. 55 to m. 56, note 1, g′ sbr–f′ dotted sbr–e′ smin–d′ smin in Segovia.

Altus. Part name, none in Segovia. M. 13, b♭ min–c′ min inserted before a dotted min in Segovia. M. 18, note 2, d′ in Segovia. M. 25, note 3 to m. 26, d′ sbr–c′ smin–b♭ smin–a sbr–g sbr in Segovia. M. 30, notes 5–7, d′ sbr in Segovia. M. 56, notes 1–2, c′ min–d′ min in Segovia. M. 57, c′ in Segovia.

Tenor. Part name, none in Segovia. Clef, C5 in Segovia. M. 9, note 2, specific flat in Segovia. M. 21, note 6, e smin–d smin in Segovia. M. 26, note 4, specific flat in Casanatense 2856, Segovia. M. 33, notes 2–3, f sbr in Segovia. M. 54, note 1, specific flat in Segovia.

Bassus. Part name, none in Segovia. M. 3, notes 1–2, F sbr in Segovia. M. 5, notes 1–2, F sbr in Segovia. M. 5, note 3 to m. 7, note 1, originally omitted and then added at the end of the folio in Segovia. M. 15, notes 1–2, F sbr in Segovia. M. 17 to m. 18, note 2, omitted in Segovia. M. 25, F sbr inserted at the beginning of the measure in Segovia. M. 36, notes 1–2, F sbr in Segovia. M. 39, note 3, c dotted min–F smin in Segovia.

10. *Fortuna disperata / Sancte Petre / Ora pro nobis (Heinrich Isaac?)*

a 5

The original superius is in the superius.

Source

Segovia, fols. 117v–118; ysaac; i–i–i–i–i; S, T, B = fortuna disperata, A = Sancte petre, Q = Ora pro nobis.

References

Inventory numbers. Meconi 10a; Picker 18; Cumming B II 3; Loeffler D2.

Modern edition. Baker, 2:840–47.

Text and Translation

Sancte Petre, ora pro nobis

Sancte Petre, ora pro nobis.
Sancte Andrea, ora pro nobis.
Sancte Jacobe, ora pro nobis.
Sancte Thoma, ora pro nobis.
Sancte Joannes, ora pro nobis.
Sancte Simon, ora pro nobis.
Sancte Philippe, ora pro nobis.
Sancte Matthaee, ora pro nobis.
Sancte Jacobe, ora pro nobis.
Sancte Thadaee, ora pro nobis.
Sancte Bartholomaee, ora pro nobis.

*

Saint Peter, pray for us.
Saint Andrew, pray for us.
Saint James, pray for us.
Saint Thomas, pray for us.
Saint John, pray for us.
Saint Simon, pray for us.
Saint Philip, pray for us.
Saint Matthew, pray for us.
Saint James, pray for us.
Saint Thaddeus, pray for us.
Saint Bartholomew, pray for us.

Text source. Segovia, fols. 117v–118, and *LU,* Appendix II, 3.

Comments

The composer places the original superius, untransposed and with original note values, in the superius of this work. Tenor and quintus also have preexistent material, the chant for the litany of the saints.[55] The two voices divide the litany so that the phrase with the saint's name is always answered by the "ora pro nobis" phrase, although the rhythms do not always permit precise underlay of the latter phrase. The names of the remaining apostles (except Judas) are added editorially to the name of Saint Peter.[56] Because of the chant used, tenor and quintus have extremely small ranges. The altus and bassus, the only freely composed voices in this work, are considerably livelier than the other three parts.

The interpretation of this work has varied considerably. For Maniates it is "mocking and slightly blasphemous," but both Loeffler and Cumming see the use of the litany as counteracting the ill effects of Fortune.[57] Picker places the work in a somewhat broader context by noting other fifteenth-century examples of combining the litany of the saints with well-known melodies, and he also argues against the charge of inauthenticity sometimes applied to this work.[58] The superius as given here differs in eight possibly significant places from the superius in Isaac's FD11, but see the introduction for a discussion of the problems in determining authenticity based on similarity of borrowed material.

Notes to the Transcription

Since none of the voices receives a designation in the manuscript, they are named here on the basis of their disposition (superius, tenor, and quintus on the verso part of the opening; altus and bassus on the recto side). I have included underlay for those wishing to sing the lines with the litany, indicating above the staff where notes must be divided to enable full texting.

11. *Fortuna / Bruder Conrat (Heinrich Isaac)*

a 4

The original superius is in the superius.

Source

Vienna 18810, fols. 22v–23, 19v–20, 20–20v, 20–20v; henricus ÿsaac (attribution given in all partbooks); i–i–i–i; S = fortuna Bruder Conrat, A = Bruder Conrat Super fortuna, T and B = Bruder conrat Super fortuna.

References

Inventory numbers. Meconi 7a; Picker 17; Cumming B II 2; Loeffler D4.

Modern edition. Isaac, 73.

Comments

Isaac places the original superius, untransposed and with original note values, in his discantus (superius). While additional material from the model is found at the beginning of the bassa vox, which quotes the first three measures of the original bassus, the three lower voices for the most part are drawn from the popular German song *Bruder Conrat* (Brother Conrad). Isaac in this work is combining two compositional traditions, both of which he has explored before. Here the *Bruder Conrat* melody has been treated freely[59] and is subordinate to *Fortuna desperata*. Isaac used the German tune in other works that have sometimes been confused with this setting, but to date no concordances have been found. Curiously, the bassa vox motive beginning in measure 27 is like the one that pervades the *Fortuna* setting attributed to both Martini and Isaac, but surely by Martini (FD9).

No complete texts are transmitted with this setting, but Cumming notes the appropriateness of the subject matter of *Bruder Conrat*, a dying man, in combination with *Fortuna desperata*.[60] This observation is especially true in light of the reference to death that appears in the full text of *Fortuna desperata*.

Notes to the Transcription

Discantus (original superius). M. 46, unique variant. M. 52, unique variant.

12. *Fortuna disperata (anonymous)*

a 4

The original superius is in the superius.

Source

Bologna Q18, fols. 28v–29; anonymous; i–x–x–x; S = fortuna disperata.

References

Inventory numbers. Meconi 6c; Picker 13.

Modern editions. Weiss, 2:454–56. Susan Forscher Weiss, "Bologna Q 18: Some Reflections on Content and Context," *Journal of the American Musicological Society* 41 (1988): 82–86.

Comments

The superius of the original song appears in the superius, untransposed and with the original note values. The bassus begins with a line that is very similar to the original bassus and returns to the model from time to time throughout the work, while the altus is composed of little besides a reiterated skipping motive. Tenor and bassus likewise make use of this motive, but their material displays greater variety. The lively and often imitative counterpoint of the lower three voices provides a striking contrast to the more sedately moving superius; Picker has noted the similarity to Martini's *Fortuna desperata* (FD9), while Weiss remarks upon the resemblance to the setting attributed to Josquin (FD8).[61] Certainly the combination of rapidly reiterated motives, sequences, runs, and fifth and octave leaps played against a slow cantus firmus is completely at home in the realm of art-song reworkings.

Notes to the Transcription

Superius. M. 32, unique variant. M. 54–55, unique variant.

13. *Fortuna disperata zibaldone*[62] *(anonymous)*

a 4

The original superius is in the superius, with the original text. The lower three voices are an Italian quodlibet and have the appropriate texts.

Sources

Primary source. **Florence 164–67**, no. 39; anonymous; t–t–t–t. This is the only complete source.[63]

Concordant sources. **Cortona/Paris,** fols. 17v–18, 17v–18, 20v–21; anonymous; t–t–t–m. **Florence 337,** fols. 42v–43 (32v–33); anonymous; m–m–m–t.

References

Inventory numbers. Meconi 6h; Picker 15; Cumming B II 1; Loeffler D21.

Modern editions. Bianca Becherini, "Tre incatenature del codice fiorentino Magl. XIX. 164–65–66–67," in *Collectanea historiae musicae*, vol. 1 (Florence: Leo S. Olschki, 1953), 79–96, 89–91 (Florence 164–67). Obrecht Masses, appendix: 138–40.

Texts and Translations

Fortuna desperata, see FD1.

Fortuna disperata zibaldone

ALTUS
Vidi la forosetta in un boschetto.
Che mangera la sposa?
Una fagiana grigia.
Ghierem.
Ballate ciascheriem.
Levantens, Donna Joanna.
Levantens, affar lo pan. Far dinderindina.
Se l'orso non ritorna,
Dammene un poco di quella mazzacrocha.
Dammene un poco et non me ne dar troppa.

*

I saw the peasant girl in a copse.
What will the bride eat?
A grey pheasant.
Ghierem.[64]
Let's dance.[65]
Rise, Lady Joanna.
Rise to make bread. Make dinderindina.[66]
If the bear doesn't return,
Give me a little of that mazzacrocha.[67]
Give me a little and don't give me too much.

TENOR
Voi m'havete svergognie.
Niente del vostro m'have done.
Che mangera la sposa la prima sera?
Dinderindina, la dinderindina.
La vita della sgalera.
Dal papa sancto et sommi confessato.
Levantens, Donna Jonna.
Noi siamo[68] a mal partito.
Chi se lo vuol saper, si se lo sappia.
Et maragnan.
Suona lo corno, capo caccia.
Chi guasta l'altrui cose fa villania.

*

You have shamed me.
You have given me nothing of yours.
What will the bride eat the first evening?
Dinderindina, la dinderindina.
The life of the convict.
I went to the pope and confessed myself.
Rise, Lady Joanna.
We're in a bad way.
Let those who wish to know, know it.
And to hell with it.
Sound the horn, huntmaster.
Who spoils what is someone else's does wrong.

BASSUS
Fortuna.
Mangio biscotti et ci che pasturava agnielli.
Voi m'avete svergognie.
Niente del vostro m'have done.
Vengho da Roma dallo giubbileo.
D'una fagana griga.
La tortorella.
Che mangera la sposa?
Una fagiana griga.
Dammene un poco di quella mazza croccha.
En chi l'aves. En ch'il sapes.
Una chucchia rasa.

*

Fortune.
I eat cookies and the one who keeps sheep.
You have shamed me.
You have given me nothing of yours.
I come from Rome from the jubilee.
From a grey pheasant.
The dove.
What will the bride eat?
A grey pheasant.
Give me a little of that mazza croccha.
And who has it. And who understands it.
An empty spoon.

Text source. Florence 164–67, no. 39.

Comments

The anonymous composer of this setting places the original superius, untransposed and with its original note values, in the cantus (superius) of the new setting. The first three measures of the new bassus are derived from the original one, but most of the rest of the material there and in the other two voices is taken from snippets of popular songs of the time, making this a quodlibet setting.[69] This is a striking setting in many ways, for it shows how far *Fortuna desperata* had come in the popular consciousness. The original song, still circulating, was about forty years old at the time this setting was written, but the new composer was clearly out to subvert the sense of the by-now classic standard. What was once a song of mourning has been draped with snippets of popular songs whose ribald natures and double meanings must have been only too clear to the listeners. The result was apparently quite popular, circulating in three Florentine (or probably Florentine) sources, a large number for a derivative setting, all fully texted. What had once marked some kind of shared Florentine tragedy was now ripe for satire with the passage of time.

NOTES TO THE TRANSCRIPTION

Cantus (original superius). The text and underlay are drawn from Florence 164–67, providing yet a third texted version for this voice (in addition to those shown in FD1 and FD2). For the superius text and underlay in Cortona/Paris, see table 1 in the introduction.

Part name, none in Cortona/Paris. Signature accidentals, none in Cortona/Paris. M. 6, a' sbr–a' sbr in Cortona/Paris. M. 7, a' br in Cortona/Paris. M. 24, e' sbr–e' sbr in Cortona/Paris. M. 27, specific flat in Cortona/Paris. M. 27 to m. 28, note 1, b♭' br–b♭' sbr in Cortona/Paris. M. 34, note 3 to m. 35, note 3, a' br in Cortona/Paris. M. 54, note 1, specific flat in Cortona/Paris. M. 55, note 2 to m. 56, f' sbr–e' dotted sbr–d' smin–e' smin in Cortona/Paris. M. 57, br in Florence 164–67.

Altus. Part name, none in Cortona/Paris. M. 56, note 3 to m. 57, c' sbr–c' long in Cortona/Paris.

Tenor. Part name, none in Cortona/Paris. M. 6, note 1, c' min–c' sbr in Cortona/Paris. M. 13, notes 1–3, c' dotted sbr in Florence 164–67; the Cortona/Paris reading is used in the edition as it permits correct underlay. M. 18, note 4 to m. 19, note 1, f' min–f' min in Cortona/Paris. M. 19, notes 3–4, e♭' sbr in Cortona/Paris. M. 25, a br in Cortona/Paris.

Bassus. Part name, Bassus/Bassus altus in Florence 337. M. 13, note 1, f sbr–f min in Florence 337. M. 16, note 2, f in Florence 337.

14. Fortuna desperata (Jean Pinarol)

a 4

The original superius is in the bassus, transposed down an eleventh.

SOURCES

Primary source. **Canti C,** fols. 68v–69; .Jo. pinarol; i–i–i–i; S and B = Fortuna desperata, A and T = fortuna. This print is considerably earlier than the Munich 1516 partbooks and provides a better reading.

Concordant source. **Munich 1516,** no. 4; anonymous; i–i–i–i; S and A = Fortuna, T = Fortuna desperata, B = fortuna.

REFERENCES

Inventory numbers. Meconi 6d; Picker 14; Cumming B II 5; Loeffler D7.

Modern edition. Whisler, 2:12–15.

COMMENTS

This setting, by the little-known Jean Pinarol, transposes the original superius down an eleventh and places it in the bassus, with unchanged note values and a short tag appended to the end. Picker views this transposition as "yet another representation of mutability" of Fortuna,[70] but it is worth pointing out that this is a technique occurring with some frequency in other families of art-song reworkings. Both Gombosi and Whisler considered the work to be of relatively low quality.[71]

NOTES TO THE TRANSCRIPTION

Munich 1516's scribe evidently copied this piece directly from Canti C.[72]

Superius. Part name, Discant in Munich 1516. M. 57, rest, sbr rest in Munich 1516. M. 60, fermata in Munich 1516.

Contra. Part name, Allt in Munich 1516. M. 32, note 1, lacking in Munich 1516. M. 60, fermata in Munich 1516.

Tenor. M. 60, fermata in Munich 1516.

Bassus. Part name, Bass in Munich 1516. M. 60, fermata in Munich 1516.

15. Fortuna desperata (Heinrich Isaac)

a 3

The tenor of the original setting appears in the superius, transposed up a fifth.

SOURCES

Primary source. **C.G. XIII.27,** fols. 91v–92 (98v–99); Ysach; i–x–x; S = Fortuna desperata. This manuscript is the earlier source and was compiled in Florence, probably while Isaac was still there.

Concordant source. **Florence 121,** fols. 37v–38; anonymous; x–x–x.

REFERENCES

Inventory numbers. Meconi 6b; Picker 19; Cumming B I 6; Loeffler D3.

Modern edition. Isaac, 74 (C.G. XIII.27).

COMMENTS

The original tenor is transposed up a fifth and placed in the superius, retaining its original note values and adding a brief coda at the end (beginning in the second half of m. 57). The coda is needed to allow the superius to form the final cadence on F with the tenor, for even though the model voice has been transposed, its original mode is used to close the piece. A certain modal ambiguity is apparent in the transmission of the work, for the borrowed melody appears with a flat in the signature in Florence 121 but with none in C.G. XIII.27; both sources provide signature flats for the lower voices. Although musica ficta requires most of the superius Bs to be flatted, this creates some modal discrepancies with the original melody, and a strict transposition would lose the flat in the key signature.

See the commentary to FD28 for a listing of the differences between this and Isaac's other tenor cantus firmus setting.

Notes to the Transcription

Superius. Clef, C2 in Florence 121. Signature accidentals, b and b' are flat in Florence 121.

Tenor. M. 28, note 5 to m. 29, note 1, e' min–c' sbr in Florence 121. M. 60, note 1, a min–c' sbr in Florence 121.

Bassus. Part name, Contr in Florence 121. Signature accidentals, B and b are flat in Florence 121. M. 12, note 1, specific flat in Florence 121.

16. Sanctus (Heinrich Isaac)

a 4

The original tenor is paraphrased in the tenor in tempus perfectum.

Source

Bologna Q17, fols. 54v–55; ysac; i–i–i–i; all incipits = Sanctus.

References

Inventory numbers. Meconi 11; Picker 22.

Comments

The original tenor is paraphrased in the tenor in tempus perfectum at the original pitch. At times, and most prominently at the beginning, the superius and tenor are in imitation. The altus and bassus are in general considerably faster moving than the superius and tenor, but occasionally have sections in longer note values; the contrast between the more rapidly moving areas and the calmer ones is reminiscent of the original song. The bassus and superius are both striking for their wide ranges of a twelfth, and the tessitura of the superius is also noteworthy.

Staehelin accepts the attribution to Isaac but thinks it is probably another secular setting rather than a mass movement, suggesting that the scribe misread "Fortuna" as "Sanctus."[73] Picker, noting the mensuration, the free treatment of the cantus firmus, and the superius/tenor imitation, is more open to the possibility of a mass origin.[74] If the piece really is a Sanctus, it is highly unusual in several ways. If it is a complete Sanctus, it is incredibly short and lacks the division into sections characteristic of contemporary Sanctus settings. If it is only the initial section, and the Pleni, Osanna, and Benedictus portions have been left out, it is still on the short side and is possibly unique as an independently circulating mass section—it is far more common for the Pleni or Benedictus to be plucked from the movement.

Notes to the Transcription

Superius. Signature accidentals, both b and b' are flatted after the first system (mm. 1–20).

17. Fortuna desperata (anonymous)

a 4

The original tenor is placed in the tenor, transposed down a fourth and paraphrased.

Source

St. Gall 462, fols. 5v–6 (pp. 18–19); anonymous; i–x–i–x; S = fortuna desperata, T = FORTUNA desperata.

References

Inventory numbers. Meconi 8a; Picker 8; Cumming B I 2; Loeffler D9.

Modern edition. Geering-Trümpy, 14–16.

Comments

The original tenor is placed in the tenor, transposed down a fourth and paraphrased. Transposition is common in art-song reworkings, and although paraphrase is not, other examples do exist. This composition is more than half again as long as the original, begins with imitation of the tenor line in all voices, and features wide ranges in the altus and bassus. The latter encompasses a twelfth even without its final optional descent to C below the staff, which would stretch the range to a full two octaves. The homorhythmic section in measures 18–29 as well as other static sections may be in reference to the original work.

The piece is distinguished in the manuscript by several features.[75] The tenor voice, the only one of the four to have a fancy calligraphic initial, places the "fortuna" of its "fortuna desperata" incipit entirely in capital letters, thereby calling attention to the preexistent melody in this part. The altus, tenor, and bassus voices all include excerpts from Latin poetry (as do several other works in the manuscript), in this case love poems by Catullus and Tibullus.[76] The copying of the piece was careless in some respects (see the transcription notes) and may account for some of the awkwardness that remains even after obvious rhythmic flaws have been corrected. The unison G–A between altus and tenor in measure 48 may be a scribal error, for example, and perhaps clashes such as the last beat of measure 32 have a similar origin.

NOTES TO THE TRANSCRIPTION

Discantus. The clef was originally written as C3 and then altered to C2.

Altus. The editorial changes enable the altus line to work in the context of the other voices.   M. 34, note 4, g sbr.   M. 54, note 3, f min.   M. 59, note 3, a sbr.   M. 85, note 1, a min.

Tenor. The clef for the first two lines was incorrectly placed as a C4 clef and then changed to C5. The first and third lines of the tenor part have B♭ in the signature. The flat on the third staff is correctly placed, but the one on the first staff was not altered along with the clef and thus appears to read as G♭, an obvious implausibility in this piece. Since the B♭ signature actually affects only measures 43–48 of the tenor line, we see certain modal changes to the melody similar to those observed in FD15.[77]   M. 49, signature flat actually drops out before note 4 of measure 48.

Bassus. Mm. 26–27, F is flatted since it is outside of the gamut and hence ficta.   M. 87, simultaneous D long and c long.

18. *Esurientes implevit bonis (anonymous)*

a 4

The original tenor is in the tenor.

SOURCE

Wrocław 428, fols. 164(a)v–164(b); anonymous; t–t–t–t; all voices = *Esurientes implevit bonis* text.

TEXT AND TRANSLATION

Esurientes implevit bonis

Esurientes implevit bonis et divites dimisit inanes.

*
He has filled the hungry with good things and the rich he has sent away empty.

Text source. Wrocław 428, fols. 164(a)v–164(b)

Liturgical source. Magnificat, v. 8

COMMENTS

This setting of verse 8 of the Magnificat text comes within a larger, anonymous *Magnificat sexti toni* that does not use *Fortuna desperata* elsewhere. The tenor, which contains the *Fortuna desperata* tenor, enters after four breves rest, at pitch and with proper note values, and then proceeds strictly. This movement simultaneously uses the Magnificat tone in D in the discantus, but once again the second borrowed melody is treated more freely than *Fortuna*. The composer uses the Magnificat tone in the discantus in other sections of the overall composition, and the resemblance of the tone's opening to the start of the *Fortuna* tenor may have inspired the use of the latter in this movement. The altus and bassus parts also mimic the tenor in their opening lines.

This setting is one of the few works using *Fortuna desperata* that does not name the tune, which was first identified by Martin Staehelin.[78] It is also the only instance within the large art-song reworking families where a voice from one of the favorite models is used in a Magnificat.[79]

NOTES TO THE TRANSCRIPTION

Very little text is given in any of the parts, and the melismas may indicate being "filled ... with good things." Performers who wish a less melismatic reading can of course repeat portions of the text.

Altus. M. 18, notes 2–3, e' min–f' sbr.   M. 36, note 4 to m. 37, note 1, e' min–d' min.

Bassus. M. 46, note 1, dotted sbr.

19. *O crux ave / Fortuna (anonymous)*

a 5

The original tenor is in the tenor.

SOURCES

Primary source. **Regensburg C120,** pp. 162–63 (in the first half of the manuscript, ca. 1518–19); anonymous; i–i–i–i–i; S = Crux ave, T = fortuna, A and B = O Crux ave, Q = O crux ave. This is the only complete source.

Concordant source. **Vatican 11953,** fols. 23v–24v; anonymous; m–m–m–m–i; B = O crux ave.

REFERENCES

Inventory numbers. Meconi 10c; Picker 30; Loeffler D19.

TEXTS AND TRANSLATIONS

O crux ave

O crux ave, spes unica
Hoc passionis tempore!
Auge piis justitiam
Reisque dona veniam.

*

Hail O cross, sole hope
In this passion time!
Advance fairness to the pious
And grant forgiveness to the guilty.

Text source. AH, 2:45.

Comments

The original tenor appears in the tenor voice, untransposed and in original note values, and the first three measures of the bassus are clearly derived from the original bassus. The preexistent melody used in the superius is an internal verse from the hymn *Vexilla regis*, which had several liturgical uses.[80] The chant is not used strictly and has several notes left out, including the distinctive B♭ normally found after the initial F–G–A rise. This means that the opening of the superius, a phrase reappearing in measure 37, follows the initial pitch sequence of the *Fortuna desperata* tenor, making the second borrowed melody doubly subservient to *Fortuna desperata*: first in being the tune that must give way rather than be used strictly, and second in having its shape altered to mirror that of the tenor.

O crux ave / Fortuna has been suggested as Senfl's, but this attribution presents problems. On the basis of the *Nester-Theorie*, which proposes that under certain circumstances an anonymous work is by the same composer as the attributable pieces that surround it in its source, Martin Staehelin assigns *O crux ave / Fortuna* to the most frequent composer of *Fortuna* settings.[81] In its two sources, the piece is indeed surrounded by works of Senfl (albeit different ones in each manuscript), but Vatican 11953 is not a particularly good source with which to apply the *Nester-Theorie*. We can demonstrate this by considering the secular work *Tantque nostre argent* that appears in both this manuscript (anonymously) and the partbooks Basel, Öffentliche Bibliothek der Universität, MS F.X.1–4 (attributed to Pierre de la Rue). This work, which is almost certainly by Johannes Japart, appears in a cluster with three chansons by Pierre de la Rue in both the Vatican 11953 and Basel sources (the same chansons in each source). The readings of all of these works are extremely close, even with such variable items as ligatures and coloration, suggesting a common exemplar. It appears as if the scribe of the Basel partbooks applied his own *Nester-Theorie* to *Tantque nostre argent*, resulting in an incorrect attribution and suggesting greater caution on our part.[82] Further, the tenor of *O crux ave / Fortuna* diverges from Senfl's *Fortuna* tenor in several crucial places, including measure 30 where it follows the reading used by Isaac rather than the one followed by Senfl.

The final cadence of the work is striking in several respects. The work ends on a D triad, and the superius provides the standard cadential motion for a D cadence before its final pitch. No voice, however, supplies the expected E to create a suspension cadence, and the last C of the superius cannot be raised by the conventional semitone without causing a horrible clash with the quintus. Meanwhile, the tenor and quintus twice set up cadential motion on G. Finally, the third of the final triad could scarcely be raised according to contemporary rules of musica ficta unless the composer wanted a real aberration of the *Fortuna desperata* tenor.

Notes to the Transcription

Superius. The text for *O crux ave* has been editorially added. I have tried to underlay the text as it fits the chant, which means that sometimes ligatures must be broken (e.g., mm. 20–21).

Bassus. Part name, Bassus in Vatican 11953. Mensuration, ₵ in Vatican 11953. M. 39, G sbr–F sbr in Regensburg C120; A sbr–F sbr reading taken from Vatican 11953.

20. Ich stund an einem Morgen / Fortuna (Ludwig Senfl)

a 5
The original tenor is in the tenor.

Sources

Primary source. **Vienna 18810,** fols. 43–44, 37, 44, 3v–4, 41–42; Ludovicus Sennfl (in discantus); i–½t–i–i–i; S = Ich stund an ainnem morgen, A = half of the text for *Ich stund an einem Morgen*, T = fortuna Ich stund an ainem morgen, B and Q = Ich stund an ainem morgen. This source is very slightly earlier than 1534[17] and may have been compiled in Munich, where Senfl lived.

Concordant source. **1534[17]**, no. 26; Ludovicus Senfflius (attribution from index); i–i–i–i–i, with seven stanzas of text in tenor book; S = Ich stund an einem morgen Quintum, A = Ich stund an einem Quintum (Vienna 18810 quintus), T = Ich stund an einem morgen (Vienna 18810 altus), B = Ich stund an einem, V = Fortuna (Vienna 18810 tenor).

References

Inventory numbers. Meconi 7b; Picker 25; Cumming B I 9; Loeffler D10.

Modern editions. Bernoulli, 42–44 (1534[17]). Senfl SW4, 12–13.

Text and Translation

Ich stund an einem Morgen

Ich stund an einem Morgen
Heimlich[83] an einem Ort
Da het ich mich verborgen.[84]
Ich hoert klegliche Wort
Von einem Frewlen hübsch und fein.
Sie sprach zu irem Buelen.
Es muß geschieden sein.

"Hertz lieb ich hab vernumen
Du wölst von hinnen schier.
Wen wiltu wider kumen?
Das soltu sagen mir."
"Nun merck, mein feins Lieb, was ich sag.
Mein Zukunft thust mich fragen.
Weis weder Stund noch Tag."

Das Freulen weinet sere;
Sein Hertz was unmuts vol.
"So gib mir Weis und Lere
Wie ich mich halten sol.
Für dich so setz ich al mein Hab
Und wiltu hie beleiben,
Verzer dich Iar und Tag.

Der Knab sprach aus seinem Muete.
"Dein Willen ich wol spüer,
Verzer ich dir dein Guete
Ein Iar wer bald hinfür
Darnach mus es gescheyden sein.
Ich wil dich freuntlich bitten:
Setz deinen Willen darein."

Das Freulein schrey laut, "Morte!
Mort uber alles Leyd!
Mich krenckin deine Worte.
Hertz lieb, nit von mir scheidt!
Für dich da setz ich Gut und Eer,
Und solt ich mit dir ziehen,
Kain Weg wer mir zu ferr."

Da sprach der Knab mit Züchten.
"Mein Schatz, ob allem Gut
Ich wil dich freuntlich bitten.
Schlag solchs aus deinem Muet.
Gedenck mer an die Frernde dein
Die dir kein Arges trawen
Und teglich bey dir sein."

Da kert er ir den Rucken
Er sprach nit mer zu ir.
Das Freilen thet sich schmucken
In einen Winckel schier
Es weinet dz sie schier verging.
Dis hat ein Schreiber gesungen,
Wie es eim Frewlen gieng.

*

I stood one morning
Secretly in a place
Where I had hidden myself.
I heard lamenting words
From a maiden beautiful and refined.
She spoke to her sweetheart.
There must be partings.

"Beloved, I have heard
That you wish to depart from here.
When will you return?
This should you tell me."
"Now note, my fair love, what I say.
You ask what my future holds.
I know neither hour nor day."

The maiden wept greatly,
Her heart filled with displeasure.
"Then advise me
As to how I should compose myself.
I will give you everything I have
And if you remain here,
I'll support you a year and a day."

The youth spoke from his heart.
"Your wish I well feel,
But even if I accept your kindness
A year will soon be past
And then we must part.
I entreat you kindly:
Accept what must be."

The maiden cried out, "Alas!
Sorrow of sorrows!
Your words grieve me.
Beloved, don't leave me!
For you I put forth goods and honor,
And were I to go with you,
No journey would be too long for me."

Here spoke the youth in propriety.
"My dear, with all goodness
I will ask you in kindness.
Banish this from your mind.
Think rather of your friends
Who think no evil of you
And are with you daily."

Then he turned his back to her
And spoke to her no more.
The maiden covered herself
And hid in a corner
And cried her eyes out.
This has a poet sung,
What happened to one maiden.

Text source. 1534[17], no. 26.

Comments

Senfl places the original tenor, untransposed and with its original note values, in the tenor of this setting. It is combined with the famous lied *Ich stund an einem Morgen*, which Senfl used in five other compositions. Here the German song is placed in the contratenor, and, as usual, is arranged around *Fortuna desperata*, which remains unchanged. The remaining three voices are considerably livelier in style. As Cumming has pointed out, the German text accords well with Fortune's notoriety for parting lovers.[85]

The difference in names for voice parts between the two sources is noteworthy. While Vienna 18810 puts *Fortuna desperata* in the tenor, its usual position, 1534[17] places it in the vagans and assigns *Ich stund an einem Morgen* the tenor part. This and the inclusion of seven full strophes of text certainly emphasizes the role of the German song in the composition, as we might expect from a print devoted to lieder.

Notes to the Transcription

Discantus. M. 29, notes 1–2, a' dotted sbr in 1534[17].

Contratenor. Part name, Tenor in 1534[17]. The text is as it appears in 1534[17].

Tenor. Part name, Vagans in 1534[17]. Mm. 46–47, e' br–f' br in 1534[17], but corrections at end of the part-book indicate these are to be a third lower, which matches Vienna 18810.

Quinta vox. Part name, Contratenor in 1534[17].

Bassa vox. Part name, Bassus in 1534[17]. Signature accidentals, B is flat except for last staff (mm. 52–58) in 1534[17]. M. 10, note 3 to m. 11, note 1, g min–g min in 1534[17]. M. 14, note 1, c sbr in 1534[17]; someone has tried to add a stem to correct it to min; this correction has also been indicated in the "Correctur" at end of the partbook. M. 31, note 2 to m. 32, note 1, B♭ min–B♭ smin in 1534[17]. M. 32, note 6 to m. 33, note 1, F min–F smin in 1534[17].

21. Es taget vor dem Walde/Fortuna (Ludwig Senfl)

a 5

The original tenor is in the tenor.

Source

1534[17], no. 30; Ludovicus Sennflius (from index in tenor book); i–i–i–i–i; S = Es taget vor dem walde fortuna, A, T, and B = Fortuna, V = Es taget vor dem walde Fortuna.

References

Inventory numbers. Meconi 7c; Picker 28; Cumming B I 12; Loeffler D11.

Modern editions. Bernoulli, 45–48. Senfl SW4, 18–20.

Texts and Translations

Es taget vor dem Walde

Es taget vor dem Walde;
Stand ûf, Kätterlîn!
Die Hasen laufen balde;
Stand ûf, Kätterlîn!
Holder Buehl, heiahô,
Du bist mîn, sô ich bin dîn;
Stand ûf, Kätterlîn!

Es taget in der Aue;
Stand ûf, Kätterlîn!
Schöns Lieb, lass' dich anschauen!
Stand ûf, Kätterlîn!
Holder Buehl, heiahô,
Du bist mîn, sô ich bin dîn;
Stand ûf, Kätterlîn!

Es taget vor dem Holze;
Stand ûf, Kätterlîn!
Die Jäger hürnen stolze;
Stand ûf, Kätterlîn!
Holder Buehl, heiahô,
Du bist mîn, sô ich bin dîn;
Stand ûf, Kätterlîn!

*

Dawn breaks by the forest;
Stand up, kitty!
The hares are soon running;
Stand up, kitty!
Darling sweetheart, heigh-a-ho,
You are mine, so I am yours;
Stand up, kitty!

Dawn breaks in the meadow;
Stand up, kitty!
Beautiful love, just look!
Stand up, kitty!
Darling sweetheart, heigh-a-ho,
You are mine, so I am yours;
Stand up, kitty!

Dawn breaks by the woods;
Stand up, kitty!
The hunters sound their horns proudly;
Stand up, kitty!
Darling sweetheart, heigh-a-ho,
You are mine, so I am yours;
Stand up, kitty!

Text source. After Senfl SW4, 18–20.

Comments

Senfl places the original tenor, untransposed and with original note values, in the tenor of this setting. He also borrows one of his favorite popular songs, *Es taget vor dem Walde*, which he used elsewhere in two settings by itself and in six other compositions with preexistent melodies such as *Kein Adler in der Welt so schön; Ich stund an einem Morgen; Ach Elslein, liebes Elselein; Wann ich des Morgens; M, dein bin ich;* and *Wiewohl viel herter Örden sind*. In the piece under discussion, Senfl places *Es taget vor dem Walde* in the discantus and vagans, and the contratenor also draws material from it. Again, *Fortuna desperata* is unchanged while *Es taget vor dem Walde* is treated flexibly.

The *Es taget vor dem Walde* text is not transmitted with the composition in its surviving source, but the subject of the famous song (lovers at dawn, presumably about to part) would have been well known to listeners. Cumming has pointed out the appropriateness of using *Fortuna*, known for separating lovers, in this context.[86] Given Senfl's fondness for both of these melodies and his penchant for combinative settings (by no means restricted to his *Fortuna desperata* works), there was doubtless also a desire to solve the compositional problem of linking up these tunes.

NOTES TO THE TRANSCRIPTION

The *Es taget vor dem Walde* text has been added editorially to the discantus and vagans.

Bassus. M. 60, note 4, A is written in by hand in the print; the correction list in the partbook also gives this note; although it also says the value should be smin, only min will work. M. 65, A in the print, but F is given in the corrections listed in partbook.

22. Herr durch dein Blut (Pange lingua) / Fortuna (Ludwig Senfl)

a 5

The original tenor is in the tenor.

SOURCE

1534[17], no. 100; Ludovicus Senfflius (name given in index); t–i–i–i–i; S = full text for *Herr durch dein Blut*, A and B = Fortuna oder Pange lingua, T = Fortuna vel herr durch dein pluet, Vagans = Fortuna vel Pange lingua.

REFERENCES

Inventory numbers. Meconi 7d; Picker 29; Cumming B I 14; Loeffler D13.

Modern editions. Bernoulli, 38–41. Senfl SW4, 132–33.

TEXTS AND TRANSLATIONS

Herr durch dein Blut

Herr, durch dein Blut,
Hilff uns Armen.
Thue durch dein Güt,
Dich erbarmen
Unser Sunden und Gebrechen.
Thue nicht, o Herr, mer rechen.
Mach uns meiden,
Durch dein Leiden,
Al Boßheit und Missethat.

*

Lord, through your blood,
Help us poor folk.
Through your goodness,
Have mercy
On our sins and failings.
Do not, O Lord, seek vengeance.
Make us avoid,
Through your suffering,
All malice and sin.

Text source. 1534[17], no. 100.

Pange lingua

Pange, lingua, gloriosi
Corporis mysterium
Sanguinisque pretiosi
Quem, in mundi pretium,
Fructus ventris generosi,
Rex effudit gentium.

Nobis natus, nobis datus
Ex intacta virgine,
Et in mundo conversatus,
Sparso verbi semine.
Sui moras incolatus
Miro clausit ordine.

In supremae nocte cenae,
Recumbens cum fratribus,
Observata lege plene
Cibis in legalibus,
Cibum turbae duodenae
Se dat suis manibus.

Verbum caro, panem verum
Verbo carnem efficit,
Fitque sanguis Christi merum.
Et si sensus deficit,
Ad firmandum cor sincerum
Sola fides sufficit.

Tantum ergo Sacramentum
Veneremur cernui,
Et antiquum documentum
Novo cedat ritui;
Praestet fides supplementum
Sensuum defectui.

Genitori genitoque
Laus et iubilatio,
Salus, honor, virtus quoque
Sit et benedictio.
Procedenti ab utroque,
Compar sit laudatio.

*

Celebrate, tongue,
The mystery of the glorious body
And of the precious blood
That, as ransom for the world,

The king of all, fruit of a noble womb,
Poured forth.

Born for us, given to us
By the virgin pure,
And dwelling in the world,
He sowed the seed of his word.
He ended his time here
In a miraculous way.

On the night of the last supper,
Reclining with his disciples,
Observing the law fully
Concerning the permitted food,
With his own hands he gave himself
As food to the group of twelve.

Word made flesh, by his word
He makes the true bread flesh,
And makes wine the blood of Christ.
And if our senses fail,
Faith alone will suffice
To strengthen the sincere heart.

Therefore, bowing, let us venerate
This great sacrament,
And let the old ways
Cede to new rites;
Faith answers for
The defects of the senses.

To the father and to the son
Be praise and rejoicing,
Health, honor, virtue,
And blessing also.
For the one who proceeds from these two,
Let there be equal praise.

Text source. AH, 50:586.

Comments

Senfl places the original tenor, untransposed and with original note values retained, in the tenor of this five-voice setting. An additional preexistent melody, the famous hymn *Pange lingua* for second vespers of Corpus Christi, is used in the discantus; it also sometimes furnishes motives for the vagans. The hymn, presented untransposed, is treated with a small amount of melodic and rhythmic freedom. As for the tenor, it is used strictly but must enter last, after a rest of six breves, as it is modally at odds with the Phrygian of the hymn and the other voices. It also has a signature flat, in contrast to the other parts. Similarly, *Fortuna desperata* must drop out once its final long has been sounded in order to avoid a dissonance at the end. This is an extremely rare instance (unique in early music?) of a piece ending without its full component of parts. Cumming's interpretation of Fortune vanquished by virtue works well because of this isolation of the tenor[87] (and the modal difference illustrates the conflict nicely), although it must be remembered that when *Fortuna desperata* is present, it is in charge; the hymn is the one that must work around *Fortuna desperata* and hence is treated flexibly, rather than the other way around.

In the sole surviving source for this setting, the chant appears with the German text *Herr durch dein Blut*. It is possible that this text was added by the publisher; Ott exchanged Catholic texts for Protestant ones more than once. Consequently the text of the first verse of *Pange lingua,* which may have been the text Senfl set, is added editorially underneath the *Herr durch* text in the discantus. In addition to the famous Josquin mass, there was a long-standing German tradition of setting this chant that dated back at least as far as the 1480s; settings appear in the Glogauer partbooks,[88] St. Gall 530, Berlin 40021, and Leipzig 1494. Senfl thus combined two compositional traditions in this work.

Notes to the Transcription

Discantus. The *Pange lingua* text has been added to conform to its chant presentation, which means that ties and ligatures in the edition must occasionally be ignored (e.g., mm. 3–4 and 25; the same is true for the German text in mm. 22–23). Performers may obviously alter the suggested underlay; they may, for example, wish to move the "-um" of measure 27 to measure 29.

Bassus. M. 43, note 1, G sbr in print, but A is given in list of corrections in the bassus partbook.

23. Virgo prudentissima / Fortuna (Ludwig Senfl)
a 5

The original tenor is in the tenor.

Source

Vienna 18810, fols. 45v–46, 5–5v, 39–39v, 45, 43v–44; Ludovicus Sennfl (attribution in all partbooks); t–t–t–i–t; T = Fortuna Virgo prudentissima, all others = *Virgo prudentissima* text.

References

Inventory numbers. Meconi 10f; Picker 27; Cumming B I 11.

Modern edition. Senfl SW6, 66–68.

Text and Translation

Virgo prudentissima

Virgo prudentissima, quo progrederis quasi aurora valde rutilans? Filia Syon, tota formosa et suavis es, pulchra ut luna, electa[89] ut sol.

*

Most prudent virgin, where are you going like dawn intensely glowing red? Daughter of Sion, you are all beautiful and charming, fair as the moon, choice as the sun.

Text source. Vienna 18810, no. 72.

Liturgical source. Antiphon before the Magnificat at first vespers on the Assumption of the Blessed Virgin Mary.

Comments

Senfl places the original tenor, untransposed and with its original note values,[90] in the tenor of the setting after an initial nine breves of rest. In the discantus secundus he uses the chant *Virgo prudentissima,* the antiphon for the Magnificat of first vespers on the feast of the Assumption of the Virgin Mary.[91] This chant also furnishes material for the remaining voices.[92] As is typical, the *Fortuna desperata* melody is treated strictly while the second borrowed melody is treated freely. As in FD22, *Fortuna desperata* retains its signature flat while the other voices have no signature accidentals.

The work is one of the four Senfl *Fortuna desperata* pieces placed back-to-back in Vienna 18810. The superius is dated "Anno dni. 1533 primo Octobris," but the significance of the date or any plausible relationship of the four contiguous works (other than sharing the *Fortuna desperata* tenor) has yet to be discovered.

Cumming has suggested that "Fortuna's instability is perhaps represented in the relatively unusual minor triad at the end (which cannot be made major without violating the cantus firmus) and her changing and uncertain character through the uniqueness of her key signature."[93] This interpretation is not completely convincing; for one thing, the tenor's usual key signature is retained and thus is actually *unchanged*. In addition, since the *Fortuna desperata* tenor is more compatible with the Dorian mode of this chant than it is, for example, with *Pange lingua* (see FD22), it is noteworthy that Senfl stops the tenor as soon as it is finished and supplies a breve rest before bringing in the F again for the final triad. He could just as easily have sustained the final note of the *Fortuna desperata* tenor were he to represent instability through the minor triad. It would seem as if Senfl intended this last F to be raised, and wanted the pause beforehand both to make this possible and to maintain the integrity of the cantus firmus. Performers, of course, are free to ignore this and any other suggested ficta.

24. *Helena desiderio plena / Fortuna* (Ludwig Senfl)

a 5
The original tenor is in the tenor.

Source

Vienna 18810, fols. 44–45, 4v, 37v–38v, 44v, 42–43; Ludovicus Sennfl (attribution in all partbooks); t–t–t–i–t; T = Fortuna Helena desiderio plena, all others = *Helena desiderio plena* text.

References

Inventory numbers. Meconi 10e; Picker 26; Cumming B I 10.

Modern edition. Senfl SW6, 62–65.

Text and Translation

Helena desiderio plena

Helena, desiderio plena, orabat cum lachrimis, dicens, "Tu, Domine, ostende lignum in quo salus nostra fuit suspensa."

*

Helena, full of longing, was praying with tears, saying, "You, Lord, reveal the cross on which our salvation was suspended."

Text source. Vienna 18810, no. 71.

Liturgical source. Psalm antiphon for the feast of the Finding of the Holy Cross.

Comments

After thirty-one breves of rest the original tenor is placed in the tenor, untransposed and in original note values. The discantus secundus enters in the same measure, presenting another preexistent melody in relatively long note values. Martin Picker has identified this as the antiphon *Helena desiderio plena*.[94] Prior to the entry of the two borrowed voices, the discantus primus, contratenor, and bassa vox all draw imitative material from the chant melody, and they present the complete text once; it is repeated upon the entry of the other two voices. As usual, the chant is treated freely while *Fortuna desperata* is treated strictly.

Once again the *Fortuna* melody is the only voice to have a signature flat, and with its Lydian mode it presents something of a contrast to the Dorian chant. Its last note forms the third of a triad on D, and although the normal rules of musica ficta would suggest a raising of this final F, the earlier B♭s in the contratenor and bassus (m. 88) prevent this.

This work is one of the four Senfl *Fortuna desperata* works placed together in Vienna 18810; the unexplained date "28. Septemb; Anno dni. 1533" appears in the superius. The text, which concerns Saint Helena, mother of the emperor Constantine and reputed finder of Christ's cross, appears to have no relation to the other three *Fortuna desperata* works with which it is placed.

NOTE TO THE TRANSCRIPTION

Discantus primus. M. 90, the f′ long is blackened in the manuscript, which may indicate an error rather than an alternative.

25. Nasci, pati, mori / Fortuna (Ludwig Senfl)

a 5

The original tenor is in the first tenor.

SOURCE

Vienna 18810, fols. 42v–43, 36–36v, 43v, 2v–3, 40v–41; Ludovicus Sennfl (in the superius); t–t–i–t–t; T = fortuna Nasci pati mori, all others = *Nasci, pati, mori* text.

REFERENCES

Inventory numbers. Meconi 10d; Picker 24; Cumming B I 8.

Modern edition. Senfl SW6, 60–62.

TEXT AND TRANSLATION

Nasci, pati, mori

Nasci, pati, mori.

*

To be born, to suffer, to die.

Text source. Vienna 18810, no. 69.

COMMENTS

The original tenor appears in the first tenor, untransposed and with original note values. All other voices make use of the motive introduced at the beginning by the tenor secundus; the discantus and contratenor employ it extensively, the tenor secundus and bassa vox less so. This motivic repetition is matched by the continual reiteration of the brief text in all parts except the first tenor.

The discantus part is dated "21. Sept. 33." without further explanation, and the piece is the first of four *Fortuna desperata* works by Senfl presented consecutively in Vienna 18810. The text, although easy to reconcile with its *Fortuna desperata* tenor, seems to bear no relationship to the other three settings. Senfl seems to be trying to show his versatility through his various settings of the *Fortuna desperata* melody.

26. Fortuna ad voces musicales (Ludwig Senfl)

a 4

The original tenor is presented twice in the tenor.

SOURCES

Primary source. **1534[17]**, no. 31; Ludovicus Senfflius (in the index to the tenor book); i–i–i–i; S and A = Fortuna ad voces Musicales, T = Fortuna / ad voces Musicales, B = Fortuna ad voces musicales. This print, a collection containing a large number of Senfl works, is the earliest source and the only one that is not a theoretical treatise.

Concordant sources. **1537 Heyden,** pp. 42–45; Ludovici Senflij (on p. 41 in the introduction to the piece); i–i–i–i; S and B = FOrtuna ad voces musicales, A and T = FOrtuna ad voces Musicales. **1540 Heyden,** pp. 46–49; Ludovici Senflij (on p. 45 in the introduction to the piece); i–i–i–x; S = FOrtuna advoces Musicales, A = FOrtuna ad voces Musical., T = FOrtuna ad voces Musicales. **1547 Glarean,** pp. 222–25; Litavico Senflio Tigurino; i–x–i–x; S = Voces Musicales ad Fortunam, T = Fortuna ad voces Musicaleis. **1553 Faber,** pp. 102–15; Ludovico Sennfflio; x–x–x–x; introduced as "Aliud vocum exercitium ad Fortunam."

REFERENCES

Inventory numbers. Meconi 6m; Picker 23; Cumming B I 13; Loeffler D12.

Modern editions. Bernoulli, 49–53 (1534[17]). Glarean, 2:295–300 (1547 Glarean). Heyden, 57–61 (1540 Heyden). Senfl SW4, 20–23 (1534[17]).

COMMENTS

In this work, whose title is sometimes translated as "Fortuna according to musical vocables,"[95] Senfl uses the original tenor, untransposed and with unchanged note values, twice in the tenor. This is reminiscent of Isaac's Phrygian setting (FD28), although Isaac has clear prima and secunda partes while Senfl continues without pausing. The discantus works gradually through the notes of the natural hexachord, ascending and descending twice (C–D, C–D–E, C–D–E–F, etc.). On the second ascent and descent, the segments are summarized (e.g. C–D, C–D–E, C–E, C–D–E–F, C–F, etc.). Senfl also occasionally ornaments the segments. Lowinsky and Loeffler connect the hexachordal rise and fall with Fortune's wheel, with the altus and bassus joining in the musical pictorialism.[96] Cumming classifies this as a combinative setting because of the use of the hexachord, but this is not the traditional understanding of that term, which is more often reserved for the use of two real melodies as preexistent material.

Heyden, Glarean (who calls the work Ionian), and Faber all use this composition in their treatises, and the combination of hexachords and extensive ligature use in this piece makes it a valuable pedagogical work.

NOTES TO THE TRANSCRIPTION

Discantus. Part name, Can. in 1547 Glarean; Cantus in 1553 Faber. Signature accidentals, b is flat in 1553

Faber.   M. 115, a' long in 1537 Heyden, 1540 Heyden.   M. 116, c' br in 1534[17]; fermata in 1553 Faber.

Contratenor. Part name, Altus in 1537 Heyden, 1540 Heyden; Alt in 1547 Glarean; Altitonans in 1553 Faber. M. 7, triplets not specifically indicated; the number 3 is placed before note 1 in 1534[17], 1537 Heyden, 1540 Heyden, 1553 Faber; ³⁄₂ in 1547 Glarean.   M. 8, ¢ is placed before note 1 in all sources.   M. 18, ³⁄₂ in 1547 Glarean. Mm. 18–20, triplets not specifically indicated; the number 3 is placed before note 1 of measure 18 in 1534[17], 1537 Heyden, 1540 Heyden, 1553 Faber.   M. 21, ¢ is placed before note 1 in all sources.   M. 116, fermata in 1553 Faber.

Tenor. Mensuration, c in 1537 Heyden. M. 30, e' br in 1553 Faber, going against the traditional Senfl tenor. M. 32, note 1 to m. 33, note 1, f' br in 1553 Faber, going against the traditional Senfl tenor (unique variant). M. 59, repeat sign is given in 1534[17]; the repeat is written out in 1537 Heyden, 1540 Heyden, 1547 Glarean, 1553 Faber.   M. 67 to m. 68, note 1, d' br in 1547 Glarean (dot lacking; error).   M. 114, g sbr in 1537 Heyden, 1540 Heyden, 1553 Faber (error).   M. 115, f br in 1534[17].   M. 116, fermata in 1553 Faber.

Bassus. Part name, BAS. in 1547 Glarean; Basis in 1553 Faber. Signature accidentals, b is flat in 1547 Glarean; B is flat in 1540 Heyden (except m. 69 to m. 80, note 2), 1547 Glarean (except m. 94, note 5 to m. 107, note 3).   M. 57, note 2 to m. 58, note 1, F sbr in 1547 Glarean.   M. 59, rest lacking in 1553 Faber.   M. 66, note 3 to m. 67, rest, e dotted sbr in 1553 Faber. M. 87, note 2, f smin in 1540 Heyden.   M. 109, triplets not specifically indicated; the number 3 is placed before note 2 in 1534[17], 1537 Heyden, 1540 Heyden, 1553 Faber; ³⁄₂ is placed before note 2 in 1547 Glarean. M. 110, ¢ is placed before note 1 in all sources.   M. 115, F br in 1534[17].   M. 116, fermata in 1553 Faber.

27. *Passibus ambiguis* (Matthias Greiter)
a 4

The first phrase of the original tenor recurs throughout the tenor.

Source

1553 Faber, pp. 140–51; Matthaeo Greitero; pars prior: t–i–t–i, pars altera: i–i–t–i; pars prior: A and B = Passibus ambiguis, pars altera: S, A, and B = Et manet; all texts = *Passibus ambiguis*.

References

Inventory numbers. Meconi 10g; Picker 11; Cumming B I 5; Loeffler D22.

Modern editions. Edward E. Lowinsky, "Matthaeus Greiter's *Fortuna*: An Experiment in Chromaticism and in Musical Iconography," *Musical Quarterly* 42 (1956): 505–8; reprinted with revisions in idem, *Music in the Culture of the Renaissance and Other Essays*, ed. Bonnie J. Blackburn (Chicago and London: University of Chicago Press, 1989), 243–48. André Pirro, *Histoire de la musique de la fin du XIVe siècle à la fin du XVIe* (Paris: Librairie Renouard, 1940), 275–77 (pars prior only).

Text and Translation

Passibus ambiguis

Passibus ambiguis fortuna volubilis errat et manet in nullo certa[97] tenaxque loco.

*

Changeable fortune roams with untrustworthy steps and stays fixed and firm in no place.

Text source. 1553 Faber, pp. 140–51.

Literary source. Ovid, *Tristia*, 5.8.15–16.

Comments

This is possibly the most striking of all the *Fortuna desperata* settings, and one for which there can be little doubt about the symbolic aspects of the work. The text of the work, from Ovid's *Tristia*, deals explicitly with the instability of Fortune, and although the *Fortuna desperata* borrowing is not identified as such in the sole surviving source for this work, a midcentury theoretical treatise, it should have been apparent to any listener. The first phrase of the *Fortuna desperata* tenor, presented in the tenor of the new work, is "fixed and firm in no place" (as the text of the new work states), entering on a new pitch at each appearance; it also briefly inspires the cantus and contratenor in measures 29–36. Further, these appearances navigate the full circle of fifths. In the pars prior the phrase is given on F, B♭, E♭ (twice), A♭, and D♭, while in the second half we have D♭ again, then G♭, C♭ (twice), and finally F♭. The basis and contratenor, meanwhile, extend as far as B♭♭. This remarkable harmonic voyage is carefully marked by accidentals and signature flats in the print. Essentially the signature flats are progressive, with the earlier flats dropping out as the more distant ones are added. Lowinsky's transcription gives the signatures that are in effect at any given point (i.e., the ones that "should" be there), but this is slightly misleading since full signature accidentals are not actually written out.

Lowinsky thinks the work was inspired by the emblematic pieces in Caspar Othmayr's *Symbola illustrissimorum principum* and thus was composed after 1547, the year that Othmayr's collection was published.[98] It comes as no surprise that the piece that most clearly uses *Fortuna desperata* symbolically should come from the middle of the sixteenth century, when humanism[99] and its concommitant concern for textual expression[100] were more clearly in vogue than at any other point in *Fortuna desperata*'s history.

Notes to the Transcription

Very little text is given in the original, and none has been added editorially. Signature flats reflect what is in the source; after a flat has dropped out of the signature in the source, it is added editorially as a ficta accidental. Accidentals before notes in the source are retained as written, even if this causes some duplication.

Cantus. M. 57 to m. 66, note 2, clef given as G4 instead of G3. I have interpreted the flats as being placed in relation to a G3 clef. Regardless of how these flats are interpreted, there is little difference in the resulting sound, as the music moves inexorably around the circle of fifths.

Contratenor. M. 76, rest, sbr rest.

Basis. M. 46, note 5 to m. 53, clef given as F3 instead of F4. I have interpreted the flats as being placed in relation to an F4 clef. Regardless of how these flats are interpreted, there is little difference in the resulting sound, as the music moves inexorably around the circle of fifths.

28. Fortuna desperata (Heinrich Isaac)

a 3

The original tenor, now in Phrygian, is in the tenor, once in each pars.

Sources

Primary source. **Zwickau 78/3,** no. 10; anonymous (both partes); i–x–i; S and B = fortuna. This is the only ensemble source to contain both partes.

Concordant source. **1538[9]**, no. 88; anonymous; x–x–x (secunda pars only). This source has a handwritten incipit (fortuna desperata) and a handwritten attribution (H. Isac), both in the tenor in a sixteenth-century hand.

Intabulations. **Basel F.IX.22,** fols. 15v–17v (prima pars), 45–47 (secunda pars); Isac (in prima pars only); keyboard tablature; both partes, but presented separately; each title = Fortuna in mi; prima pars copied in 1513, secunda pars copied in 1515.[101] **Berlin 40026,** fols. 8–9v; anonymous; keyboard tablature; secunda pars only, title = Fortuna in mi.

References

Inventory numbers. Meconi 6g; Picker 20, 21; Cumming B III 5; Loeffler D17, E2, E3.

Modern editions. Berg-Kotterba, 1:9–12 (Berlin 40026). Isaac, 134 (secunda pars only; 1538[9]), 143 (secunda pars only; Berlin 40026), 144–45 (prima pars only; Basel F.IX.22). Marx, 14–15 (prima pars; Basel F.IX.22), 40–41 (secunda pars; Basel F.IX.22). Formschneyder, 2:127 (secunda pars only; 1538[9]).

Comments

The two partes of this work each place the original tenor, now in Phrygian, in the tenor voice with unmodified note values. Only in Zwickau 78/3 are the two sections of the work contiguous; in the Basel F.IX.22 keyboard tablature, the earliest surviving source, they are separated, and the other two sources contain the secunda pars only. Each of the partes has been independently attributed to Isaac, and although the attribution for the secunda pars is only a contemporary, handwritten addition to 1538[9], it appears in both surviving copies of the print. The close stylistic similarity of the two partes, both of which are imitative and highly motivic, show that they clearly belong together, and Picker has noted how the opening descending motive in the bassus of the prima pars is inverted to form the opening ascending motive in the superius of the secunda pars.[102] There seems to be no reason, stylistic or otherwise, to doubt Isaac's authorship—as Johannes Wolf did for the secunda pars[103]—and the work, except for measures 7 and 26, follows the version of the tenor line used in Isaac's FD15.

The piece presents a good example of the dangers inherent in correcting "mistakes" in the sources. Two readings in Zwickau 78/3, the only ensemble source for the prima pars, appear to be faulty. In measure 52 the second note in the superius was originally a C, which generated a dissonance with the bassus B; the former has been changed here to a D, the reading in Basel F.IX.22. That tablature also changes the final bassus pitch in measure 52 to G to avoid dissonance with the superius line, but I have retained the Zwickau 78/3 reading since it is part of a recurring bassus motive. More difficult to resolve is measure 28, where the second note of the bassus (A) sounds against a B in the superius, creating a semibreve clash. While it might initially seem as if the bassus note is at fault— one can more easily imagine a pitch error creeping in when a leap is involved than when stepwise motion is in order—changing the bassus pitch creates a fresh set of problems. Turning it into a G or B eliminates the dissonance, but at the expense of the melodic line, which now must leap either a seventh or a ninth. Neither of these intervals was in common use melodically. In addition, altering the bassus pitch also mars the construction of the entire bassus line, which is built on a series of reiterated motives, each concluding on A. Finally, if further evidence were needed that the A is the intended bassus pitch, it is found in the intabulation in Basel F.IX.22, where the A is clearly maintained.

In the intabulation the dissonance is avoided by providing a rest in place of the superius B, and that is the solution followed here. A closer look at the superius line reveals that it, too, reiterates melodic material, and the B found in Zwickau 78/3 in measure 28 links two statements of a recurring motive. This motive is elsewhere followed by a rest, so substituting a rest here does no harm to the structure of the line.

Based on this example, one may be tempted to think that intabulations are to be trusted over ensemble sources, but a look at measure 30 (and remembering the bassus in measure 52) suggests that this is not always the case. Here we seem to have the same problem that we saw in measure 28, for the first sonority pits a superius B against a bassus A. In Basel F.IX.22 the intabulator again avoids the dissonance, this time by altering the bassus pitch to G. This is not all that is altered, however; the previous note has also been changed, in this case from G to A. The dissonance is thus avoided, but only by destroying the bassus motive. In this instance I have retained the reading in Zwickau 78/3, for it marks the congruence of bassus and superius motives. Moreover, the supposedly offending dissonance, despite being on a strong beat, actually sounds quite different from that of measure 28. This is for several reasons: it is of shorter duration and all voices immediately move to a new pitch, the A is approached by step rather than leap, and the entire sonority occurs within a ninth rather than a sixteenth.

Measures 30 and 52, then, appear to be yet other examples of what we have already seen in *Fortuna desperata* itself: compositional "errors" sanitized by contemporary hands in a concordant source. If we similarly edit out all casual dissonance we will present only a partial picture of the music of the time.

Notes to the Transcription

Superius (prima pars). M. 6, note 3, specific sharp in Basel F.IX.22. M. 8, note 4, specific sharp in Basel F.IX.22. M. 17, note 2, specific sharp in Basel F.IX.22. M. 20, note 3, specific sharp in Basel F.IX.22. M. 28, rest, b' sbr in Zwickau 78/3; reading is from Basel F.IX.22. M. 29, note 1, dot lacking in Zwickau 78/3. M. 30, note 3, specific sharp in Basel F.IX.22. M. 35, notes 2 and 4, specific sharps in Basel F.IX.22. M. 37, note 3, specific sharp in Basel F.IX.22. M. 41, note 4, specific sharp in Basel F.IX.22. M. 43, note 4, specific sharp in Basel F.IX.22. M. 52, note 2, c' in Zwickau 78/3; reading is from Basel F.IX.22. M. 53, note 2, specific sharp in Basel F.IX.22. M. 55, note 2, specific sharp in Basel F.IX.22.

Tenor (prima pars). M. 23, note 1 and rest, unique variant; given the overall sloppiness of Zwickau 78/3's scribe, it is possible that he intended to write a dot rather than a minim rest after the semibreve. M. 48, note 4, unique variant; again, this is possibly a scribal error.

Bassus (prima pars). M. 17, note 3, specific sharp in Basel F.IX.22. M. 40, note 3, f is fusa in Zwickau 78/3, but the mark under it turns it into smin. M. 46, note 3, specific sharp in Basel F.IX.22.

Superius (secunda pars). Part name, Discantus in 1538[9]. M. 61, note 2, specific sharp in Basel F.IX.22. M. 65, notes 1–3, c' min–b smin–a smin in 1538[9]. M. 66, note 4, specific sharp in Basel F.IX.22, Berlin 40026. M. 67, note 3, specific sharp in Berlin 40026. M. 73, note 2, specific sharp in Berlin 40026. M. 73, notes 5–7, g' min–f' smin–e' smin in 1538[9]. M. 77, note 4, specific sharp in Basel F.IX.22, Berlin 40026. M. 83, f' min–e' smin–d' smin–a' sbr in 1538[9]. M. 84, note 1, sbr rest in 1538[9]. M. 89 to m. 90, note 4, a' dotted min–g' smin–f' min–a' min–g' smin–f' smin–e' min in 1538[9]. M. 96, note 2, specific sharp in Basel F.IX.22. M. 97, note 3, specific sharp in Basel F.IX.22, Berlin 40026. M. 111 to m. 112, note 2, c" sbr–b' min–a' dotted min–g' smin–f' smin–e' smin. M. 113, note 2, specific sharp in Basel F.IX.22, Berlin 40026. M. 114, sbr rest–min rest–e' dotted sbr–a' min–g' min (effectively adding an extra measure before m. 115, which throws off the final cadence) in 1538[9]. M. 115, note 2, specific sharp in Basel F.IX.22, Berlin 40026. M. 115, notes 3–5, g' min–f' smin–e' smin in 1538[9].

Tenor (secunda pars). The tenor is not written out in the secunda pars of Zwickau 78/3; it is instead indicated with the words "Secunda pars tenor" followed by an indecipherable word. The edition has repeated the tenor as it appears in the prima pars. The following is a comparison of the secunda pars of 1538[9] with the prima pars of Zwickau 78/3. Measure numbers are given for the tenor as it appears in the secunda pars of the edition, followed in parentheses by the measure numbers for the equivalent place in the prima pars.

Part name, Tenor in 1538[9]. Mensuration, ¢ in 1538[9]. M. 61 to m. 62, note 1 (m. 1 to m. 2, note 1), e dotted br in 1538[9]. M. 83, note 1 and rest (m. 23, note 1 and rest), unique variant in Zwickau 78/3; d' dotted sbr in 1538[9]. M. 108, note 4, (m. 48, note 4), g min in 1538[9]. M. 119 (m. 60), no fermata in 1538[9].

Bassus (secunda pars). Part name, Bassus in 1538[9]. M. 68, note 2, specific sharp in Basel F.IX.22. M. 99, note 1, e min in Zwickau 78/3; the edition follows the reading in 1538[9]. M. 108, note 1, e sbr (hence adding an extra beat). M. 116, rest and note 2, sbr rest in 1538[9]. M. 117 to end, a considerably different reading, which can be substituted for Zwickau 78/3's version by those who prefer a more flamboyant close, appears in 1538[9]:

29. *Fortuna desperata* (anonymous)

a 4

The original tenor, now in Phrygian, is in the tenor.

SOURCES

Primary source. **Regensburg C120,** pp. 284–85 (in the second half of the manuscript, ca. 1520–21); anonymous; x–i–i–i; A and B = fortuna, T = fortuna desperata. This is the only complete source.

Concordant source. **Munich 328–31,** fols. 15–15v, 50v, 8v–9; anonymous; i–m–i–i; S and T = Fortuna, B = Fortuna b.

Intabulation. **St. Gall 530,** fols. 45v–46; Maister Hansen Buchnerus; keyboard tablature; title = Fortuna in mi.

REFERENCES

Inventory numbers. Meconi 6f; Picker 31; Cumming B III 1; Loeffler D8.

Modern editions. Buchner, 2:70–73 (St. Gall 530). Marx-Warburton, 124–25 (St. Gall 530). Moser, 62–64 (St. Gall 530).

COMMENTS

This setting places the original tenor, now in Phrygian, in the tenor with the original note values. Its author is unknown; Hans Buchner is more probably the intabulator than the composer. The work circulated in more sources than usual for this type of setting. In St. Gall 530 it is one of only two pieces labeled "pedaliter," and in Munich 328–31 the "Fortuna b" reference distinguishes it from an earlier "Fortuna a" setting (FD35). Bente has given Senfl's name with a question mark for this piece,[104] but that is an unlikely attribution. Senfl composed no known settings using the tenor in mi, and the work is not especially skillful in its writing. Similarly, Birkendorf wondered whether Isaac was the composer.[105] The Munich 328–31 reading is closer to Isaac's tenor than the Regensburg C120 reading is. Both follow FD28 rather than FD15 at measure 7, but Munich 328–31 also follows Isaac at measures 23, 24, 29, and 53, whereas Regensburg C120 does not. Both differ from Isaac, however, at the crucial measures 30 and 48, where Munich 328–31 follows an early reading found in Perugia 431 (FD2) and Regensburg C120 has an unusual variant found only in the Josquin and Obrecht masses.

NOTES TO THE TRANSCRIPTION

Superius. Part name, Discantus in Munich 328–31. M. 33, note 2, the tritone between the superius and altus has been left because flatting the b' destroys both the motivic and harmonic unity in this section; the offending interval is ameliorated somewhat by the distance between the two voices and the intervening d' provided by the tenor voice. M. 35, notes 2 and 4, specific sharps in St. Gall 530. M. 35, notes 4–5, f' dotted min–e' smin in Munich 328–31; Regensburg C120 is unusual in including the number 3 below these pitches, evidently to prevent them from being interpreted as minor color. M. 39, note 3, d" smin–e" smin in Munich 328–31; this slightly increases the range of the superius. M. 40, notes 5–8, g' sbr in Munich 328–31. M. 43, note 4, specific sharp in St. Gall 530. M. 50, notes 2 and 4, specific sharps in St. Gall 530. M. 59, note 3, specific sharp in St. Gall 530.

Altus. Part is missing in Munich 328–31. M. 6, notes 3–4, specific sharps in St. Gall 530. M. 38, note 4, specific sharp in St. Gall 530. M. 46, note 4, specific sharp in St. Gall 530.

Tenor. Part name, Tenor in Munich 328–31. M. 23, d' dotted sbr–e' min in Munich 328–31. M. 24, f' dotted sbr–e' smin–d' smin in Munich 328–31. M. 29, e' dotted sbr–d' smin–c' smin in Munich 328–31. M. 48, c' dotted sbr–b smin–a smin in Munich 328–31. M. 52, g br in Munich 328–31. M. 53, note 2, unique variant in Regensburg C120; g sbr in Munich 328–31.

Bassus. Part name, Bassus in Munich 328–31. M. 54 to m. 55, rest, c dotted br in Munich 328–31.

30. *Ave mater matris Dei / Fortuna disperata* (Jacquet of Mantua)

a 5

The original tenor, now in Phrygian, is in the tenor.

SOURCE

Bologna Q19, fols. 106v–107; Jachet; t–t–i–t–t; all texts = *Ave mater matris Dei,* incipit = Fortuna disperata.

REFERENCES

Inventory numbers. Meconi 10b; Picker 32; Cumming B III 4.

Modern edition. Sherr Selections, 2:28–34.

TEXT AND TRANSLATION

Ave mater matris Dei

Ave mater matris Dei,
Per quam salvi fiunt rei.
Ave prole fecundata,
Anna Deo dedicata.
Pro fideli plebe tota,
Apud Christum sis devota.
Alleluia.

Hail mother of the mother of God,
Through whom the guilty are saved.
Hail fruitful in your progeny,
Anna, dedicated to God.
For all faithful people,
May you be devoted in the presence of Christ.
Alleluia.

Text source. Bologna Q19, fols. 106v–107.

COMMENTS

The original tenor, now in Phrygian, is placed in the tenor with its original note values. The tenor matches that used by Isaac; in measure 7 it follows the FD28 reading. Isaac, of course, spent long periods in Italy, and it is likely that his work was known to Jacquet.[106] The motet, one of the composer's earliest,[107] is unusual in its relatively low tessitura; tenor clef is used for the top three voices and bass clef for the bottom two. The work is also rather short for a motet, continuing just a few breves beyond the presentation of the cantus firmus, and the closing melodic motion in the bassus prevents the expected raising of the G of the final triad.

For Cumming, the text shows the association of Fortune with the Virgin,[108] but it is actually only peripherally concerned with Mary. Its subject matter, rather, is her mother, Saint Anne, who conceived her child only in old age. A more likely interpretation of this text-music juxtaposition is suggested by George Nugent, who notes the wry commentary on Saint Anne's delayed good fortune that the use of the borrowed melody makes here.[109]

31. *Consideres mes incessantes plaintes / Fortuna desperata* (anonymous)

a 5

The first phrase of the original tenor, now in Phrygian, appears twice in the tenor.

SOURCE

Vienna 18746, fols. 22–22v, 24–24v, 20v, 23–23v, 21v–22; anonymous; i–i–i–i–i; S and A = Consideres, T 1 = Consideres mes incessantes plaintes. Fortuna desperata, T 2 = Consideres mes incessantes, B = Consideres mes incessantes plaintes.

REFERENCES

Inventory numbers. Meconi 6i; Picker 34; Cumming B III 2; Loeffler D20.

COMMENTS

The first fifteen breves of the original tenor, now in Phrygian, are presented twice in the tenor, the first time at double the original note values and the second time in its usual form. According to Cumming, this is probably an example of the two wheels of fortune (slow and fast, bad and good).[110] The surviving textual incipit ("regard my unceasing laments"), however, reads exactly like a standard courtly love complaint, and it is doubtful that the text would have switched to joyful sentiments halfway through. The complaining text at least accords well with the Phrygian version of the cantus firmus, and Picker's suggestion that it was composed for Marguerite of Austria is certainly plausible.[111]

The treatment of the tenor in this piece is also, of course, a standard technique of cantus firmus manipulation since the Middle Ages. As stated in the introduction, Josquin uses this technique in his mass, which was copied in another manuscript from the same scriptorium as Vienna 18746 at almost the same time, and it is likely that the composer of FD31 was inspired by the mass. Similarly, the Josquin mass (or FD31 itself) probably inspired Cabilliau's motet *Anima mea liquefacta est / Amica mea* (FD32), which is constructed in exactly the same manner. FD31 is also apparently related to the piece that immediately precedes it in the manuscript, the anonymous *A moy seule / Comme femme*, which has the same underlying structure, albeit one built on a different model.[112] It seems likely, then, that compositional play more than symbolic imagery was the driving force here.

Although the piece is transmitted anonymously, Jaap van Benthem has attributed it to Josquin on the basis of its style, and Picker speculates that Josquin may have composed this "Fortuna in mi" setting in rivalry with Isaac.[113] This is unlikely given Josquin's standard procedures for borrowing,[114] and scholars have not generally accepted the attribution; Noble lists the work under "Doubtful and Misattributed Works" in *The New Grove,* and Charles does not even include it in *Josquin des Prez: A Guide to Research*.[115]

A final unusual aspect of the work is its combination of a (now lost) French text with the model. Only one other work, the anonymous si placet setting *Fortune esperee* (FD5)—also on a lost text—did that as well.

NOTES TO THE TRANSCRIPTION

Tenor. The tenor line is not written out completely, but instead has a repeat sign at the end of measure 32; at this point the melody must be repeated in ¢, although this mensuration sign is given only at the beginning of the part.

32. *Anima mea liquefacta est / Amica mea* (Cabilliau)[116]

a 5

The first fifteen breves of the original tenor, now in Phrygian, appear twice in the tenor.

Source

1554[9], fol. VI in each partbook; Cabbiliau; t–t–i–t–t; SAQB = full text of *Anima mea liquefacta est*, T = AMica mea Amica mea ij / Fortuna desperata.

References

Inventory number. Picker 35.

Modern edition. Sherr Susato, 45–50.

Texts and translations

Anima mea liquefacta est

Anima mea liquefacta est ut dilectus locutus est. Quaesivi et non inveni illum; vocavi et non respondit mihi. Adiuro vos, filie Ierusalem, nunciate dilecte quia amore langueo.

*

My soul failed when he spake. I sought him, but I could not find him; I called him, but he gave me no answer. I charge you, O daughters of Jerusalem, that ye tell him that I am sick of love.

Text source. 1554[9].

Biblical source. Song of Songs, 5:6, 8.

Translation. King James Bible.

Amica mea

Amica mea.

*

My friend.

Text source. 1554[9].

Comments

This motet has exactly the same foundation as *Consideres mes incessantes plaintes / Fortuna desperata*, with the first fifteen breves of the original tenor first appearing in doubled note values and then at integer valor. The notation of the tenor voice of each piece is identical, even down to the rest of two breves at the opening of the work. Martin Picker is undoubtedly correct in suggesting that of the several composers named Cabbiliau, the most likely to be the author of this work is Joachim de Tollenaere *dit* Cabilliau, who was a choirboy for Charles V in 1528.[117] Cabilliau thus surely drew on the earlier piece for inspiration—if not from the Josquin mass that inspired it—working now with a biblical text from the Song of Songs. Although the tenor is noted in the print as being that of *Fortuna desperata*, the words underlaid in the source are "amica mea" (my friend), making a textual connection with "anima mea."

Notes to the Transcription

Tenor. The tenor line is not written out completely, but instead has a repeat sign at the end of measure 32. At this point the melody must be repeated in ¢, although this mensuration sign is given only at the beginning of the part.

33. Fortuna (Wilhelm Breitengraser)

a 4

The original tenor, now in Phrygian, provides material for the tenor and bassus.

Source

1534[17], no. 121; Guiliel. Breitteng. (in discantus);[118] i–i–i–i; all incipits = Fortuna.

References

Inventory numbers. Meconi 8b; Picker 33; Cumming B III 3; Loeffler D18.

Comments

Wilhelm Breitengraser's setting draws on the Phrygian version of the original tenor to provide material for the tenor as well as the contratenor (at the beginning) and bassus. The tenor and bassus are often imitative, but references to the original melody are increasingly difficult to trace as the composition progresses. According to Cumming,

> Here the composer has sacrificed a completely faithful rendition of the cantus prius factus in order to present a more thorough representation of the concept associated with the melody; the idea of the "melos" has become more important than its integrity.[119]

She also posits that the descending motives as well as the final melodic motion of the piece, the octave descent of the bassus to the E below the staff, demonstrate Fortune's customary practice of debasing.[120] It is also possible, this late in the game, that Breitengraser was merely writing a kind of instrumental fantasia on a by-now well-known melody without intending any symbolic meaning at all. Also, this setting is another work where the closing melodic motion precludes the raising of the third in the final triad.

Notes to the Transcription

Discantus. M. 24, note 5 to m. 25, note 1, f' smin–g' smin; corrections given at the end of the vagans book indicate that this passage should be g' smin–f' smin.

Bassus. M. 66, the print has an additional c sbr after note 1, but this repetition is an error evidently caused by the line break that occurs here.

34. Fortuna desperata quae te dementia coepit? (anonymous)

a 3

The original tenor fits (as tenor) with the sole surviving voice (the discantus) of this piece.

SOURCE

St. Gall 463, fol. 13v (no. 29); anonymous; ½t–m–m; text = *Fortuna desperata quae te dementia coepit? Solemur contrariis.*

REFERENCES

Inventory numbers. Meconi 6n; Picker 6; Cumming B I 3.

Modern edition. Loach, 2:48–50.

TEXT AND TRANSLATION

Fortuna desperata quae te dementia coepit [vertit], see FD2.

COMMENTS

Although only the discantus of this setting remains, the work is marked in the index as being for three voices and appears in the manuscript in the section of three-voice Latin works. The surviving voice has the wide range of a thirteenth, and the original tenor fits perfectly underneath it, although neither the superius nor the bassus of the original do. The two voices are not structurally complete, however, and those wishing to improvise a third part will need to observe the implied cadences at points such as measures 4–5, 20–21, 30–31, 46–47 and at the very end of the work. This work is one of only two surviving three-voice, non-Phrygian, tenor cantus firmus settings; the other is by Isaac (FD15).

The composition evidently uses the same classical Latin text compilation that other *Fortuna* works in the St. Gall manuscripts do. The mode of the work is given in the manuscript as "Ionici Hÿpoionicique connexio."

NOTES TO THE TRANSCRIPTION

Discantus. The additional text in the discantus is supplied from FD2 in St. Gall 462. M. 7, note 4, specific flat. None of the other b' pitches are flatted in the source, but all are flatted in the edition by virtue of the modern key signature. Performers wishing to play it exactly as written in the manuscript should thus raise b♭' in measures 17–19, 27, 36, 56, and 61.

Tenor. The version of the tenor used by Senfl has been chosen to add to the discantus, both because it comes from Germanic circles and because its variants fit perfectly with the discantus in measures 27–29.

35. *Fortuna* (anonymous)

a 4?

The original tenor is in the tenor.

SOURCE

Munich 328–31, fols. 13, 45v, 6v; anonymous; i–m–i–i; S = Fortuna a, T and B = Fortuna.

REFERENCES

Inventory numbers. Meconi 6l; Picker 7; Cumming B I 1.

COMMENTS

This work places the original tenor, untransposed and retaining the original note values, in the tenor voice, making this a tenor cantus firmus setting. Since the new discantus and bassus are written entirely in breves, the result is a static composition that lacks any proper cadential motion. The composition as it survives provides a perfect foil for improvising a lively altus part, which is surely what has been left out of the original partbooks. The work is identified as "Fortuna a" in contrast to "Fortuna b" (FD29), which appears later in the same partbooks. Martin Bente, without further elaboration, offers "Senfl?" as a possible author, and it is true that the tenor of this work exactly matches the version used by that composer.[121]

36. *Fortuna desperata quae te dementia vertit?* (Robertus Fabri)

a 6

The original superius is in the discantus (superius).

SOURCES

St. Gall 463, fols. 76v, 141v–142[122] (no. 214); Robertus Fabri (attribution with the discantus and altus parts); ½t–i–i–m–m–m; S = Fortuna desperata quae te dementia vertit? Solemur contrariis, A and V = Fortuna desperata. **St. Gall 464,** fols. 3 and 3; Robertus Fabri (attribution in each partbook);[123] i–m–m–m–m–i; S and B = F fortuna.

REFERENCES

Inventory numbers. Meconi 6e; Picker 16; Cumming B I 4; Loeffler D16.

Modern edition. Loach, 2:400–403.

TEXT AND TRANSLATION

Fortuna desperata quae te dementia coepit [vertit], see FD2.

COMMENTS

Robertus Fabri, of whom nothing is known, places the original superius, untransposed and with original note values, in the discantus of his six-voice setting, making this a superius cantus firmus setting. Although two voices of the work are missing, several inscriptions in both sources indicate that it is a six-voice composition and classify it modally as Hypoionian ("Hÿpoionicus, id est sextus tonus").[124] The surviving voices are reminiscent of the original setting in their frequent use of homorhythm. The original tenor and bassus are not the lost voices; in the first fifteen measures alone using the original bassus would provide harsh dissonances in measures 4, 5, 7, and 13, while the tenor would cause clashes in measures 7 and 8 and create parallel octaves with the vagans in measures 12–13.

The text of this piece, from Virgil, is evidently the same as that used in the other *Fortuna* settings in St. Gall 462, 463, and 464. These three manuscripts likewise share the superius variant in measure 14. Fabri's work also has a unique reading of measure 45.

NOTES TO THE TRANSCRIPTION

Discantus. The discantus reading in St. Gall 464 is the same as in St. Gall 463. The additional text in the discantus is supplied from FD2 in St. Gall 462. M. 45, unique variant.

Altus. M. 4, note 1, specific flat in St. Gall 463.

Notes

1. For the dating of the various sections of this manuscript, see John Kmetz, *Die Handschriften der Universitätsbibliothek Basel: Katalog der Musikhandschriften des 16. Jahrhunderts: Quellen kritische und historische Untersuchung* (Basel: Verlag der Universitätsbibliothek Basel, 1988), 76–77.

2. See Rainer Birkendorf, *Der Codex Pernner: Quellenkundliche Studien zu einer Musikhandschrift des frühen 16. Jahrhunderts (Regensburg, Bischöfliche Zentralbibliothek, Sammlung Proske, Ms. C 120)*, 3 vols., Collectanea musicologica, no. 6 (Augsburg: Bernd Wißner, 1994), 1:121–24.

3. On this date, see Honey Meconi, "The Manuscript Basevi 2439 and Chanson Transmission in Italy," in *Atti del XIV congresso della Società Internazionale di Musicologia (Bologna 1987): Trasmissione e recezione delle forme di cultura musicale*, 3 vols., ed. by Angelo Pompilio (Turin: Edizioni di Turino, 1990), 3:171.

4. For this date, see Anthony M. Cummings, "Guilio de' Medici's Music Books," *Early Music History* 10 (1991): 93.

5. Date from *Florence, Biblioteca Nazionale Centrale, MSS Magl. XIX, 164–167*, 4 vols., introduction by Howard Mayer Brown, Renaissance Music in Facsimile, vol. 5 (New York: Garland, 1987), 1:vi.

6. This is a printed lauda collection that is currently missing its title page. See Giulio Cattin, "I 'Cantasi come' in una stampa di laude della Biblioteca riccardiana (Ed. r. 196)," *Quadrivium* 19, no. 2 (1978): 5–52; on the date, see page 7. According to Cattin the *cantasi come* is "Fortuna desperata." I would like to thank David Fallows for bringing this print to my attention.

7. On this manuscript, see David Fallows, *A Catalogue of Polyphonic Songs, 1415–1480* (Oxford: Oxford University Press, 1999), 19. I am grateful to Professor Fallows for kindly bringing this manuscript to my attention and sharing material about it.

8. On this manuscript and its date see Meconi, "Poliziano, *Primavera*, and Perguia 431: New Light on *Fortuna desperata*," in *Antoine Busnoys: Method, Meaning, and Context in Late Medieval Music*, ed. Paula Higgins (Oxford: Clarendon Press; New York: Oxford University Press, 1999), 466–78.

9. Fallows, *A Catalogue of Polyphonic Songs*, 520.

10. See Honey Meconi, "Style and Authenticity in the Secular Music of Pierre de la Rue" (Ph.D. diss., Harvard University, 1986), 33–34. I have since traced the original owner to Augsburg and discuss his career in a forthcoming essay.

11. See Ian Woodfield, *The Early History of the Viol* (Cambridge: Cambridge University Press, 1984), 111–14. I would like to thank Dr. Hiroyuki Minamino for providing me with a copy of his unpublished study and transcription of this manuscript. The information on this manuscript cited in the critical commentary for FD1 comes from Dr. Minamino's work.

12. See François Lesure, introduction to *Tablature de luth italienne: Cent dix pièces pour luth seul et accompagnements pour luth d'oeuvres vocales: Fac-similé du ms. de la Bibliothèque nationale, Paris. Rés. Vmd. ms. 27., ca. 1505* (Geneva: Minkoff Reprint, 1981).

13. According to Fallows, *A Catalogue of Polyphonic Songs*, 518, the piece is dated "8 Octubris."

14. See Walter H. Rubsamen, "The Earliest French Tablature," *Journal of the American Musicological Society* 21 (1968): 286–99; David Fallows, "15th-Century Tablatures for Plucked Instruments: A Summary, a Revision, and a Suggestion," *Lute Society Journal* 19 (1977): 10–18; and Vladimir Ivanoff, *Das Pesaro-Manuskript: Ein Beitrag zur Frühgeschichte der Lautentabulatur*, Münchener Veröffentlichungen zur Musikgeschichte, vol. 45 (Tutzing: Hans Schneider, 1988).

15. See Birkendorf, *Der Codex Pernner*, 1:27.

16. Ibid.

17. For the dating of Segovia's repertoire, see Honey Meconi, "Art-Song Reworkings: An Overview," *Journal of the Royal Musical Association* 119 (1994): 14–16.

18. See Marx-Warburton, 14–15.

19. See Birkendorf, *Der Codex Pernner*, 3:39 and 101–4.

20. This date appears several times in the partbooks.

21. For information on this source, Josquin CW, 8:66 (critical commentary).

22. The si placet altus was added by a later hand.

23. According to Fallows, *A Catalogue of Polyphonic Songs*, 519, this is all that remains of the title.

24. This is the only two-lute intabulation in this print.

25. The reading is from Perugia 431. Paris 676 reads "la fama tua hai denigrata," but the "tua," which appears in no other textual source, is obviously incorrect and spoils the

line's rhythm. Most sources read "denigata" here; see the introduction for further discussion of this issue.

26. From Perugia 431; Paris 676 has only the syllable "ta."

27. This abbreviation for the refrain is from Perugia 431; lacking in Paris 676.

28. For the readings of Perugia 431 for stanzas 1 and 2, see table 1 in the introduction. All other sources have stanza 1 only; see table 1 for those readings as well.

29. Stanza 3 is found only in Perugia 431.

30. *AH* is used as the text source instead of Frankfurt 20, fol. 1, as the latter is both difficult to read and incomplete.

31. It is possible that this is a signature flat and hence holds for the whole system. In any event, solmization would flat the remaining Bs in the system (mm. 26–48).

32. This text is not the same as the sequence in *AH*, 34:99–100.

33. Although it is impossible to tell which of the versions using the original bassus is contained in this source since only a sole partbook remains, it is likely to be one of the si placet settings. Other pieces contained in this manuscript are four-voice works such as Adam von Fulda's *Ach hulff mich leid* and Paul Hofhaimer's *Fro bin ich* setting. The Basel partbook has been placed under FD2 since this setting was the most widely-circulated of the si placet versions.

34. The second "che" is crossed out in the manuscript.

35. Florence Pan. 27 reads "te hebi" here, which is not as good for the poetic structure but preferable for the underlay.

36. "Vertit" in St. Gall 462 (FD2) and St. Gall 463 (FD36); "cepit" in St. Gall 463 (FD2); "coepit" in St. Gall 463 (FD34).

37. Text ends here in FD2 (St. Gall 463) and FD34 (St. Gall 463).

38. The text ends here in FD36 (St. Gall 463).

39. "Sociis" in St. Gall 462.

40. "Ah, Corydon, Corydon, quae te dementia cepit?"

41. "Solabar, fatis contraria fata rependens."

42. For these texts and their identification, see Geering-Trümpy, 179 (items A19–20). The poem by Beroaldus is appropriately from his elegy *Fortuna*.

43. This is the original foliation; the modern foliation is given variously as 131v–132 (Brooks, 3:312); 132v–133 (Fallows, *A Catalogue of Polyphonic Songs*, 519); and 133v–134 (Edward Pease, "A Report on Codex Q16 of the Civico Museo Bibliografico Musicale, Bologna," *Musica disciplina* 20 [1966]: 57–94, 75).

44. Loeffler erroneously lists Florence 2439 as the sole source for this work.

45. Other pieces in the manuscript are similarly numbered.

46. See John Dunstable, *Complete Works*, 2d, rev. ed., prepared by Margaret Bent, Ian Bent, and Brian Trowell, Musica Britannica, vol. 8 (Royal Musical Association and American Musicological Society; London: Stainer and Bell, 1970), 133–34.

47. It is not clear whether this attribution refers to the original superius, tenor, and bassus voices, the si placet altus, or the new contratenor replacement bassus.

48. For information on this practice in the *O rosa bella* family, see Meconi, "Art-Song Reworkings," 12–14.

49. On Felice, see Frank A. D'Accone, "Some Neglected Composers in the Florentine Chapels, ca. 1475–1525," in *Viator* 1 (1970): 280–81.

50. See the introduction for more discussion of this issue.

51. Cumming erroneously lists this source as Florence 2439.

52. This setting is the first piece in the original section of four-voice works in the manuscript; there is another number 102, a piece added later to the folios that were originally left blank between the sections of three- and four-voice works.

53. "Nichtsagende, erfindungslose und uninteressante." Otto Johannes Gombosi, *Jacob Obrecht: Eine stilkritische Studie*, Sammlung musikwissenschaftlicher Einzeldarstellungen, no. 4 (Leipzig: Breitkopf & Härtel, 1925), 102.

54. Picker, 437; Edward E. Lowinsky, "The Goddess Fortuna in Music, with a Special Study of Josquin's *Fortuna d'un gran tempo*," *Musical Quarterly* 29 (1943): 74–75; reprinted with revisions in idem, *Music in the Culture of the Renaissance and Other Essays*, ed. Bonnie J. Blackburn (Chicago and London: University of Chicago Press, 1989), 238 (subsequent references are to the revised version).

55. *LU*, Appendix II, 3 shows a slightly different form of this litany.

56. I would like to thank Pamela Whitcomb for this ingenious suggestion (private communication, 29 November 2000).

57. Maria Rika Maniates, "Quodlibet Revisum," *Acta musicologica* 38 (1966): 174; Loeffler, 12; Cumming, 17.

58. Picker, 438.

59. For some discussion of this treatment, see Gombosi, *Jacob Obrecht*, 104–5.

60. Cumming, 15.

61. Picker, 437; Susan Forscher Weiss, "Bologna Q 18: Some Reflections on Content and Context," *Journal of the American Musicological Society* 41 (1988): 81.

62. The title is taken from the index to the cantus partbook for Florence 164–67.

63. Cumming erroneously lists Florence 121 as the sole source for this work. In Florence 164–67, it is followed by two other zibaldone.

64. This is first person plural, future tense, but of which verb is unknown.

65. The meaning of the Italian is not completely clear.

66. Nonsense word.

67. The most likely meaning in this context is a kind of long pastry that is shaped like a stick with a knob on one end; see *A Florentine Chansonnier from the Time of Lorenzo the Magnificent: Florence, Biblioteca Nazionale Centrale MS Banco Rari 229*, 2 vols., ed. Howard Mayer Brown, Monuments of Renaissance Music, vol. 7 (Chicago: University of Chicago Press, 1983), text volume:268. The obvious obscene overtones fit well with the general nature of the patchwork texts. I am grateful to Allan Atlas for bringing this reference to my attention.

68. "Siano" in Florence 164–67.

69. The exception seems to be the tenor, measures 49–53, which prefigures the cantus firmus in measures 52–55.

70. Picker, 437.

71. Gombosi, *Jacob Obrecht*, 101–2; Whisler, 1:88–89.

72. For more on Munich 1516's reliance on Petrucci's Canti C, see Whisler, 1:19–23.

73. Martin Staehelin, *Die Messen Heinrich Isaacs*, 3 vols., Publikation der Schweizerischen Musikforschenden Gesellschaft, ser. 2, vol. 28 (Bern and Stuttgart: Paul Haupt, 1977), 1:47–48.

74. Picker, 440.

75. For a facsimile of fol. 5v, see Geering-Trümpy, xix.

76. See ibid., 179 (entries A15–A18) for complete citations.

77. Geering and Trümpy ignore the accidental signs and thus retain the modal purity of the line; see ibid., 14–16.

78. Martin Staehelin, *Der Grüne Codex der Viadrina: Eine wenig beachtete Quelle zur Musik des späten 15. und frühen 16. Jahrhunderts in Deutschland*, Abhandlung der geistes- und sozialwissenschaftlichen Klasse, no. 10 (Mainz: Verlag der

Akademie der Wissenschaften und der Literatur; Wiesbaden: Franz Steiner, 1971), [47].

79. For a list of the major families and their components, see Meconi, "Art Song Reworkings," 26–36.

80. See the list provided in Birkendorf, *Der Codex Pernner*, 3:83. The tune was first identified in Picker, 440.

81. See Martin Staehelin, "Möglichkeiten und praktische Anwendung der Verfasserbestimmung an anonym überlieferten Kompositionen der Josquin-Zeit," *Tijdschrift van de Vereniging voor Nederlandse Muziekgeschiedenis* 23 (1973): 86.

82. See Meconi, "Style and Authenticity," 36–37 and 114–16.

83. "Heimlch" in 1534[17].

84. End of text in Vienna 18810.

85. Cumming, 15–16.

86. Ibid., 16. She gives here the first verse of the *Es taget vor dem Walde* text and a translation.

87. Ibid., 17.

88. Berlin, Staatsbibliothek zu Berlin Preussischer Kulturbesitz (formerly Preussische Staatsbibliothek), MS Mus. 40098 (olim Z 98 and Z 8037).

89. The discantus, contratenor, and bassa vox all have "electa es, electa ut sol" (or varied repetitions thereof).

90. It is not "stretched out into long notes," as Cumming, 16, claims, although it is usually slower moving than the surrounding voices.

91. Found in *LU*, 1600.

92. The chant was also used in motets by Senfl and other composers, including Isaac and Josquin. Matthias Schneider has suggested that the work is a parody of Senfl's own *Virgo prudentissima* motet; see *Collection of German, French, and Instrumental Pieces: Wien, Österreichische Nationalbibliothek MS 18 810*, introduction by Matthias Schneider (Peer, Belgium: Musica Alamire, 1987), discantus volume:14.

93. Cumming, 16.

94. Picker, 445, and private communication, 9 February 2000. The antiphon is found in *Antiphonale Pataviense (Vienna 1519): Faksimile*, ed. Karlheinz Schlager, Das Erbe deutscher Musik, vol. 88 (Kassel: Bärenreiter, 1985), fol. 75.

95. For example, Heyden, 57.

96. Lowinsky, "The Goddess Fortuna," 238; Loeffler, 11–12.

97. "Certata" in 1553 Faber.

98. For a full discussion of this work and its cultural context, see Edward E. Lowinsky, "Matthaeus Greiter's *Fortuna*: An Experiment in Chromaticism and in Musical Iconography," *Musical Quarterly* 42 (1956): 500–519; 43 (1957): 68–85; reprinted with revisions in idem, *Music in the Culture of the Renaissance*, 240–61.

99. The choice of a classical text underlines this connection.

100. Uses of chromaticism for textual expression, however, can be traced back at least as far as La Rue's *Pourquoy non* and *Absalon fili mi*.

101. For the dating of the various sections of this manuscript, see Kmetz, *Die Handschriften der Universitätsbibliothek Basel*, 76–77.

102. Picker, 440.

103. Wolf places it in the doubtful works section of Isaac, 134.

104. Martin Bente, *Neue Wege der Quellenkritik und die Biographie Ludwig Senfls: Ein Beitrag zur Musikgeschichte des Reformationszeitalters* (Wiesbaden: Breitkopf & Härtel, 1968), 258.

105. Birkendorf, *Der Codex Pernner*, 1:69 and passim.

106. Picker, 441.

107. For a discussion of Jacquet's early motet style, see George Nugent, "The Jacquet Motets and Their Authors" (Ph.D. diss., Princeton University, 1973), 235–41.

108. Cumming, 16. The text was also set by Gombert and Lhéritier.

109. Nugent, "The Jacquet Motets," 238.

110. Cumming, 15. Lowinsky, "The Goddess Fortuna," 238, has a completely different interpretation of the passage—which appears only in the *Roman de Fauvel*—on which Cumming is basing her interpretation.

111. Picker, 441.

112. Meconi, "Poliziano, *Primavera*, and Perguia," 495. It is unusual for *Comme femme* to be coupled with a chanson text; see the list in Meconi, "Art-Song Reworkings," 26. Perhaps here too *Consideres mes incessantes plaintes* provided the inspiration.

113. Jaap van Benthem, "Einige wiedererkannte Josquin-Chansons im Codex 18746 der Österreichischen Nationalbibliothek," *Tijdschrift van de Vereniging voor Nederlandse Muziekgeschiedenis* 22 (1971): 32–36; Picker, 442.

114. Meconi, "Poliziano, *Primavera*, and Perugia," 496.

115. *The New Grove Dictionary of Music and Musicians*, s.v. "Josquin Desprez," by Gustave Reese and Jeremy Noble; and Sydney Robinson Charles, *Josquin des Prez: A Guide to Research*, Garland Composer Resource Manuals, vol. 2 (New York and London: Garland, 1983).

116. This setting was discovered by Bonnie J. Blackburn, who kindly brought it to my attention.

117. Picker, 442.

118. The entry in the index to the tenor partbook is "Fortuna Guil. Breitt.," but it is curiously listed under "Incerti Auctoris."

119. Cumming, 13.

120. Ibid.

121. Bente, *Neue Wege der Quellenkritik*, 258.

122. The vagans part is on fol. 141v in the altus partbook; the altus part is on fol. 142.

123. The discantus book indicates Fabri as "Robertus bri."

124. On the modal organization of St. Gall 463 and the derivation of classifications from tenors, see Loach, 1:214–46.

Recent Researches in the Music of the Middle Ages and Early Renaissance
Charles M. Atkinson, general editor

Vol.	Composer: Title
1	Johannes Martini: *Secular Pieces*
2–3	*The Montpellier Codex. Part I: Critical Commentary; Fascicles 1 and 2*
4–5	*The Montpellier Codex. Part II: Fascicles 3, 4, and 5*
6–7	*The Montpellier Codex. Part III: Fascicles 6, 7, and 8*
8	*The Montpellier Codex. Part IV: Texts and Translations*
9–10	Johannes Vincenet: *The Collected Works*
11–13	*The Conductus Collections of MS Wolfenbüttel 1099*
14	*Fors seulement: Thirty Compositions for Three and Five Voices or Instruments from the Fifteenth and Sixteenth Centuries*
15	Johannes Cornago: *Complete Works*
16–18	*Beneventanum Troporum Corpus I. Tropes of the Proper of the Mass from Southern Italy, A.D. 1000–1250*
19–21	*Beneventanum Troporum Corpus II. Ordinary Chants and Tropes for the Mass from Southern Italy, A.D. 1000–1250. Part 1: Kyrie eleison*
22–24	*Beneventanum Troporum Corpus II. Ordinary Chants and Tropes for the Mass from Southern Italy, A.D. 1000–1250. Part 2: Gloria in excelsis*
25–26	*Beneventanum Troporum Corpus II. Ordinary Chants and Tropes for the Mass from Southern Italy, A.D. 1000–1250. Part 3: Preface Chants and Sanctus*
27	*Beneventanum Troporum Corpus II. Ordinary Chants and Tropes for the Mass from Southern Italy, A.D. 1000–1250. Part 4: Agnus Dei* [Not yet published.]
28	*Beneventanum Troporum Corpus III. Indexes, Inventories, and Analytical Studies* [Not yet published.]
29	*The Florence Laudario: An Edition of Florence, Biblioteca Nazionale Centrale, Banco Rari 18*
30	*Early Medieval Chants from Nonantola. Part I: Ordinary Chants and Tropes*
31	*Early Medieval Chants from Nonantola. Part II: Proper Chants and Tropes*
32	*Early Medieval Chants from Nonantola. Part III: Processional Chants*
33	*Early Medieval Chants from Nonantola. Part IV: Sequences*
34	Johannes Martini: *Masses. Part 1: Masses without Known Polyphonic Models*
35	Johannes Martini: *Masses. Part 2: Masses with Known Polyphonic Models*
36	*De tous biens plaine: Twenty-Eight Settings of Hayne van Ghizeghem's Chanson*
37	*Fortuna desperata: Thirty-Six Settings of an Italian Song*